PENGUIN BOOKS

# THE DREAM OF THE GOLDEN MOUNTAINS

Malcolm Cowley grew up in Pittsburgh, Pennsylvania, and interrupted his undergraduate career at Harvard to drive an ambulance during World War I. He moved to New York City in 1919 and worked as an editor of *The New Republic* from 1929 to 1944. He served as president of the National Institute of Arts and Letters from 1956 to 1959 and 1962 to 1965 and was chancellor of the American Academy of Arts and Letters from 1966 to 1976. Penguin Books also publishes Malcolm Cowley's *Exile's Return: A Literary Odyssey of the 1920s; The Faulkner-Cowley File: Letters and Memories, 1944–1962; A Second Flowering: Works and Days of the Lost Generation;* and *—And I Worked at the Writer's Trade: Chapters of Literary History, 1918–1978.* He is also the editor of *The Portable Faulkner* and *The Portable Hawthorne* and coeditor of *The Portable Emerson,* also published by Penguin. His most recent book is *The View from 80.* Mr. Cowley lives with his wife in Sherman, Connecticut, in a remodeled barn on the seven acres he bought for $1,300 in 1936.

# THE
# DREAM
## OF THE
# GOLDEN
# MOUNTAINS
*Remembering the 1930s*

### BY
# MALCOLM COWLEY

PENGUIN BOOKS

Penguin Books Ltd, Harmondsworth, Middlesex, England
Penguin Books, 625 Madison Avenue, New York, New York 10022, U.S.A.
Penguin Books Australia Ltd, Ringwood, Victoria, Australia
Penguin Books Canada Limited, 2801 John Street,
Markham, Ontario, Canada L3R 1B4
Penguin Books (N.Z.) Ltd, 182-190 Wairau Road, Auckland 10, New Zealand

First published in the United States of America by The Viking Press 1980
Published in Penguin Books 1981

LIBRARY OF CONGRESS CATALOGING IN PUBLICATION DATA
Cowley, Malcolm, 1898–
The dream of the golden mountains.
Includes index.
1. Cowley, Malcolm, 1898–          —Biography.
2. United States—Civilization—1918–1945.
3. Communism and literature.    4. Authors,
American—20th century—Biography.    I. Title.
PS3505.O956Z464    1981      811'.52    [B]   81-5900
ISBN 0 14 00.5919 9           AACR2

Printed in the United States of America by
Offset Paperback Mfrs., Inc., Dallas, Pennsylvania
Set in Linotype Janson

ACKNOWLEDGMENTS

Thanks are owed to *Saturday Review, The Carleton Miscellany, The Sewanee Review, The New Republic, The Michigan Quarterly Review,* and *The Los Angeles Times,* which published portions of this narrative, usually in different forms. Special thanks are owed to *Esquire,* which serialized some of the early chapters ("A Remembrance of the Red Romance") and one later chapter ("The High 1930's"), and also to the editors of *The Southern Review,* which published "The Meriwether Connection" as well as two later chapters, these under the joint title of "1935: The Year of Congresses." "Lullaby" and "Dirge" from *New and Selected Poems* by Kenneth Fearing reprinted by permission of Indiana University Press and the Estate of Kenneth Fearing; copyright © Kenneth Fearing, 1956. Selections from "A Primer on the Thirties" by John Steinbeck, published in the June 1960 issue of *Esquire,* reprinted by permission of the Estate of John Steinbeck; copyright © John Steinbeck, 1960. Selections from *Travels in Two Democracies* by Edmund Wilson reprinted by permission of Farrar, Straus and Giroux, Inc.; copyright 1936 by Edmund Wilson; copyright renewed © Edmund Wilson, 1964. Selections from the play *Waiting for Lefty* by Clifford Odets reprinted by permission of Brandt and Brandt Literary Agency; copyright 1935 by Clifford Odets; copyright renewed © Clifford Odets, 1962. Selections from "In a Coffee Pot" from *The Big Time* by Alfred Hayes, published by Howell, Soskin Publishing Company, used by permission; copyright 1944 by Alfred Hayes.

Illustration on title page courtesy Radio City Music Hall Entertainment Center

For Robert Penn Warren

# Contents

# A Foreword

This is the story of the early depression years as one man lived out and observed them. The book was started a long time ago and it changed in the writing. At first I had planned to make it a sequel to *Exile's Return*, which had recounted the adventures in literature, in Montparnasse, and in Manhattan of the World War I generation. That book had a great deal to say about young writers of my acquaintance and the ideas they discussed or brooded over, or wordlessly accepted as guides to conduct. It had ended with the year 1930, which seemed to me a watershed between two ages. Now I was continuing the story into a more turbulent era, one that demanded—or so it seemed to me—a different choice of topics. As I slowly worked ahead on the manuscript, sometimes setting it aside for long periods, I found that public events were intruding into the narrative—and why not, considering that they had intruded day by day into our private lives? That was a characteristic of the 1930s.

"There has never been a period," I wrote years ago, "when literary events followed so close on the flying coattails of social events. In ordinary times it takes a man of long memory to recognize that such and such a book may have been inspired by such and such a political struggle, now generally forgotten. . . . But during the 1930s, the time between event and expression was so short that no one could miss their connection—and least of all the author." Many writers had the feeling (I more than some others) that we were living in history. Perhaps the fact was that we were living much of our lives in the daily and weekly press, which we followed with strained attention. This was especially true after the winter of 1933, when American banks were closing in the same month that Hitler became chancellor. Two years later Clifford Odets, to mention one writer, read a report from Hitler's Germany printed in *The New Masses*. He was so stirred by it that immediately, in one night, he wrote a short play, *Till the Day I Die*. It was hortatory and simplified, as might have been expected, but during 1935 it was applauded in more than thirty American cities. To make a theater evening, it was almost always combined with a better short play by Odets, *Waiting for Lefty*, that one inspired by what he had read about the New York taxi drivers' strike of 1934.

Odets was quicker than others in his response to printed reports, but all of us read them and, with what we saw in the streets, they created a mood of anger and apprehension. Great changes would surely take place; they *must* take place, and many of us felt—most of us felt at one time or another—that it was our duty as writers to take part in them, at least by coming forward to bear witness. I say "we" and "us" while conscious of their being treacherous pronouns; any reader is entitled to ask, "Who is *we*?" The question had been fairly simple to answer in *Exile's Return*, where the first person plural usually referred to those of my own age group with literary ambitions—by no means all of them, but many. After 1930 most of my coevals were going their separate ways, and they also had younger rivals in the writing community, which by then was more than usually rife and riddled with dissensions. There were still general statements to be made about the climate of opinion as it changed for all of us, but plainly the author of this new book would have to be more careful with his "we's," replacing many of them with a straightforward "I"—or even with "they," when he was thinking about the larger community of puzzled Americans. He would have to be more objective—and more subjective too, out of a feeling that one man is always representative when he gives honest testimony about what he has felt and observed. Scholars working from the record can be more dispassionate, but also, not having taken part in events, they can go subtly wrong.

And that author, that observer who is trying to be candid about himself: what sort of person was he in 1930? If one looks back at him he seems less typical, even of his own age group, than he once fancied himself to be. He was still a country boy after spending most of his life in cities; he had a farmer's blunt hands. "Look at the hands if you get a chance," that man of elegant letters, John Peale Bishop, wrote to his Princeton friend Edmund Wilson. "The plowboy of the western world who has been to Paris." The plowboy admitted that he was awkward, credulous, either rash or exuberant at moments, and usually persistent (or would you call it stubborn?). He never forgot that he came of people without pretensions, not quite members of the respectable middle class. He was slow of speech and had a farmer's large silences, though he was not slow-witted; people were fooled sometimes. He mentally revised his words, often until the moment had passed to utter them. Perhaps one might call him a wordsmith essentially, working at his forge and anvil, devoted to the craft of hammering his thoughts into what he hoped would be lasting shapes.

As compared with many of his colleagues he had few worldly ambitions; that is, he didn't want to be rich or famous too soon, or occupy a place of influence, or be a leader; he simply wanted to write better than others. A second ambition was to survive as a free man, an independent observer, though he was also loyal to friends and institutions (sometimes too loyal, it seems in retrospect). As an observer he was especially curious about the behavior of people in groups: how they came together and how they tried to win each other's approval; "That's the way things work," he said to himself. He also said that the behavior of individuals could often be explained by the image that each of them had formed of his future place in the community: know a man by his daydreams.

That was the author as he saw himself in the early depression years. As I look back at him among his associates of those days, it seems to me that many of these were possessed, and all were affected in some fashion, by a daydream of revolutionary brotherhood. American society, and business society over the world, and the trade of writing had all been stumbling downhill since the Wall Street crash, and might soon be plunged into the abyss. But there was hope as well, the apocalyptic hope that a City of Man would rise on the other side of disaster. By surrendering their middle-class identities, by joining the workers in an idealized army, writers might help to overthrow "the system" and might go marching with comrades, shoulder to shoulder, out of injustice and illogic into the golden mountains. That was the dream in an exalted form; I remember reading it in the shining eyes of younger people. As I worked ahead on the manuscript, the daydream and its temporary power became a central theme of the story.

Sherman, Connecticut,
July 1979

*There is a great destiny which comes in with this as with every age, which is colossal in its traits, terrible in its strength, which cannot be tamed, or criticised, or subdued. It is shared by every man and woman of the time, for it is by it they live. As a vast, solid phalanx the generation comes on, they have the same features, and their pattern is new in the world. All wear the same expression, but it is that which they do not detect in each other. It is this one life which ponders in the philosophers, which drudges in the laborers, which basks in the poets, which dilates in the love of the women. . . . The strong persons look at themselves as facts, in which the involuntary part is so much as to fill all their wonder, and leave them no countenance to say anything of what is so trivial as their private thinking and doing. I can well speak of myself as a figure in a panorama so absorbing.*

*Journals of Ralph Waldo Emerson,* 1841


*One generation abandons the enterprises of another like stranded vessels.*

Thoreau

# THE
# DREAM
## OF THE
# GOLDEN
# MOUNTAINS

# 1.
# The Old House
# in Chelsea

It happened that I had a better-than-usual post from which to observe the changing moods and intellectual crosscurrents of the depression years. In the fall of 1929, three weeks before the Wall Street crash, I went to work for *The New Republic*, which had been appearing since 1914 as "a weekly journal of opinion." Although the journal was in one sense unaffected by the depression, living as it did on a subsidy that was not withdrawn, it was in other ways profoundly shaken. Its editors were forced to question and revise their own opinions. Its readers, including many new ones, were articulate as well as being worried, and their ideas passed in a stream across our desks.

In those days the *New Republic* office was an old brownstone house on a side street in Chelsea, between the Ninth Avenue Elevated and the docks. It was actually a row of three old houses, but we seldom entered one of them, which was occupied by the business department, and never entered the third, which was divided into flats except for a double roomful of filing cabinets. Next door to it was the House of the Good Shepherd, where some of the young women arrested for prostitution were kept under religious supervision until their trials. We could see

them being taken down the street by plainclothesmen, and sometimes one of them made a dash for freedom. Across from us was
the General Theological Seminary, a group of low red-brick
buildings around a court. They needed cleaning and painting, as
did most of the houses that faced them. The general effect was
shabby-genteel, like that of a side street in Dublin.

Inside the *New Republic* house, the atmosphere was of a
home where one family had been living for a long time, while the
carpets went threadbare without being replaced and the furniture, originally a mixture of heirlooms with practical objects
picked up in a secondhand shop, acquired a uniform look of
age and daily use. The reception room was a parlor furnished
with moth-eaten upholstered chairs and had a big steel engrav-
ing of Lincoln's cabinet over the fireplace. The dining room had
an enormous round table surmounted with a lazy susan. There we
gathered for luncheon two or three times a week and sometimes
for a rather stuffy dinner, when changes in policy were to be
discussed. Although the luncheons were less solemn than they
had been in the days of Herbert Croly, the founding editor,
strangers were likely to be intimidated. A painter's wife, invited
for the first time, was so nervous that she kept rubbing her
hands on her skirt; then she looked down and discovered that her
thighs were bare. That day she didn't enjoy the good French
cooking. Lucie the cook, who was actually North Italian, lived
in the basement with her husband, Etienne the butler. Upstairs
each of three editors had a big room to himself, the two assistant
editors shared another, and the secretaries had cubbyholes that
used to be hall bedrooms. There was also a backyard where we
played deck tennis late on Wednesday afternoons, like a big suburban family.

The moral atmosphere, too, was that of a family rather than
of a business office. There were family jokes and mild family
quarrels and the sound of laughter in the hallways, sometimes
mingled with the smell of cooking. Bruce Bliven, the managing
editor, would emerge from his front room like an angry paterfa-

milias to ask whether people wouldn't please not talk so loud. To anyone familiar with New York business life, the comparative absence of office politics was refreshing and extraordinary. Everyone felt sure of his job and hardly anyone was angling for a better one. It sounds tremendously old-fashioned and inefficient, as compared with some bright new office full of business machines, where the desks are in straight rows, and everyone has to look hurried on pain of being fired. But here everyone knew what had to be done, and did it without waste motions; and later when we compared our costs with those of two other magazines supposedly run on the principles of scientific management, we were surprised to find that the comparison was in our favor.

Meanwhile the work itself seemed to us more and more important as the depression grew deeper. This musty house on a side street, where the stairs creaked and the radiators pounded, was for a time curiously close to the center of what was happening in America.

People were hurt and bewildered and were trying to puzzle things out. When they listened to the men supposed to be charged with maintaining the financial welfare of the country— the business leaders, the bankers, the government administrators —they did not find answers to the questions they were asking. When they turned to the daily press, they hardly even found the questions: "But why?" and "How much longer?" and "What should be done?" In those years the press was afflicted with a lofty sense of its own responsibilities. Its function of telling people what happened was being subordinated to the apparently greater function of saving the nation's business. Having adopted the official doctrine that business was fundamentally sound and that the only trouble was lack of confidence, most of the newspapers were trying to make their readers confident again and abolish the depression by printing very little news about it.

That was especially true in the big and small industrial cities. There any sign of better times ahead was spotted on the front page, if it was only the hiring of a few extra clerks for Christmas or a temporary rise in common stocks. But the closing of a bank, the boarding up of a factory, the failure of a department store, the loss of homes by foreclosed mortgages, all the news that meant the life or death of a community was reported on the inside pages, and sometimes it wasn't reported at all. Nor did movies and radio take over a function that was being inadequately performed by newspapers. In those early years of the depression, Hollywood was avoiding "controversial topics," including all those that directly concerned its audience, and the radio was chiefly devoted to name bands, advertising, and Amos 'n' Andy. People were turning more and more to books, not only for interpretation but for actual news of what was happening to the country. They were also turning to magazines like *The New Republic*, which carried so little advertising that they were in a sense outside the American business system.

Week after week more mail was being delivered to the old house in Chelsea. The correspondents of former years had been mostly teachers, writers, and professional liberals, but the letters we now received came from all sorts of people all over the nation. One day it would be a Chicago brakeman out of work for two years, sitting down in a public library to write his life history on a five-cent school pad and to ask us what was going to happen to millions like himself. Another day it would be a morally bewildered small businessman who had just been forced to discharge half his working force; he begged us not to print his name. A bank clerk would tell us how he happened to be watching a demonstration of the unemployed when the police charged in with nightsticks. His skull was fractured—and worse than that, his bank had closed three weeks later and he was now unemployed himself. A Missouri housewife would write us by the kerosene lamp in her kitchen, after the children had each been given a bowl of mush without milk—for the cow was dry—and sent off to bed; in six pages she told the whole story of a marginal farm. Some of the letters developed into articles we could print. In ordinary times a magazine gets almost all its material from persons known to the editors, at least by name, but there was no telling in those days who would next be sending us a fresh idea or a revealing incident.

More and more people were coming to see us, in spite of our inconvenient location. I seem to remember dozens of correspondents back from Russia, either inspired by the Five Year Plan or else disturbed by the omnipresence of the political police and the signs of hunger. "In the provinces people are dying by thousands," one of them said. His wife took another helping of Lucie's *boeuf bourguignon.* "Yes, and in Moscow," she added, "they gave us nothing but just chicken, chicken, chicken." At another luncheon we had among our guests the former presidents of two Latin American republics and the foreign secretary of another; all three were liberals who had been forced out of office by military revolts. On still another day it was a German professor, among the first of the intellectual refugees, who had left Berlin in 1931 because he was tired of hearing crowds in the streets singing "Grease the Guillotine"; he could see nothing but violence ahead, no matter which side won. There were occasions when we listened to Hungarian democrats, Italian Socialists, Chinese Communists, Arab and Indian nationalists, a whole assortment of rebels who had risked their lives before going into exile; apparently most of the world beyond our borders was given over to civil war, and our own country was no longer at peace. People now came to see us on their return from Pennsylvania mining towns or the Imperial Valley or the textile mills of the South. The stories they told were of incredible poverty leading to strikes and demonstrations that were suppressed by clubbing, flogging, kidnapping, sometimes lynching—in other words, by the criminal violence of the "better people" and the lawlessness of the law. We listened and took notes for editorials, wishing there were something more we could do.

Together with these correspondents home from the battlefronts, we found ourselves entertaining more than our share of cranks and crazy people. One of the less agreeable tasks assigned to a junior editor was that of listening to a man who suffered from homicidal mania. His powerful enemies had tracked him to the door, he said, but we could save him by printing his story, as we would certainly do unless—he looked hard at everything in the room—we too were part of the conspiracy. The junior editor was afraid to reach for the telephone. There was nothing to do but keep watching his hands until he had talked himself out and was ready to say good-bye. The cranks were much more common, especially in those days when everyone was seeking or propounding a cure for the depression. Some of the worst began by talking sensibly and only betrayed themselves by the glint in their eyes when they told us how the world could be saved by just a slight change in the paper currency. Others untied a roll of soiled manuscript and urgently requested us to read it in their presence. One woman carried a big sealed envelope in which she said was a series of articles that would shake the nation. She wouldn't let us open the envelope unless we accepted and paid for its entire contents in advance. "I know you editors," she said. "You'd steal my ideas and print them under a different name. You'd steal the pennies from a dead man's eyes."

We had more persuasive visitors, also with schemes for remaking America. Ralph Borsodi appeared with his project for resettling millions of families on five-acre subsistence homesteads. He explained to us how they could install labor-saving machinery and live in comfort on what they produced themselves, as he and Mrs. Borsodi had been doing for years. The difficulty with the project was that it required capital to start with, a part-time office job, and a wife like Mrs. Borsodi in every household. Another day Howard Scott, soon to be famous for a time as the high priest of Technocracy, crossed his long legs and drawled out his dream of a society ruled by engineers, where nobody would have to work more than two or three hours a day and everybody would be rich in terms of products to be bought with paper money based on units of energy: ergs and joules.

A gray-haired man named Edgar Chambless unrolled a blue-print of what he called Roadtown, extending from New York to Los Angeles. It would have a tunnel for rapid transit, another tunnel for automobiles, and a landscaped mall with apartment houses that would accommodate the entire population of the country. The plan was immensely detailed, practical from an engineering standpoint, and I thought it was a diagram of Hell rolled out in a shiny ribbon. But we listened to all our visitors if we had the time: stamped-scrip enthusiasts, self-help and barter enthusiasts, silver enthusiasts, single taxers, Townsendites, Social Crediters, Technocrats, primitive Christians, primitive communists, and more and more disciples of Marx and Lenin. Perhaps there was part of the truth in what each of them had to say. The tangled moods and emotions of those years, the bewilderment, the sense of personal guilt, the religious exaltation centered on economic doctrines, and the despair mingled with dreams of a better world that was soon and surely to be achieved: all these swept in through the door of the old house in Chelsea.

# 2.
# The American Jitters

The New Republic had its own somewhat less utopian plans for reshaping the nation; in fact it had a variety of plans, since its editors did not always agree with one another. Any issue of the paper, in those early depression years, was likely to be a chorus of discordant voices.

If Herbert Croly had been there, the voices would have been more in harmony. Croly had founded the paper in 1914, with money provided by Willard Straight, an idealistic young Morgan partner who had been impressed by Croly's book, *The Promise of American Life* (1909). After Straight died, the subsidy had been continued by his widow Dorothy, who had a much larger fortune of her own, part of the Whitney estate, and who later married an Englishman, Leonard Elmhirst. In theory the paper had always been run by a council of editors, a sort of soviet, but in practice all the editors but one were like the members of a military staff, with Croly as the commanding general; he listened attentively to their opinions, then chose his own policy. He was a short man with gray hair who wore conservative gray clothes (with just a glimpse of flamboyant socks) and kept retreating into what I pictured as gray silences; he was shy and at times inarticulate, but he had a gift for establishing communication with others, especially younger journalists, on a level below that of the spoken word. He commanded the editorial board not so much by his friendship with Dorothy and Leonard Elmhirst, who provided the money, as by simple force of intellect and depth of conviction. If any of the others disagreed with him fundamentally, they left the paper—though their names might still be carried on the masthead, as Robert Morss Lovett's name was carried for a dozen years after Croly urged him out of the office in 1928.

Croly's policy for the paper had changed more than once. At first *The New Republic* had been loosely allied with Theodore Roosevelt; then during the Great War it had supported Wilson (and had been attentively read on the false assumption that it spoke for the administration). The Treaty of Versailles, with the staggering reparations imposed on the vanquished, had been a moral crisis for Croly. He walked the floor for three nights before deciding that, as a betrayal by Wilson of his own ideals, the treaty should not be ratified. During the years that followed, Croly became more and more disillusioned with politics. He was considering the notion of transforming *The New Republic* into a journal of literature, the arts, and moral philosophy, but in the fall of 1928—shortly after Bob Lovett's departure—he was crippled by a stroke and the notion had to be abandoned. It seemed to me when I came on the paper the following year that it had no guiding policy beyond what Croly suggested in letters or in conversations with one or two editors summoned to his apartment. Then he went to California, where he died in May 1930, and his junior colleagues were left to hammer out a policy for themselves.

It was the sort of opportunity that journalists dream of having. The colleagues now had their own paper, a weekly of thirty-two pages concerned with whatever they chose to regard as the crucial issues of the day. The issues were exciting and seemed unprecedented, as the national economy bumped and jolted its way downhill. There was a distinguished body of contributing editors, often generous with advice, and the paper had a faithful body of readers in spite of Croly's disregard for the public. One year, not listening to everybody's warning, he had serialized a long messianic book by Waldo Frank, *The Rediscovery of America*, that killed off subscribers like flies, but the serial went on and so did the paper.

In 1929 it had a paid circulation of probably no more than twelve thousand; the exact figure was a secret of the business office. Advertisers were tolerated, but there was no attempt to please them. The Elmhirsts had promised to continue paying the deficits, and they were ideal patrons, eager to hear about everything that happened, inviting the editors to their camp in the Adirondacks every summer for a weekend discussion of policies, but not attempting to guide the discussion and never dictating what should be printed. The editors were free to say anything, at least in theory, though it was understood that what they said in those critical times should be clear and persuasive. Nothing in print would influence Mr. Hoover's administration—that much had become certain—but changes must come in spite of him, and the dream was that *The New Republic* might have its share in projecting the future.

Meanwhile the colleagues each pictured a different future and argued politely with one another. Bruce Bliven was the managing editor, as he had been under Croly; he presided at editorial meetings and put the paper together each Thursday from the barrel, as we called it, of accepted articles. The barrel was always full, and an article accepted against his will was likely to stay at the bottom until it became too moldy to use; but otherwise he did not impose his opinions on the other editors. Bruce was the only professional newspaperman on the staff—he had been managing editor of *The New York Globe* before it went under—and he was chiefly interested in news stories and technological developments. I suspected that his dream was of a universally prosperous world in which everybody would have a home and every home would be full of ingenious gadgets, turned in for new models each year.

George Soule was the staff economist, though he had started in life as a poet. Under his calm Connecticut Yankee look, he was then keeping a good deal of excitement under control. It seemed to him that the financial disasters of those years were forcing America closer to his dream of a planned society in which production would be exactly balanced by consumption and nobody would be unemployed. Week after week he put forward suggestions for economic measures that would later, in many cases, become part of the New Deal. I sometimes stood waiting for him to finish a last-minute editorial while I envied his gift for writing without apparent effort. The words flowed from the tip of his pencil to a pad of legal-size paper at an unhurried and absolutely even rate, with no pauses or erasures, and his manuscripts went to the printer without being typed. The prose was simple, logical, and clear, but somewhat lacking in heat, like steam generated in a vacuum.

Stark Young, the drama editor, was less excited by national bankruptcy than by the American visit of performers from the Peking Opera Company, with their star the handsome Mei-lan Fang. The literary editor, Edmund Wilson, was more shaken than others by the crisis. He began reading history and economics instead of symbolist poetry, and his second wife, a friendly woman without strong convictions, complained that he used to wake her in the middle of the night to discuss the political situation. "You see, it's this way," he would tell her as he paced up and down the bedroom. In the fall of 1930 he announced that he was going to travel over the country and send back a series of articles. Wilson, then thirty-five years old, had always been a reader first (and the best in America), then a writer inspired by Dean Gauss of Princeton with the lifelong ambition of producing "something in which," as Wilson says in his essay on Gauss, "every word, every cadence, every detail, should perform a definite function in producing an intense effect," and only in the third place a man in the world of living creatures. Inclined to be shy then brusque with strangers; used to getting his information from print rather than people, so that he often paged through a book while asking questions to which one suspected that he wouldn't hear the answers (but write him a letter and he could read it between the lines); an innocent in politics because he never bothered to understand how people act in groups, he seemed the last person, at the time, whom a sensible magazine would have chosen as its roving reporter. Yet partly because of that same innocence, his reports had a freshness of detail and a vigor of interpretation that nobody else could have achieved. They were later published as a book, *The American Jitters* (1932), and they are still the most vivid picture of this country in the second year of the depression.

I hadn't taken much part in discussions of policy, and at first I wasn't invited to the editorial meetings that followed a staff luncheon every Tuesday. Bruce Bliven had hired me chiefly as a copyeditor and proofreader, two fields in which I had some experience; I was replacing T. S. Matthews, who had lately resigned. Just then the paper badly needed someone with a passion for getting words right. It had been printing some abominably written articles among the competent or brilliant ones, and it sometimes appeared with typographical errors like those in the bulldog edition of *The New York Times*. One of my first assignments was editing a new series of articles by John Dewey, a philosopher I had admired from a distance; now I was appalled by reading his prose in the raw. Timidly at first, then recklessly, I found myself untangling his sentences and changing his words to others that were closer to what I rather guessed he intended to say. He saw proof of the articles, which he returned without comments, almost without corrections, and all my changes went into the text of his book *Individualism, Old and New* (1930). When I next saw Tom Matthews, who had joined the staff of *Time*, I told him about Dewey's articles. "You're not the first," he said. "Every junior editor of *The New Republic* has to cut his teeth on John Dewey. That's one of the reasons I left the paper."

While the editors were meeting on Tuesday afternoon, I went to the Steinberg Press to put each issue to bed. I had an assistant, Martha Gellhorn, a Bryn Mawr girl with literary ambitions and a lot of yellow hair. Years later, after being divorced from Ernest Hemingway, she married Tom Matthews as a delayed sequel to those *New Republic* days. I met her at a bad time, for she had announced that she too was leaving the paper in a few weeks, and meanwhile she was exhibiting a fine disdain for punctuation, spelling, and the whole mechanics of printing editorials about the economic crisis. "If there's too much copy," she told me, "I just kill a few paragraphs of George Soule's leader. He never misses them." It must have been on my third weekly visit to the printer's that I sent her home early, then had the forms unlocked and reread the issue from beginning to end, holding the presses until late at night while I made corrections on every page.

With Martha leaving, another assistant had to be found, and I remembered a friend of friends, Betty Huling, who had impressed me with her knowledge of books and her explosive laughter. She had never worked for a magazine, but my theory was that anyone who cared about the language could learn to read copy and proof in a few hours. I went to see her one Saturday afternoon with a lecture prepared and half a dozen corrected galleys to serve as a textbook. Either my theory was correct or Betty was an exceptionally good student. She started to work on Monday, and the next issue of *The New Republic* came out, for a miracle, with no typographical errors.

Soon Betty took over the work at the press, and I was asked to attend the editorial meetings, though at first without having much to say. I was the youngest editor, after all, and like most writers of my own generation I had rather prided myself on being ignorant of economics and contemptuous of politicians. My attitude resembled Martha Gellhorn's, except that for me the contempt didn't extend to the text of an editorial; that had to be right, for the honor of the paper and of the written language. Writing was my field, and I was concerned with everything in it, from the comma before a nonrestrictive clause to the status of the literary profession and the right way of managing the climax of a novel. About writing problems I did speak up in meeting, besides discussing them in reviews and editorials, and my opinionatedness had one happy result for me. Edmund Wilson, even before he started on his travels, had been staying out of the office to finish his book on the Symbolist movement, *Axel's Castle* (1931), which we were publishing by installments, and I was regarded as the logical person to take over his desk upstairs in the book department.

There, in a big room under the roof, with its windows looking over a double rank of backyards, I could lead a sheltered life in the midst of the hurricane, almost as if I had been given a post in the General Theological Seminary across the street. For perquisites there were more books than I could read, so many more that they became a burden, there was Lucie's good cooking, and there was a salary of $100 a week, comfortable for those years when food was cheap and rents were falling; even bootleg liquor had come down in price, and one could buy Jersey applejack in five-gallon casks at the new rate of four dollars a gallon (paying extra for the cask). For excitement there were the literary battles of the time: first over Irving Babbitt's New Humanism, then over the Southern Agrarians and their symposium, *I'll Take My Stand*, then over Michael Gold's polemic against Thornton Wilder (whom he called the "Prophet of the Genteel Christ"), and then over Sinclair Lewis's address in Stockholm; as the first American writer to win the Nobel Prize, in December 1930, he had made a furious attack on the American Academy of Arts and Letters.

The battles were good fun, and I charged into most of them like a halfback into a scrimmage, but I began to note that real blows were being exchanged by others. These were not college teams, eager to shake hands after the game; the writers who quarreled were revealing themselves as the spokesmen for social interests in deadly combat. Thus, Irving Babbitt had announced for the New Humanists that "The remedy for the evils of competition is found in the moderation and magnanimity of the strong and successful, and not in any sickly sentimentalizing over the lot of the underdog." Babbitt was on the side of the rulers, whoever they might be, while most of his opponents pictured themselves as defending the underdog. The Southern Agrarians were fighting the last skirmish of a lost campaign against Northern industrialism. Mike Gold was proudly a Communist, and he attacked Wilder not so much for taking refuge in the past as for being the representative "of a small sophisticated class that has recently arisen in America—our genteel bourgeoisie." When Gold's article appeared in *The New Republic* and was answered by hundreds of letters from anguished subscribers, the class war was bursting forth in literature. But it had already appeared in many other departments of American life, as we kept hearing from our guests at luncheon and observing for ourselves when we walked in the streets past closed banks and boarded-up shops and lines of gray-faced men waiting for a hand-out. As the months passed I began to feel that there was no refuge from the storm, that the profession I loved was involved in the fate of everything else, and that everything, including literature, would have to be changed.

Meanwhile Edmund Wilson was sending back reports of his travels, and they impressed me probably more than anything else I read at the time. That was partly because they were *written*, not hammered out to meet a deadline, and partly because Wilson and I had been trained to see much of the world through the same sort of glasses. When he described a political rally, for example, I too might have been sitting on a folding wooden chair while listening over loudspeakers to Dwight Morrow, then Republican candidate for senator from New Jersey, and I was ready to share Wilson's conclusions that "the giant ventriloquial voice which emanates from the nice little man is merely the voice of American capitalism."

After the rally in Newark, Wilson made a visit to Washington, where he was favorably impressed by the Communists summoned to testify before a House committee. Back in New York, he witnessed a bloody riot in City Hall Park, where the police broke up the first large Communist-led demonstration of the unemployed. He made a tour of the Ford plant at River Rouge and visited a Red Cross relief station in the drought-stricken hills of Kentucky. He attended the dedication of the Empire State Building, last memorial of the boom years; at first it was almost as empty of living tenants as a mausoleum. Then he started south and west: to the gun-ruled mining camps of West Virginia; to Scottsboro, Alabama, where eight young Negroes had been sentenced to death for a crime that was committed by others, if it was committed at all; to a dude ranch in New Mexico and an Indian corn dance; to Hollywood, which he described in Joycean prose, and finally to San Diego, the southwesternmost city, where wanderers stopped because they could go no farther.

In writing his reports, Wilson utilized the same methods that he had developed in writing criticism. That is, he began each of them by describing a scene and a situation, much as if he were expounding the subject matter of a book little known to his readers; then he told about the events he witnessed and the comments he heard, as if he were summarizing a plot and suggesting its moral atmosphere; then finally he made his critical comments, which were brief and sometimes expressed by his choice of concrete details. His report on Dwight Morrow was like a short book review; his section on the Ford plant was a formal essay based on parallels and contrasts: first an account of how old cars were stripped down, squashed in a press like beetles, and fed into an open-hearth furnace to make new cars; then various stories to illustrate how Ford's working force was treated in almost the same fashion; then by contrast a biographical sketch of Henry Ford himself, the mechanical genius at sea in a new age. Wilson's emphasis, like that of Sainte-Beuve and many other good critics, was on the human element. "The place to study the present crisis and its causes and probable consequences," he said, "is not in the charts of the compilers of statistics, but in one's self and the people one sees."

What Wilson conveyed to his readers, after making those human studies, was chiefly a sense of widespread despair and bewilderment. He was trying to speak for millions, including the middle classes as well as the poor, whose lives were not reflected in the newspapers. "It seems to me," he said in "An Appeal to Progressives," an article written at the same time as the travel pieces, but not reprinted in *The American Jitters*, "that at the present time the optimism of the Americans is flagging, that the morale of our society is weak . . . a dreadful apathy, unsureness and discouragement seem to have fallen upon our life. It is as if people were afraid to go on with what they have been doing or as if they no longer had any real heart for it." This sense of something ending was confirmed in a report (this one reprinted) that he called "The Jumping-off Place"; it dealt with San Diego, which he presented not only as the southwestern limit of American migration but also as the city with the highest suicide rate. Here, he said after reading the coroner's reports,

> . . . you seem to see the last blind futile effervescence of the great burst of the American adventure. Here this people, so long told to "go West" to escape from poverty, ill health, maladjustment, industrialism and oppression, discover that, having come West, their problems and diseases still remain and there is no further to go. . . . Ill, retired or down on their luck, they stuff up the cracks of their doors in the little boarding houses that take in invalids, and turn on the gas; they go into their back sheds or into back kitchens and swallow Lysol or eat ant-paste; they drive their cars into dark alleys and shoot themselves in the back seat; they hang themselves in hotel bedrooms, take overdoses of sulphonal or barbital, stab themselves

with carving-knives on the municipal golf course; or they throw themselves into the placid blue bay, where the gray battleships and cruisers of the government guard the limits of their enormous nation. . . .

One element in the picture that Wilson's travel reports and his subsequent book failed to emphasize was the hopefulness and eagerness for change that had begun to appear in the midst of general discouragement. But this element had already been supplied in "An Appeal to Progressives," the article he wrote midway in his travels to embody his tentative conclusions. It was printed in *The New Republic* of January 14, 1931, and it continued to be discussed during the whole decade.

The article began by saying that the liberalism which the magazine had represented in the past was derived primarily from Herbert Croly's book *The Promise of American Life*. Croly had put forward a new democratic goal, which he pictured as a return to the strong centralized government advocated by Alexander Hamilton, but administered as Jefferson would have liked it to be administered, in the interest not of a propertied class but of the people as a whole. He thought that such a return, though it would require a reorganization as drastic as that produced by the Civil War, might now be accomplished without violence, by an orderly series of reforms. "He expressly repudiated the ideal of an international working-class movement to fight international capitalism. It was still possible," Wilson said, "for him to feel that America constituted an ideal in itself—something isolated, unique and almost mystic. And to the extent that he believed in America, he thus believed not only in nationalism but in capitalism. He thought that the American spirit would be strong enough to compel American capitalism to restrain and reform itself."

Wilson went on to explain that Croly had lost some of this faith as the years passed and had become increasingly skeptical and indifferent about politics. At present, in the midst of the worst depression in our history, it seemed impossible "for people of Croly's general aims and convictions"—including Wilson himself—"to continue to believe in the salvation of our society by the gradual and natural approximation to socialism which he himself called progressivism, but which has generally come to be known as liberalism. . . . May we not well fear that what this year has broken down is not simply the machinery of representative government, but the capitalist system itself?—and that, even with the best will in the world, it may be impossible for capitalism to guarantee not merely social justice but even security and order?"

American liberals and progressives—again including Wilson—had all been betting on capitalism. "And now," he said, "in the abyss of starvation and bankruptcy into which the country has fallen, with no sign of any political leadership which will be able to pull us out, our liberalism seems to have little to offer beyond a discreet recommendation of public ownership of water power and certain other public utilities, a cordial feeling that labor ought to organize in a non-social revolutionary way and a protest, invariably ineffective, against a few of the more obviously atrocious of the jailings, beatings-up and murders with which the industrialists have been trying to keep the working class docile."

At this point, however, the note of hopefulness began to sound and swell. "It may be that the whole money-making and spending psychology has definitely played itself out," Wilson said, "and that Americans would be willing now for the first time to put their idealism and their genius for organization behind a radical social experiment. . . . After all, the Communist project has almost all the qualities that Americans glorify—the extreme of efficiency and economy combined with the ideal of a herculean feat to be accomplished by common action in an atmosphere of enthusiastic boosting—like a Liberty Loan drive—the idea of putting over something big in five years." Then Wilson grandly put forward his own slogan. "I believe," he said, "that if the American radicals and progressives who repudiate the Marxian dogma and the strategy of the Communist Party hope to accomplish anything valuable, they must take communism away from the Communists, and take it without ambiguities or reservations."

In the following issue of *The New Republic* George Soule published an answer to Wilson. He agreed that there was a new psychological atmosphere in the country which offered a possibility of drastic changes. He did not believe, however, that the capitalist system was on the point of collapse. The duty of the progressives, he said, was to stimulate the process of social learning, and "what is required on their part is not a complete break with their previous activity, but more vigorous steps toward its fulfillment." In that respect he proved to be a good prophet, since many of those steps would be taken by the Roosevelt administration, which moved consciously toward Croly's idea of a centralized and Hamiltonian democracy.

Other writers entered the discussion, which continued through the spring, gradually losing its hard outlines in a haze of conflicting moral exhortations. But Wilson's challenge to progressives was not forgotten: "They must take communism away from the Communists." What would that mean in practice, people were asking, and who would do all the dull but essential work that Communists seemed eager to perform? Would it be any easier to take communism away from them than to take Roman Catholicism away from Rome? In that second year of the depression, hundreds or thousands of intellectuals decided that a more effective step would be to cooperate with the Communists, accepting their leadership, or even to become Communists themselves.

# 3.
## Almost Nobody
## Starved

Among all the curious features of the 1930s, those mass conversions to communism seem hardest for a new generation to understand. Why did so many Americans of more than average intelligence accept a body of doctrine that predicted (rather than preached) the violent overthrow of American institutions and looked forward to a dictatorship of the proletariat? There were not so many converts as the Communists then implied in their reports to Moscow, which were like inflated sales reports from the road—"Grand prospects for business here in Oshkosh"—nor were there so many as the House Committee on Un-American Activities later claimed when submitting body counts like those of field commanders in Vietnam, but still there was a considerable number. Included in the number were hundreds of writers, mostly beginners, but with a sprinkling of older persons successful in their profession. That suggests another question: Why did they support a movement that cost them much financially and would cost them more, as they gradually discovered, in terms of their literary freedom?

We know why they left the movement, since that story has been told at length in dozens of books, American and European

—most effectively, I think, in a symposium edited by Richard Crossman, *The God That Failed* (1950). But why did Americans join the movement in the beginning? The answers that writers make to that question are usually briefer, as if the experience had become too painful to be remembered. "It was the depression," many of them say before dismissing the subject. For others, converted in the following years, it was the fight against Hitler, or against racial prejudice, or it was the civil war in Spain; the Communists always had good issues. In most of these they were widely supported by liberal opinion, but they also had the advantage of proposing to do something about the issues, instead of just being indignant like the liberals. "We must . . ." the liberals often said, meaning "We should, but probably we shan't." "We will," said the Communists, appealing to one's idealism as each new crisis arose by offering an opportunity for hard work and self-sacrifice. The depression, however, was truly their best American issue and the one that produced the greatest number of converts.

But merely to say "It was the depression" is not very illuminating in a new age. To men and women of a younger generation, brought up in the longest period of continued prosperity this country had ever enjoyed, the depression is hardly more than a topic hurried over in their school histories. Even the gray-haired survivors find it hard to remember that there was a time in this century when millions of American families, with their savings exhausted, were living not far from the edge of starvation. It was the time when relief was said to be a local problem, for which the national government could and should accept no responsibility, even when the localities ran out of money. Although New York was one of the more fortunate cities during the winter of 1931–32, whole families there were receiving a weekly average of $2.39 for relief; that was for food, rent, clothing, everything. In Toledo that same winter, the municipal commissary could allow only 2.14 cents per meal per person. Not every needy person was certified for such relief as could be doled out, and one got used to seeing older men and women scrounging in garbage cans for their next meal. Already there had been talk of institutionalizing the garbage can, so that the unemployed could be fed without increasing taxes. That is a fact of which I was reminded by reading *The Crisis of the Old Order* (1957), by Arthur M. Schlesinger, Jr., a book that contains the best account of those early depression years. Schlesinger says:

> Some devised even more unusual schemes to supplement local relief. Thus John B. Nichlos of the Oklahoma Gas Utilities Company wrote his friend Patrick J. Hurley, the Secretary of War, about an idea that he was trying out in Chickasha, Oklahoma. By the Nichlos plan, restaurants were asked to dump food left on plates into five-gallon containers; the unemployed could then qualify for these scraps by chopping wood donated by farmers. "We expect a little trouble now and then from those who are not worthy of the support of the citizens," wrote Nichlos philosophically, "but we must contend with such cases in order to take care of those who are worthy." Hurley was sufficiently impressed by the plan of feeding garbage to the jobless that he personally urged it on Colonel Woods.

That was during the winter of 1930–31, when Colonel Arthur Woods was directing the President's Committee for Employment. Woods was an experienced relief administrator, and he did not accept Hurley's recommendation; instead he went to the president with a public-works program for increased employment in such new fields as slum clearance, low-cost housing, and rural electrification. Mr. Hoover rejected the program, and Woods resigned in the spring of 1931, leaving the federal government with the clean record—or so it seemed to us then—of having done nothing to solve the problems of the unemployed.

It is no wonder that Americans prefer to forget those fantastic times. Mr. Hoover would not even authorize an accurate census of the unemployed, perhaps out of apprehension that it would furnish new arguments for direct government aid. The result was that various private agencies made their own estimates; usually these ran to somewhere in the neighborhood of five million unemployed in the spring of 1930, ten million in 1931, and fifteen million at the end of 1932, or roughly one-third of the nation's working force. All but one-fifth of the steel furnaces had banked their fires, and the building industry had come to an almost complete halt. Farmers had work as always, but no money to buy clothes or machinery; the total farm income fell to less than one-third of what it had been in 1929. Cotton was five or six cents a pound, as against thirty cents in good years, and wheat was selling on the Chicago Board of Trade for less than fifty cents a bushel. On Kansas farms it brought only twenty-five cents, making it cheaper to burn in the parlor stove than coal shipped in by rail.

Meanwhile it seemed to us that the government did nothing but issue statements designed to restore confidence among its hungry sheep by feeding them with wind. In reality the government had been taking other measures; the trouble was that they either came too late or else were misdirected and produced the wrong effects. One famous example of misdirected effort was the Smoot-Hawley Tariff of 1930. When Congress first discussed the bill, we had been told that its purpose was simply to rationalize the tariff system; many rates would be lowered and some would be raised, with the aim in both cases of giving equal protection to American industries. It soon transpired, however, that each industry wanted more protection than others, that they all had lobbies in Washington, and that Congress was giving them everything they asked for. The assumption of the legislators seemed to be that raising the tariff to the highest level in history would somehow lift us out of the depression.

Economists believed, on the contrary, that it would plunge us deeper into the depression. In May 1930 a statement on the tariff was issued by 1028 members of the American Economic Association. They included both liberals and conservatives on the faculties of all the big universities, and for once they agreed on a policy: Mr. Hoover should veto the tariff bill if it passed Congress. They said that it would reduce exports as well as imports. They said that European nations could not pay their war debts, or the interest on their loans from American bankers, or buy the goods produced by American farms and factories, unless we bought European goods in turn. Mr. Hoover, who was known to believe that Congress had gone too far, took their statement under consideration.

Early in June he received a delegation that had come to Washington on another errand; like Colonel Woods it was pleading for an immediate program of federal public works. Mr. Hoover listened impatiently, then told the delegates that public works were no longer needed. "Gentlemen," he said, "you have come sixty days too late. The depression is over." A few days later Congress passed the tariff bill, and Mr. Hoover announced on June 16 that he would sign it. The bill might have been better, he said in effect, but at least there was now a reformed tariff commission empowered to change rates when they proved inequitable. But Wall Street put no faith in the tariff commission. The news that Mr. Hoover was signing the bill produced what *The New York Times* called a "torrent of liquidation," affecting the whole market and leading to the broadest and steepest decline in values since November 1929. Within a few days after the new tariff went into effect, import trade had fallen to its lowest point since the Great War. Exports also declined, as Wall Street expected and the economists had prophesied; still more factories closed down; and the depression, instead of ending, went into a second and intensified phase.

That was not the last result of a mistimed and misdirected effort to bring back prosperity; Europe suffered from it too. For some years before 1930, German manufacturers had been thriving on loans from American bankers and sales to the American market. There were no more loans after the crash, and German factories closed down in great numbers. Then the new tariff raised a higher wall around the American market, with the result that still more German workers lost their jobs that summer. They looked for a saviour, and in the election of September 4, 1930, millions of desperate men voted for Hitler's party, which received eight times as many votes as in the last previous election, that of 1928.

The depression was spreading through Central Europe, and the banking systems of several countries threatened to collapse after the failure in May 1931 of the Creditanstalt in Vienna. In June of that year Mr. Hoover called for a moratorium on inter-governmental debts, most of which were owed to the United States; it was a generous measure, but it came too late to save one of the largest banks in Germany. When the Darmstädter und Nationalbank stopped payments on July 13, Chancellor Brüning was forced to declare a bank holiday, during which the Germans who were still employed received only a trickle of wages. Brüning was a gloomy and upright man, like Mr. Hoover, and he had been following the same policy of financial retrenchment, with even more disastrous results—that is, except for the Nazis. In the midst of a national catastrophe, Hitler declared in his party newspapers, "Never in my life have I been as well disposed and inwardly contented as in these days."

Brüning was partly to be thanked for that inner contentment and for having opened a path toward the seizure of power, but there seems to be no doubt that Hitler owed another debt—one cannot say how small or great—to the Smoot-Hawley Tariff. There is also no doubt that the economic disasters in Europe, for which this country was partly to blame, helped to spread confusion in the United States. Another such disaster was announced on September 20, 1931, when Great Britain went off the gold standard and all the European stock exchanges closed down to forestall a panic. In this country the depression thereupon entered a third phase. While the breadlines grew longer, Mr. Hoover was now trying to save the banks—more than a thousand of them went under during the last three months of the year—

the insurance companies, which were already menaced, and the whole system of currency and credit.

For comic relief, there was Mr. Hoover's tariff commission, on which he had placed such extravagant hopes. It had been working hard for more than a year to adjust inequities. Undisturbed by the financial crisis, it had investigated the relative cost of producing several articles here and abroad, it had held a series of hearings in Washington, and—as George Soule pointed out in *The New Republic*—it had succeeded in changing just eleven duties out of 3300 specified in the Smoot-Hawley Act. Three of the duties had been raised and eight had been lowered. One result of its unceasing labors was that the American consumer might now pay a somewhat lower price for "hats, bonnets and hoods of straw, chip, paper, grass, palm-leaf, willow, osier, rattan, real horsehair, cuba bark, ramie, or manila hemp, wholly or partly manufactured, *if sewed*," but not for unsewed hats of those materials, the duty on which was not changed.

I have to apologize for this digression into economic matters, grand or ridiculous, in what started out as a literary memoir. But I am trying to explain a state of mind among writers, and it was largely produced by events in the economic world. In those days almost everyone was trying to be an economist of sorts. Writers studied "conditions," as they called them, in various cities or industries and tried to publish their findings as pamphlets. They were hardly more affected in their thinking by the depression itself than they were by the futility of the measures adopted for ending it or for mitigating its worst effects. All those measures were limited in scope, and they all seemed to be drawn from very old textbooks that prescribed what the government should or shouldn't do in an economic crisis. Thus, it shouldn't pass laws that might throw the budget out of balance. It shouldn't help the unemployed, whether or not they were hungry, since letting them suffer like heroes was better in the end than destroying their self-reliance by giving them a dole. The depression was an economic disease, and the government should keep away from the field of economic medicine. It was privileged to do a little toward helping the victims of a natural as opposed to an economic disaster, but even this help should be free of "sickly sentimentalizing," in Professor Babbitt's phrase, and should be kept within the limits of a sound business policy. All these doctrines were presented to us day by day, with assurances that anyhow no American was starving, and writers had begun to feel that they were all outrageous and cruel nonsense.

The natural disaster of those years was the 1930 drought, which had afflicted most of the South from Oklahoma to Virginia, as well as sections of Pennsylvania and Ohio. I had driven through much of the area in October of that year, and I remember being disheartened by the dry streambeds, the gaunt ribs of the cattle, and the fields that had the uniform color of old straw matting. At a general store where I stopped for cigarettes, the proprietor couldn't change a $5 bill. Three farms, along with their stock, implements, and household furnishings, were being advertised for sale in handbills tacked to the wall. Across the road an ice-cream parlor was closed; the owner explained that he wouldn't sell city-made ice cream, and there wasn't enough milk in the county to make his own. That was near Belleville, Pennsylvania, in a limestone valley as rich as any farming land in the East. On reaching Tennessee, I found that the rains had fallen in time to save most of the tobacco crop, but the corn was ruined and there would be no hay to carry the cattle through the winter. In the Shenandoah Valley, through which I passed six weeks later, the autumn rains had still not fallen in early November. The great barns, which carried the look of Pennsylvania deep into the South, were almost empty of hay. An old man told me that fodder hadn't been so scarce since Sheridan laid waste the valley. "They'll be hungry people too," he said. "Maybe not here, but back in the hills."

It wasn't only back in the hills that people went hungry. By December we began to hear that something close to a famine was spreading among the small farmers and sharecroppers of Kentucky, Mississippi, and Arkansas, among other states. Mr. Hoover promptly took action of a sort, but he did not show the zeal or decisiveness he had shown in feeding the Belgians during the Great War and the Russian peasants during the famine of 1921. This time he was inhibited by one of his textbook theories, and he would not go beyond recommending that the Department of Agriculture should be given a small extra appropriation, so that it could lend the farmers money "for the purpose," as he said, "of seed and feed for animals." As for feeding the farmers themselves, he held that it was not a governmental function, and he urged the Red Cross to take care of them with its own funds.

The Red Cross was willing, but its directors did not appreciate the extent of the disaster, and at first they allotted only $5 million to feed the victims of drought in twelve states. They had experienced administrators in the field, but these were hampered both by insufficient funds and by an abundance of paperwork. A family had to prove beyond doubt that it needed food before receiving a requisition on a local merchant for an average of forty-two cents' worth of groceries per person per week. In England, Arkansas, five hundred hungry farmers went to the Red Cross in a body and asked for food; that was early in January 1931. The local administrator told them that his supply of requisition blanks had run out. "We don't want requisition blanks," the farmers said, "we want something to eat." With rifles and shotguns produced from hiding, they marched on the stores to seize what they needed. The merchants, almost as poor that winter as the farmers, stopped them by distributing something like $900 worth of free groceries, with which the farmers went home. It was the first successful and publicized example, during those years, of what the Communists called "direct action," and it had echoes over the country. "Paul Revere just woke up Concord," Will Rogers said in his syndicated column. "Those birds woke up America."

Meanwhile the government was having trouble with its program of making loans to drought-stricken farmers for the sole purpose of buying seed grain and feed for their stock. There was a brief scandal when it was discovered that some farmers had been stealing feed from their mules and using it to keep their families alive. Some congressmen couldn't understand why the distinction had to be made between "feed" and "food," and later it was abandoned quietly. The distinction was based, however, on a theory widely held at the time, namely, that a government should never help its own citizens in their simple role as consumers. On occasion it could help them *as producers,* but only by offering loans on good security and on condition that the loans should be used to put them back into production. Not only was the theory hard to explain, and hard to justify at a time of widespread hunger, but it also had the practical weakness that the country was then suffering from overproduction and underconsumption: helping citizens merely as producers would throw the market further out of balance.

But the theory had another practical weakness that became more obvious as it was extended to other fields besides farm relief. It intensified the old hostility between the rich and the poor. Men who produce goods for the market with their own capital are much richer, on the average, than men regarded simply as consumers, and therefore it was the richer citizens who received government loans. That was true even in Arkansas during the winter of 1930–31, when everyone in the countryside was poor, and most of the local banks had failed. Some of the farmers, however, still had unmortgaged land or implements or cattle that they could offer as security for government loans. God knows they needed the money, but they didn't need it more than those others who had nothing to eat and nothing to pledge, not even a broken-down mule. In Arkansas the government was helping only the least impoverished farmers, as elsewhere it would soon be helping some of the richest men in the nation, while refusing as before to help the unemployed.

# 4.
# Act of Conversion

Those were the days when public libraries, while trying to get along on reduced budgets, were crowded as never before. Partly that was because they served as a daytime refuge for the unemployed, but they were also patronized by worried businessmen. In Muncie, Indiana, chosen by Robert S. Lynd as the middlemost American city, the library circulation of adult books rose by 145 percent between 1929 and 1933. "Big things were happening that were upsetting us, our businesses and a lot of our ideas," a Muncie businessman told Lynd when he was preparing to write *Middletown in Transition* (1937), "and we wanted to try to understand them."

Later the man from Muncie began to be frightened. "I waked up to the fact," he said, "that my business was in immediate danger. We small businessmen began to see that we had to save our own necks. And so we stopped trying to understand the big issues and kind of lost touch with them." He might have added that merchants who became known for holding radical ideas were likely to find that wholesalers and bankers had stopped giving them credit; that was another reason why they decided that the issues were "too big for us anyway." But writers were less directly threatened by public opinion, were less afraid of pecuniary failure—if it didn't interfere with their work—and many of them were willing to follow their chain of thought as far as it might lead.

The more they studied American capitalism, the less logical it seemed to be. It had gathered together the wealth of a continent, but only at the cost of going partially bankrupt every ten or fifteen years. The present depression was one of a series that had started early in the nineteenth century, but it was also the worst of the series, for the line of business activity seemed to be climbing toward higher peaks by continually falling into deeper gullies. That was only the first of the contradictions that writers found when they entered the unfamiliar field of economic behavior. All during the 1920s American bankers had been lending money abroad on doubtful security, thus making it possible for Europe and South America to buy North American commodities; in effect, the bankers had been trying to increase our national wealth by exchanging part of it for worthless paper. American citizens had been urged during the same years to get rich by wasting their money. The adjuration was never stated in those blunt words—except by Kenneth Burke in a satirical essay called "Waste: The Future of Prosperity"—but still it was the message implied by masses of advertising. Buy more and more, we were told; buy things on credit without needing them; throw things away before wearing them out. That is the magic formula by which our factories will keep busy seven days a week and the nation will always prosper. Something was wrong in the formula. Neither foreign loans nor domestic wastefulness had furnished the vaster market that business needed, with the result that the country now suffered from poverty in the midst of plenty.

That greatest paradox was best described by William Z. Foster, still the leader of American Communists (though he was soon to be deposed). "Millions of workers," he said, "must go hungry because there is too much wheat. Millions of workers must go without clothes because the warehouses are full to overflowing with everything that is needed. Millions of workers must freeze because there is too much coal. This is the logic of the capitalist system." Foster was in Washington testifying before a House committee late in 1930. It was the first time that a great many writers found themselves in agreement with what the Communists were saying.

The writers continued their efforts to puzzle things out, and soon they were reading Karl Marx. They found that the early chapters of *Das Kapital* were hard going for anyone not trained in abstract economics, and I doubt whether many of them were ever clear in their minds as to the all-important distinction between constant and variable capital ($c$ and $v$), not to mention the much finer distinction between surplus value ($s$) and profit. But the historical passages were easier to understand, especially the "terrible chapter," as Scott Fitzgerald called it, on "The Working Day" and the still more terrible chapter on "Primary Accumulation," with its tragic story of how the English and Scottish peasants had been hunted from their fathers' lands. Equally impressive to writers were Marx's historical pamphlets on the class struggle in France from 1848 to 1871, with their analysis of political actions in terms of material interests. As for *The Communist Manifesto*, it not only described the maladies of capitalism, in words nearly all of which could be applied to what was happening in our time, but also offered a simple and grandiose program for the future.

The effect on many readers was overwhelming. Here at last were the answers they had been seeking to most of the questions raised by the depression: why capitalism had progressed by a series of financial panics, why the panics had been growing worse as the world grew richer, why the government had rushed to the aid of bankers and factory owners while letting the workers go hungry, and finally what must be done by each of us to halt this worst of panics and prevent another. Marx made it possible—as Edmund Wilson was saying at the time—to look at the capitalist system from the outside, to judge it historically, to realize that it had a beginning and would therefore have an end. Marx even provided a sort of answer to the question "How much longer?" by saying time and again that the system would be overthrown by a revolution of the workers. "Revolution" had always been a magical word in this country, and Marx's social aims, as opposed to his economic theories, were most of them familiar to American readers. The emotions underlying his works—the fierce passion for justice and equality, the faith in ordinary persons, the belief that all human difficulties could be solved by the human reason, with science as its tool, and the stubborn optimism that allowed him to face exultantly the prospects of riots and executions and civil war—all these were expressed in terms more darkly vindictive than Americans were used to hearing, but otherwise they could be fitted into the system of ideals that was taught in the public schools.

Marx's plans for reorganizing society were then being tested in Russia, a vast country that resembled our own in its pioneering spirit. Apparently their success had been amazing. A year before the crash in Wall Street, Russia had adopted her Five Year Plan, the first attempt in history to control in advance the economic output and living standards of a nation. Reports of its progress had been appearing not only in popular magazines but also in widely read books like *New Russia's Primer*, distributed in 1931 by the Book-of-the-Month Club, and in impressive films like Eisenstein's *The Old and the New*. Those were the Russian years in middle-class circles. Eisenstein was invited to make a film in Hollywood (though his visit there would end by producing nothing but recriminations). Ray Long, editor of *The Cosmopolitan*, went scouting for new talent in Moscow. He brought back Boris Pilnyak (one of many Russian authors who would disappear in the great purge) and gave him what was almost a state dinner at the Metropolitan Club in New York. It was the dinner at which Sinclair Lewis accused Theodore Dreiser of having stolen three thousand words from his wife's book about Russia, whereupon Dreiser slapped his face twice.

Everybody quarreled about Russia, and almost everybody wanted to see and judge the new civilization for himself. Amtorg, the Soviet trading corporation that served as an informal consulate in those days before this country had recognized the Russian government, was receiving 350 applications a day from Americans eager to work for the Five Year Plan. The burden of most reports about the Plan was that it had enabled Russia to move in an opposite direction from the rest of the world. Under capitalism, everything had been going downhill; less and less of every vital commodity was being distributed each year. Under communism, everything was climbing dizzily upward; each year there was more wheat, more steel, more machinery, more electric power, and there was an unfailing market for everything that could be produced. Nobody walked the streets looking for a job. Under communism, it seemed that the epic of American pioneering was being repeated, not for the profit of a few robber barons, but for the people as a whole.

It is true that stories of a different sort were also coming out of Russia. Some of the newspapers reported that the fine new Russian factories were being wrecked by mismanagement and deliberate sabotage. In the winter of 1932–33 they reported that the result of collectivizing the Russian farms had been a famine in the Ukraine with millions of peasants starving to death. Other millions, they claimed, had been reduced to slavery in labor camps—but were reports like these to be accepted? Many writers remembered that the newspapers, particularly those in the Hearst chain, had a long record of printing falsehoods about the Communists. There was undoubtedly much suffering in Russia, the writers said among themselves, and they were ready to admit that most of the unemployed in America got more to eat than skilled workers in Russia. But Americans, they also said, had to face the prospect of eating less and less as their savings were exhausted, whereas the Russians were fighting and suffering to build a world in which no one would go hungry.

What could writers contribute toward building a new society in their own country? They had learned from experience that they were almost powerless so long as they stood alone. They had learned from Marx that they could act and write with vastly greater effect by allying themselves with the working class. They had learned from Russia, so they believed, that the working class was capable of running the government more effectively than the capitalists and of putting an end to the whole series of depressions. Although the writers were trying to move slowly and have no illusions, knowing that black days were in front of them, by now their course of action seemed clear. At least that is what many of them were saying, in public speeches and personal confessions that were like the testimony of converts at revival meetings.

But something was missing from those generally honest statements of belief, so that they failed to explain two stages in the process of self-persuasion. There was in reality a long step between agreeing with Marx about the inevitable collapse of the capitalist system and agreeing with Lenin that the system should and must be overthrown by a single, disciplined revolutionary party. The first conception could be reached by purely intellectual means; the second involved at least the partial surrender of one's intellect to party dogma. Again there was a long step between choosing the workers' side in the class struggle and deciding that the Communist International was the voice of the workers. It was certainly not entitled to speak for them by statistical evidence or popular vote; its claim depended on a philosophy of revolution and a dream of the future. And the question remains why many writers, and many more Americans in other professions, accepted both the party philosophy and, to a lesser extent, the party discipline.

The answer is, of course, that we are dealing here with what was essentially a religious experience. The problems of the time were not only political but also moral and personal. In order to solve them, writers were trying to find a new set of ideas; but that was not the whole story. Many of them were also unconsciously seeking a religious solution, a faith that would supply certain elements heretofore lacking in their private and professional lives as middle-class Americans.

I suspect that the element most acutely missed was a sense of comradeship or cooperation or, to use the religious word, communion. In a business society like ours, the relations among individuals were being confined more and more to business transactions. Almost all the organizations that had brought people together during the Middle Ages—the guilds, colleges, congregations, and confraternities; the fields held in common, the joint labors, the pilgrimages and crusades—had by now died out and been forgotten. It is true that other institutions had partially replaced them. The business classes had their country clubs and women's clubs, their Rotary and chambers of commerce, while workingmen had their own churches, their lodges (mostly for burial insurance), and their labor unions. But some of those institutions, especially the unions, had declined in importance during the boom years, and even the family was becoming a smaller and less cohesive group. More and more the individual was forced to stand alone.

Writers were peculiarly alone; they were cut off from other people both by their working habits and by a professional snobbishness that made them say they were "not joiners." Then too, the literary doctrines popular for more than a century had contributed to their sense of isolation. One school had succeeded another, from Gothic Romance to Surrealism, but the hero picked out for admiration by almost all the schools was the individual defying a hostile universe; he was the artist retiring from society, obeying only the laws of art, and creating a separate world out of his dreams. But it is not in the nature of the human species to live each man by and for himself. There are penalties for drawing apart from others, and the artist's penalty, if he persisted in living for art alone, was to be deprived of his power to depict other living persons. More and more he found his attention turned inward, concentrated on his technical problems and physical ailments, until he was left at the center of his make-believe world with death as the only alien reality. His independence, instead of being a matter for pride, was becoming an intolerable burden.

It seems to me in retrospect that many writers were also disturbed by the decline and confusion of moral standards in American life, though the subject would not be widely discussed until the end of the decade. It was already clear, however, that the Protestant churches were losing their moral authority. Partly that was because they had staked too much of it on the Prohibition Amendment, of which they refused to admit the outrageous failure. Prohibition still had support in the countryside, where the old-time religion continued to flourish, but many of the big-town ministers were becoming ashamed to talk about it; instead they preached a watered-down gospel that amounted to little more than the Golden Rule. Hardly anyone in literary circles listened to what they were saying; in fact I remember that among my close acquaintances there was only one churchgoing writer, John Brooks Wheelwright, or "Wheels" as he called himself, taking pride in his eccentricity.

Anthropologists, sociologists, and even mathematical physicists had a more attentive audience than clergymen when they talked about moral problems, as many of them did in those days, but the general effect of their pronouncements was to upset the old standards without providing new ones. Freudian psychology was another upsetting influence. Many writers formerly hostile to Freud were learning more about him by the costly process of being treated for nervous breakdowns, of which there seemed to be an epidemic in 1930, but his theories were more discussed at the time than they were understood. Often they were still reduced to the simple notion that it was suicidal to suppress one's desires. That fitted in with the older romantic notion, also popular among writers, that people should follow their instincts in utter defiance of social conventions, the assumption being that most men were instinctively good. On the same assumption, the two virtues most admiringly presented in the fiction of the late 1920s were naturalness and candor. Writers were trying to achieve the same virtues in their lives. They often found, however, that their natural desires conflicted with one another, as when the sexual instinct collided with the parental instinct, and that complete candor between lovers was a refined form of cruelty. Thus, they were continually involved in moral dilemmas, even though they avoided using the word "moral." In the end they grew tired of always having to choose between two courses of action neither of which was sanctioned for them by dogma and neither of which was "right." Moral liberty, like personal isolation, was becoming a greater burden than some of them could bear.

When nothing seemed very evil, the corollary was that almost nothing seemed heroic. There are young men in every age who want to be heroes if they can; who want to distinguish themselves in some great cause, preferably against bitter opposition and at the risk of their lives—for some of them feel a physical need for running risks. In America during the boom years, there had seemed to be an appalling lack of difficulties and dangers. That is why millions identified themselves with Lindbergh, who had invented a new danger and triumphed over it. His laundry never came back, he tells us, because it was stolen and shared out as souvenirs (and one was reminded of savages eating the heart of a brave warrior). Rich people, unable to fly alone across the Atlantic, had been traveling over the world for the privilege of matching their wits against a mountain or a man-eating tiger and thus earning, for a moment at least, the sensation of being alive. Among those who stayed safely at home, one had the impression of potential abilities that were shriveling like unused muscles.

"Success" was still the magic word for most Americans, just as "failure" was the confession they made to themselves in moments of blank despair. Except by a few dedicated persons—most of them artists, scientists, or teachers—success and failure were judged in pecuniary terms. That made everything simple: a man with $50,000 a year was exactly five times as successful as a man with $10,000. "The business of America is business," as Calvin Coolidge had announced, and everybody seemed to be in it for what he could get out of it. But had the successful men, let alone the failures, been getting anything of human value? Edmund Wilson was speaking for most writers of our generation when he said in his "Appeal to Progressives," "The Buicks and Cadillacs, the bad gin and Scotch, the radio concerts interrupted by advertising talks, the golf and bridge of the suburban household, which the bond salesman can get for his money, can hardly compensate him for daily work of a kind in which it is utterly impossible to imagine a normal human being taking satisfaction or pride—and the bond salesman is the type of the whole urban office class. The brokers and bankers who are shooting themselves and jumping out of windows have been disheartened by the precariousness of their profession—but would they be killing themselves if they loved it? Who today, in fact, in the United States, can really love our meaningless life?"

"Nobody," we others answered with a mixture of anger, pity, self-pity, glee at the defeat of our enemies, and also concern for the nation. Financially, writers were less disturbed than those in other professions; most of us were used to being poor; but much as we had tried to stand apart from our pecuniary culture, we could not help feeling involved when the whole edifice, as it seemed to us, was about to collapse in the wind like a circus tent.

That sense of social collapse would be expressed in many novels of the 1930s—most directly in Dos Passos's *The Big Money*, where everybody and everything go to pieces, but also at the end of Fitzgerald's *Tender Is the Night* and in the Key West chapters of Hemingway's *To Have and Have Not*. Less clearly expressed, but present as an undertone in these books and others, was the feeling that if the society was at fault, so too were the individuals composing it, and even the rebel writers. Ours was still a Protestant country in those days, for all the loss of authority by the Protestant churches. Even the American Catholics and to a lesser extent the Jews had acquired a somewhat Puritan cast of mind that distinguished them from their coreligionists in Europe. Most of the writers under forty were trying hard to be pagan, yet they retained enough of the Calvinist background to have a sense of personal guilt for the sorrows of the unemployed. They had been too idle, so it seemed to them, and perhaps too fortunate. Poor as most of them were, they had profited indirectly from the bond-salesmen's racket. They had let themselves be bribed into acquiescence by publishers' contracts and penthouse parties and weekends on the north shore of Long Island. Even when they escaped to Europe, they had been corrupted by the mood of the times, and now, back in New York, they dreamed of changing everything in the world and in their hearts. They wanted to bury the corrupt past and be reborn into a new life. After all, that is one of the oldest dreams, expressed in the rituals of great religions.

This state of feeling, not confined to writers, might have led at other times to a widespread religious revival. Most of the churches, however, had only the old answers to new questions. The Catholics gained a few distinguished converts during the early depression years, and they would gain others, including several of my friends, at the end of the decade. Among the Protestants there was a rash of storefront churches in poor neighborhoods, but the only new proselyting sect that writers heard about was Buchmanism, or the Oxford Group, which appealed, as Edmund Wilson said, "to the best people and their butlers." On the whole there was no movement toward the Christian churches.

Communism was not Christian and it was not a church in the ordinary sense of the word. It proclaimed its opposition to all existing religions from shamanism to Christian Science, explaining that they were allied with the ruling classes and that their principal function was to make people tolerate their present sorrows in the hope of being recompensed hereafter. The head of the Communist Party in this country had recently told a congressional committee that if a person didn't cease to be religious soon after joining the party, he would probably be a poor Communist. Yet the party performed for its members the social and institutional functions of a church, and communism was, in effect and at the moment, the only crusading religion. Certainly it was the only one that appealed widely to Americans of the professional classes.

Even those who would accept it for a time began by having a host of reservations. Its doctrines seemed harsh and rigid to persons trained in the liberal tradition of tolerance and skepticism. Its language was barbarous and abounded in doctrinal terms that were especially distasteful to poets used to expressing themselves in concrete images. In Communist terminology men lost their personal traits and were presented simply as doctrines: instead of talking about leaders named Lenin or Trotsky, the party members discussed Leninism, Trotskyism, Stalinism, Bukharinism, as well as Cannonism, Lovestonism, and Gitlowism. When Communists talked about "the workers," with a hoarse note of reverence in their voices, a friend of mine used to say that they were lamenting the hardships of an exiled and persecuted Breton aristocrat: de Voykaz. At best one suspected a masquerade, for the Communists one met were mostly intellectuals and politicians disguised in workingmen's clothes (cap, blue or checked shirt, army shoes, leather jacket). The real Communist workers were at the time largely concentrated in New York and in the needle trades. There was an air of foreignness about the whole movement, and a smell of the closed sect, and worst of all there were echoes of bitter factional struggles that disheartened those in sympathy with its professed aims. Some of the sympathizers, including John Dos Passos, would sing in mockery:

> Oh, the right-wing pants makers
> And the Socialist fakers,
> They make by de Voykaz
>     Double cross;

*They preach Social-ism,*
*But practice Fasc-ism,*
*To keep capitalism*
*By the boss.*

Dos Passos was an old hand "in the movement," though never a party member, and we thought he had earned the right to be cynical among friends. Even the newcomers were learning that the Communist Party had other characteristics besides its single-minded revolutionary zeal. Many of them continued to draw closer, however, for reasons strong enough to make them adjourn their doubts. For communism not only furnished a clear answer to the problems raised by the depression—that was the economic side of it—and not only promised to draw writers from their isolation by creating a vital new audience for the fine arts in general—that was its professional side—but it also seemed capable of supplying the moral qualities that writers had missed in bourgeois society: the comradeship in struggle, the self-imposed discipline, the ultimate purpose (any action being justified insofar as it contributed to the proletarian revolution), the opportunity for heroism, and the human dignity. Communism offered at least the possibility of being reborn into a new life.

Yet the process of conversion was not rapid or easy. There were discussions, doubts, quarrels, lonely meditations, and sleepless nights. A novelist—I think it was Waldo Frank—told me that he reached his decision after a trip to Russia, where he watched a parade and heard the schoolgirls chanting as they marched, "We are changing the world." Granville Hicks says that night after night he used to walk the streets of a college town with his closest friend—another young instructor, Newton Arvin—while they talked about the disasters at home and abroad and wondered what they should do. If a stenographic record had been kept of their conversations about communism, he says, it would have filled several big volumes. They could find no escape from the logic of it. A letter from Arvin written in the crazy summer of

1932 suggests the tone of the conversations and the goal toward which they had been leading. "It is a bad world in which we live," Arvin said, "and so even the revolutionary movement is anything but what (poetically and philosophically speaking) it 'ought' to be: God knows, I realize this, as you do, and God knows it makes my heart sick at times: from one angle it seems nothing but grime and stink and sweat and obscene noises and the language of beasts. But surely this is what *history* is."

History was the cruel God that the young instructor was learning to worship, and he was ready to accept the Communist leaders as His wrathful and lice-ridden prophets coming down from the mountains clad in goatskins. "I believe we can spare ourselves a great deal of pain and disenchantment and even worse (treachery to ourselves)," his letter continued, "if we discipline ourselves to accept proletarian and revolutionary leaders and even theorists for what they are and must be: grim fighters in about the most dreadful and desperate struggle in all history— *not* reasonable and 'critically-minded' and forbearing and infinitely far-seeing men. . . . Let's salvage as much as we can of the rather abstract things we care for, but, golly, let's realize that there are far more basic and primitive things that have to be taken care of first (as long as men are starving and exploited), and do absolutely nothing, at any moment, to impede the work of the men who are fighting what is really our battle *for us*."

Whittaker Chambers had been converted to communism at a much earlier date, but his account of the conversion reveals the same mixture of emotions. It took place, he says, on a cold spring day in 1925. Huddled in his overcoat, Chambers sat alone on a bench outside the Columbia University Library while he tried to answer two obsessive questions. First he wondered whether he could go on living in a world that was dying, then he asked himself what a man should do in the crisis of the twentieth century. It seemed to him that communism was the only workable answer to the crisis. "It was not an attractive answer," he says, "just as the Communist Party was not an attractive party. Neither was the problem which had called it forth, and which it proposed to solve, attractive. But it had one ultimate appeal. In place of desperation, it set the word: hope." With that gift of his, which was also a weakness, for always finding a manichaean conflict between Light and Darkness, he tells us that the choice he made

> . . . was not for a theory or a party. It was—and I submit this is true for almost every man and woman who has made it—a choice against death and for life. I asked only the privilege of serving humbly and selflessly that force which from death could evoke life, that might save, as I then supposed, what was savable in a society that had lost the will to save itself. I was willing to accept Communism in whatever terms it presented itself, to follow the logic of its course wherever it might lead me, and to suffer the penalties without which nothing in life can be achieved. For it offered me what nothing else in the dying world had power to offer at the same intensity—faith and a vision, something for which to live and something for which to die. It demanded of me those things which have always stirred what is best in men—courage, poverty, self-sacrifice, discipline, intelligence, my life, and, at need, my death.

That same day he had his first disillusionment. He went to the campus friends who had worked long and patiently to convert him to communism and said that at last he was ready. He asked them where the Communist Party could be found, and, to his amazement, they did not know. But word was passed along, a real Communist inspected him at the New York Public Library, and finally he was taken to a party meeting.

# 5.
# The Church on Earth

If Whittaker Chambers had waited until 1931 to join the party, he would have had no trouble finding it; by that time the Communist Party of the United States (CPUSA) was listed respectably in the telephone book. Its national office, moved to New York from Chicago, was at 50 East Thirteenth Street, on the ninth floor of a loft building that the party had managed to buy for itself. In the same building was the Workers Bookshop, which had branches in other cities, and the offices of *The Daily Worker*. The party was beginning to grow, after twelve years of struggle, but it still had fewer than twenty thousand dues-paying members. Sympathizers were more numerous, as various congressional committees kept announcing with horror, and they could fill Madison Square Garden on two days' notice whenever a protest meeting was called; but without bringing their children along they would have had a hard time filling the Yale Bowl. Two presidential elections had given a partial tally of their numbers. In 1924 the Communists had received 33,361 votes, and in 1928, when they were on the ballot in many more states and made a vigorous campaign, they received 48,770, as against 21 million votes for Herbert Hoover and 15 million for Al Smith.

The party members were like the brothers of a preaching order, working hard and traveling widely on party orders, so that each man counted for ten or a dozen, and yet they had made hardly any impression on what they were always invoking as "the broad masses." That was true even among the labor unions, where the Communists were especially eager to make a showing. In 1926 and 1929 the party had led several famous strikes, including those of the New York fur workers and cloakmakers, the Passaic silk weavers, and the Gastonia, North Carolina, cotton-mill hands. All these had been bitterly fought and had attracted wide support among liberals, but all except the fur strike had been disastrous for those who took part in them, and the results of that one successful effort had been frittered away. By the end of the decade, the party had lost the marginal influence it once possessed in the American Federation of Labor. It controlled only a handful of small independent unions, most of them penniless and powerless. Except for the support of a few mine workers, it had no foothold in the basic industries, and it was making steady progress only among the unemployed.

One cause of its failure to win or hold more adherents had been its persistent factionalism. That was not usually the vice of its rank-and-file members, most of whom did their work with an admirable self-forgetfulness. The leaders, however, seemed less concerned with fighting the capitalists than with fighting other leaders for all-power in the Soviet world of the future. The energies of the party were being consumed internally. All during the 1920s there had been two rival factions, or caucuses, of almost equal numbers. One was led by Charles E. Ruthenberg until his death in 1926, and then by two of his former lieutenants, Jay Lovestone and Benjamin Gitlow. The other, which had been forced out of office in 1925, was led by William Z. Foster, James G. Cannon, and Earl Browder. Both factions maneuvered to win the support of the Communist International. As the fight between them grew fiercer, there were secret bulletins, rifled mailboxes, stolen briefcases, desks with their drawers jimmied open, and an endless series of cablegrams to and from "Mecca," or Moscow. People said that the party was like the Brooklyn Bridge, entirely suspended on cables.

The Foster caucus lost one of its leaders in 1928, when Cannon was expelled from the party for leftist heresy. He promptly founded a Trotskyist organization that started out with a hundred members: the Workers Party of the United States. Lovestone and Gitlow had never seemed more secure in their leadership of the orthodox Communists; at the national convention of 1929 they controlled the votes of ninety delegates out of a hundred. Brusquely a cablegram from Stalin deposed them from office and ordered them to report in Moscow. They returned from a disastrous visit to find that none of their old friends would speak to them. Soon expelled from the party like Cannon and his followers the year before, but this time for rightist heresy, they too founded an organization of their own. It started with forty members and a name that celebrated the past: Communist Party (Majority Group).

All that was an old story by 1931, and it was partly forgotten in the midst of great events. The heretical groups on the left and right of the Communist movement had both remained small, though the Trotskyists had begun to make converts among the younger intellectuals. The orthodox or Stalinist center of the movement had mildly prospered under its new leaders, most of whom would stay in office all during the depression. Foster himself was one exception; he would give place to Earl Browder in 1932, but without a public dispute. United as it now appeared to be and subjected to an even sterner discipline than before, the party had resumed its assault on the whole capitalist world, which seemed at the moment to be crumbling from within. The American leaders of the party, because of their close connection with international leaders in Moscow, enjoyed a greater reputation than they had earned by their own efforts. They shared in the moral prestige of the innumerable martyrs who had died for communism on five continents, and the intellectual prestige of a doctrine that had been handed down from Marx to Engels to Lenin to Stalin as if by apostolic succession, and finally they shared in the political prestige of the strong young Soviet state.

That is why the Communist leaders, not one of whom was an outstanding person—or brilliant or magnetic or easy to talk with —made a deep impression on the writers who were then approaching the movement. The writers were unfamiliar with politics and were not much interested in hearing about political intrigues. Some of them argued at the time that as novelists or poets or critics their concern was with the great spectacle before them, the difficult march of humankind toward a new society. Among the leaders of that march were doubtless many self-seekers and a few traitors. That was to be expected, considering the nature of men in the mass, but the march would continue, and before many years the unworthy leaders would desert or be exposed. Meanwhile it would be a mistake—the writers told themselves— to mingle in backstairs intrigues or even to fight against the intriguers. Men who got themselves involved in factional struggles soon lost their balance and were afflicted with a violent sort of madness. A far wiser course would be to cooperate with the recognized leadership from a distance—to sign petitions and join delegations and write about the struggles of the working class— while always retaining one's independence and one's right to criticize.

It was a position for which a name was invented in those years: the men who adopted it were known as fellow travelers. It seemed to have many advantages, both for writers and for politicians who didn't want to have them meddling in party affairs. What the fellow travelers did not realize at the time is that they were accepting responsibility for decisions which they had no share in making and which might be changed overnight by a cablegram from Moscow. Neither did they realize that, as a result of their deep concern for human values, they were acting under instructions from a party that consistently disregarded human values for the greater good of the movement, or that the greater good might be confused with some momentary advantage to be gained in a factional or personal struggle for power. Dangers like these were slow to make themselves apparent. The prospect at the moment was for an era of primitive faith and enthusiasm.

# 6.
# An Evening at Theodore Dreiser's

I first became involved in "the movement" after an evening in Theodore Dreiser's studio in April 1931. Not long before that evening there had been two events in my nonpolitical life that had helped to prepare me for new convictions. I had separated from my first wife, Peggy Baird Johns, after twelve years together, and I had said good-bye to Hart Crane.

The separation from Peggy was friendly, but painful to both of us. Our marriage had cracked in pieces during the late 1920s, like many others among our friends, but it had been held together for three years more by the frayed ends of an old affection. Suddenly the string broke, as many others did at the time; there was an epidemic of divorces in the literary world. Perhaps the depression had something to do with those crises in private lives. Many people felt that they were setting out on journeys, and that first they had to put their houses in order by cleaning out the breakage of the past.

It may be that the experience was more painful for me than for others. My Swedenborgian father had instilled into me a belief in the sacredness of marital or, to use the word that Swedenborg spelled in his own fashion, "conjugial" love. I hated the notion of divorce, but Peggy and I had tortured each other in many heedless fashions. As time went on she had casual affairs, and I had less casual ones. She was a heavy drinker, though not an alcoholic like Hart Crane. I felt responsible for Peggy, but after I went to work for *The New Republic* I could no longer lead the old bohemian life. Often when I came home from the office I found the apartment full of her boon companions; bottles galore, but nothing to eat. I worried. Night after night I lay in bed staring at the shadows on the ceiling, then dressed to roam the streets or stand alone at a crowded bar.

In those days the respectable speakeasies closed at three o'clock, by order of Mayor Jimmy Walker, but there were some tougher ones that stayed open till six after paying extra-large bribes to the police. Sometimes they recouped the bribes from customers by forcing them to sign personal checks for extra-large sums and then holding them prisoners until the checks were cashed. I never had that experience, since I didn't look prosperous, but once I was forced to pay double prices for a lot of drinks I hadn't ordered or consumed, while an extra-large man stood over me with a blackjack. Afterward I complained to the policeman on the beat. "You ought to close up that place," I said. "It's a gyp joint."

The policeman put a fatherly hand on my shoulder. "Son," he said, "you shouldn't go *in* to places like that."

I went home sober and lay awake until it was time to get dressed for the office. There was, I had learned, a special world in New York for men who couldn't sleep; it consisted of speakeasies, all-night lunchrooms, and the waiting room of Grand Central Station, where one sat on snowy nights and read the bulldog edition of the morning papers; but it wasn't a world designed for permanent habitation. I began to feel that my only choice was between getting a divorce, much as I hated to do so, and going off to a sanitarium. Some time in February, Peggy and I moved into separate lodgings.

As for Hart Crane, I saw him late in March; it was in Sherman, Connecticut, not far from the Tory Hill neighborhood across the New York state line where Hart and I had both lived. Peter and Ebie Blume, who were very poor that year—pictures weren't selling—had been spending the winter in Matthew Josephson's comfortable farmhouse. They had asked me up for the weekend and had also asked their friend Muriel Maurer, a fashion editor, who came out on the same train. When we reached the Josephson house on Saturday afternoon, I was surprised to find Hart waiting there. He had left the neighborhood at the end of the previous summer, after a riotous period during which he had been evicted from the two rooms that were as close to being a fixed home for him as anywhere he had lived since boyhood. He was in Sherman for the weekend, but merely to collect some of his possessions before sailing for France on a newly awarded Guggenheim fellowship.

Elsewhere I have recalled that weekend at length,[1] but there are features of it that bear repeating. There is, for example, the sharing out of gifts. Having brought forth his possessions, Hart found among them something for each of us: a dress suit for Peter (handed down from Hart's father), a pea jacket for Ebie, a broad red-flannel sash for Muriel, and for me a woven leather belt embossed with a brass anchor, the nautical touch that Hart loved. Everything was considerate, everything was warm, but still one had a feeling of last things, as if we were Roman soldiers casting dice for his garments.

There is my walk with Hart on Sunday morning, when he wondered where he should spend the year of his fellowship. France, he had said on his application, but now he was beginning to be doubtful, remembering the months he had wasted there in 1929.

"What about Mexico?" I asked him.

I had spent October in Mexico, and I spoke with enthusiasm about its somber landscapes, its baroque churches, and its mixture

1. See *A Second Flowering*, pp. 211–15.

of Spanish and Indian cultures. Life there was even cheaper than in Europe. One heard of sexual customs not unlike those of the Arabs.

Hart walked on in silence for a moment, on the frozen road. Then he said, "Maybe I'll go to Mexico if the Guggenheim people don't mind." He suddenly began talking about a project he had in mind, a long poem with Cortes and Montezuma as its heroes.

Finally there is the comic episode of the bottle containing the only liquor in the house (and no more to be had for miles around). At dinner on Saturday the Blumes poured one drink for each of us, then put the bottle away. Hart watched it go, knowing that it was being hidden to keep him sober. At lunch on Sunday there was nothing to drink and Hart didn't complain; his face was red and he was chuckling at his own jokes one after another. Ebie, usually attentive to her guests, made only a pretense of listening. Once she went out to the pantry and came back with a worried look. Hart had found the bottle and had hidden it somewhere else.

For the rest of us, sober and thirsty, the afternoon was like a theatrical performance that we had sat through often. Hart was repeating a series of inevitable phases. First came the outgoing phase in which he paid warm compliments to each of us and left all blushing. Then, after another visit to the bottle, came the phase of wild metaphors and brilliant monologues in which he listened only to his own voice. The bottle must have been empty by now and a third phase supervened, during which he sank into himself and muttered darkly about "betrayal." It was the phase that sometimes led to his smashing other people's furniture, but everything remained peaceful that late afternoon; I think he was a little afraid of Peter, who did not tolerate nonsense.

We were driven twenty miles to the station in Peter's open touring car, an old Stutz, while the lights picked out board fences and an occasional white farmhouse. Hart shivered all the way and tried to bury himself in Muriel's thick-piled coat. Sometimes he wailed, "Oh, the white fences . . . the interminable white Connecticut fences." He slept in the train, then roused himself as it crawled into Grand Central. In the concourse he said good-bye to us, warmly but decisively, before hurrying off with his two heavy bags to find a taxi. I surmised that a fourth phase was about to begin, though I had never seen more than the beginning of it: the phase in which he cruised the Brooklyn waterfront in search of compliant sailors and was often beaten up or jailed. Something in my own life had ended. Hart and I had been close friends for seven years, but now he was not so much a friend as something more distant, an object of care and apprehension. He was living now by the iron laws of another country than ours.

During the week that followed, Hart went to see Waldo Frank, whose advice he sometimes followed, and asked him about going to Mexico. Waldo approved the notion, though he warned Hart against drinking anything stronger than beer at the high altitude of Mexico City. Henry Allen Moe of the Guggenheim Foundation also gave him a warning, but otherwise made no difficulty about the changed destination. Hart bought passage on the *Orizaba*, which was sailing the first Saturday in April. I wasn't sorry to miss his uproarious farewell party.

About that time I received an invitation—it was almost a royal command—to a meeting in Theodore Dreiser's studio. The address on West Fifty-seventh Street turned out to be a big apartment building, an ornate pile. When I arrived at the meeting not very late, a butler took my coat and gave me a drink of scotch from a row of bottles that looked impressive in those days when we were used to nothing better than Jersey lightning or bathtub gin. The big studio was already crowded. There were novelists, critics, liberal editors, crusading journalists, almost everyone in the literary world—except Red Lewis and Dorothy Thompson, I noted—who had expressed an interest in the fate of American society. Nobody but Dreiser could have assembled them.

Dreiser, then fifty-nine, had been fighting our battles since his first book, *Sister Carrie*, had been encouraged to die of neglect in 1900. The younger writers were proud of his later success, and most of them felt that he and not Lewis should have been the first American to be awarded the Nobel Prize; but they also felt that he groped and fumbled more than anyone had a right to do. His mind, it often seemed to us, was like an attic in an earthquake, full of big trunks that slithered about and popped open one after another, so that he spoke sometimes as a Social Darwinist, sometimes as a Marxist, sometimes as almost a fascist, and sometimes as a sentimental reformer. Always he spoke, though, with an uncalculating candor that gave him a large sort of bumbling dignity.

It was so that evening in the clatter of glasses and gossip. Dreiser stood behind a table and rapped on it with his knuckles. He unfolded a very large, very white linen handkerchief and began drawing it first through his left hand, then through his right hand, as if for reassurance of his worldly success. He mumbled something we couldn't catch and then launched into a prepared statement. Things were in a terrible state, he said, and what were we going to do about it? Nobody knew how many millions were unemployed, starving, hiding in their holes. The situation among the coal miners in Western Pennsylvania and in Harlan County, Kentucky, was a disgrace. The politicians from Hoover down and the big financiers had no idea of what was going on. As for the writers and artists—

Dreiser looked up shyly from his prepared text, revealing his scrubbed lobster-pink cheeks and his chins in retreating terraces. For a moment the handkerchief stopped moving. "The time is ripe," he said, "for American intellectuals to render some service to the American worker." He wondered—as again he drew the big white handkerchief from one hand to the other—whether we shouldn't join a committee that was being organized to collaborate with the International Labor Defense in opposing political persecutions, lynchings, and the deportation of labor organizers; also in keeping the public informed and in helping workers to build their own unions. Then, after some inaudible remarks, he declared that he was through speaking and that we were now to have a discussion.

A meeting like this was strange to all of us under forty; there had been nothing like it since the hopeful days before the Great War. We felt that writers should do their part, but we had no suggestions to volunteer. Louis Adamic, a plainspoken man who wrote an account of the evening, thought that Dreiser's great honesty and bewilderment had engulfed everyone present. At last Lincoln Steffens, who had just finished writing his *Autobiography*, rose in a quiet fashion and began telling us what he knew about labor warfare. Small, trim, with a little white chin-beard and a Windsor tie tucked loosely into his collar, Steffens looked like a cartoonist's notion of a dapper French artist, an Aristide Duval, but he spoke with a flat-toned Western reticence. "Then they took him to the police station and beat him to death," he said in an unemphatic voice. "After the other leaders were run out of town and a few children starved to death, the strike was broken. The newspapers didn't print a word about it, naturally." He had a theory that facts should speak for themselves—a good theory for journalists, but less good for speakers trying to hold the attention of a restless audience. Adamic said in his diary (from which he quotes in his book *My America*, 1938): "Lincoln Steffens got up and spoke; what about I don't know. He rambled about in his own past and tried to be sage. By-and-by the meeting closed and people began to leave."

But the evening had more of a sequel than Adamic expected. Many of the writers present agreed with Dreiser that it was their duty to "do something" about the depression, since the politicians and financiers had done nothing whatever. The Communist Party, under its new leaders, was planning to make use of their enthusiasm, and it had assigned one of its organizers to the task of assembling a writers' committee. Joe Pass was the organizer, a young man with a flattened boxer's nose and a crooked engaging smile. He had been spending a good deal of time with Dreiser, and now he began making calls on other writers to reinforce Dreiser's hesitant plea. Partly as a result of his efforts, the new organization took shape; it was to be called the National Committee for the Defense of Political Prisoners. The committee was endorsed by an alphabetical list of sponsors beginning with an anthropologist, Franz Boas, and ending with a sculptor, William Zorach, but mostly consisting of literary men. Dreiser was its first chairman and Lincoln Steffens its treasurer.

According to a statement of purpose, "The National Committee recognizes the right of workers to organize, strike and picket, their right to freedom of speech, press and assembly, and it will aid in combating any violation of those rights, through legal means, and above all, by stimulating a wide public interest and protest." It invited "writers, artists, scientists, teachers and professional people" from the United States and other countries "to join its ranks and aid its work." In effect, the committee was a writers' and artists' branch of the International Labor Defense, which in turn was an auxiliary created by the Communist Party for legal work and propaganda; there was no secret about the connection. The NCDPP—to use its imposing row of initials in the manner of the period—was I think the first among hundreds of "front organizations" designed to enroll middle-class sympathizers. For me it was the first organization of any sort (except three or four editorial staffs) that I had joined since getting out of college.

At first I was not a very active member. I was writing a series of articles for *The New Republic*, and besides I had family problems that kept me occupied. Late in June Peggy sailed for Mexico to get a divorce. I wrote to Hart asking him to help her in cashing checks and getting settled. When she arrived in Mexico City, Hart had gone north to attend his father's funeral. He left a note for her offering the use of his house, staffed with servants, but instead she accepted another invitation, from Katherine Anne Porter. The fact was, as she wrote me, that she felt some trepidation about seeing Hart again. He had fallen into the habit of reviling his friends in public; also he had been spending nights in Mexican jails, usually as the result of a drunken fight with a taxi driver. Peggy was a little relieved to find that he was temporarily absent.

Meanwhile Dreiser was going ahead with his effort "to render some service to the American worker." In July he made an expedition to the Western Pennsylvania coalfields, where the National Miners Union, organized by the Communists, was conducting a hopeless strike. He issued a violent and merited rebuke to the American Federation of Labor for neglecting the miners. Early in November, in his capacity as chairman of the NCDPP, he led a delegation of writers into Harlan County, Kentucky, another area that the Communist union was trying hard to organize.

Harlan was a classical example of labor warfare in a depressed industry. The market for coal had been shrinking, with the result that the operators had tried to protect their investments by cutting wages, and also—since the miners were paid for each ton they produced—by using crooked scales to weigh the coal. In 1931 very few of the eastern Kentucky miners were earning as much as $35 a month, after deductions. Even that miserable wage was paid, not in cash, but in scrip, good only at the company store and worth no more, in most cases, than fifty or sixty cents on the dollar. The United Mine Workers—John L. Lewis's union —had withdrawn from the field, apparently on the ground that the situation was hopeless and that the miners couldn't afford to pay their union dues. Then the Communists had stepped in, as they often did in hopeless situations, but their meetings were broken up by deputized thugs armed with Browning guns.

It was much the same story as in western Pennsylvania and in Gastonia, North Carolina, but Harlan had its special features too. All the miners there were of English or Scottish descent, tall, lean mountaineers whose faces, Dos Passos said, "were out of early American history." They had come down from the hills with their Elizabethan turns of speech and also with their hillmen's custom of settling disputes with rifles. Harlan County at the time had the highest incidence of death by gunshot wounds in the United States. Mountain feuds had been transformed into battles between striking miners and gun thugs first hired by the coal operators, then deputized by the high sheriff. During one such battle, at the town of Evarts in May 1931, heavy firing lasted for half an hour. Three deputies and one miner were killed, according to the district attorney, but the miners counted ten coffins shipped out of town on the evening train. After that the deputies were hot for revenge, and a union sympathizer who ventured into Harlan County was likely to have a shorter life than a federal revenue agent in search of a corn-liquor still.

For a wonder the writers' delegation came into the county and conducted a series of public hearings without so much as a bullet wound or a broken head. Besides Dreiser and among others, the writers included Charles Rumford Walker and his wife Adelaide, the novelist Samuel Ornitz, and John Dos Passos. They were saved from injury partly by their innocence and partly by a major of the Kentucky National Guard, who was assigned to accompany them after Dreiser telegraphed to the governor of the state and requested military protection. Dreiser, who presided over the hearings, had a massive presence—"like a goofy old senator," Dos Passos said—that compelled the respect of friends and enemies. The hearings were stage-managed by Ornitz—later successful in Hollywood, until he was placed on the blacklist—and he gave them the professional air of courtroom dramas.

Followed by carloads of gun thugs, the delegation moved from Pineville, the county seat of Bell County, to Harlan town, and then to mining camps back in the hills. Everywhere it heard the same stories from witnesses: miserable wages (or none at all, after the deductions had been made), only two meals a day of only beans and bulldog gravy (flour and water with a teaspoonful of lard), houses broken into and searched without warrants, miners thrown into jail and held for weeks without being arraigned, and a general terror of "the law." Dreiser asked one witness, a Harlan miner's wife, what the law meant to her. "The law," she said, "is a gun thug in a big automobile." At Straight Creek a volunteer nurse, Aunt Molly Jackson, sixty-five years old, testified that from three to seven babies in the camp were dying each week from malnutrition and "the bloody flux." Then she sang a song of her own composition, "The Kentucky Miner's Wife's Ragged Hungry Blues":

> *All the women in this coalcamp*
> *    are a-sittin' with bowed-down heads,*
> *Ragged and barefooted*
> *    and their children a-cryin' for bread.*
> *No food, no clothes for our children,*
> *    I'm sure this ain't no lie.*
> *If we can't get no more for our labor*
> *    we will starve to death and die.*

After a final night in Pineville the writers went back to New York with their stenographic records of the hearings. "The law" and the coal operators, sometimes indistinguishable one from the other, let the delegation go in peace; perhaps they had been confounded by Dreiser's self-assurance, but they soon rallied their wits. All the writers were indicted for criminal syndicalism, and Dreiser was charged with the additional crime of misconduct in the Pineville hotel with an otherwise unidentified woman named Marie Pergain. The deputies who had been watching his room testified that they had seen the woman go into it and had then leaned toothpicks against the door; the toothpicks were still leaning there in the morning. Dreiser answered indignantly that it would have been impossible for him to commit the offense, because he was "at this writing completely and finally impotent." The Communists, who were looking hard for martyrs, urged Dreiser and Dos Passos to go back to Kentucky and stand

trial (for criminal syndicalism, not adultery), but they both refused the crown of thorns. All the indictments were later dismissed. The stenographic records of the delegation appeared in
a book edited by Dos Passos, *Harlan Miners Speak* (1932), and
some of them were read into the minutes of a Senate hearing. But
the war continued in Harlan and Bell counties, and the miners'
wives that winter were as ragged, hungry, and barefoot as before.

# 7.
# Cumberland Gap

Meanwhile Peggy was leading a busy life in Mexico City, where she was being squired about by a Mexican artist. So as not to abuse Katherine Anne Porter's hospitality, she had moved out of her house as soon as she found a furnished room. Late in August Katherine Anne sailed from Veracruz on the German boat that she used as a setting for her novel published thirty years later, *Ship of Fools*. Peggy's determinedly brave letters of the following months might have been another novel appearing serially, with Hart Crane as the central character. Here are some extracts that tell part of the story:

> *September 8.*
> . . . Hart tracked me down last night just before the meeting [of a library committee that Peggy was trying to organize]. Lord, it was good to see him, although I had only a moment. He thought I was out of town and hadn't even tried to look me up before. He was rather pathetic and very subdued. I told him you were hurt at not having been looked up while he was in New York, and he said he wasn't sure you would want to see him. . . . I did one

of "My darling Hart" stunts and we flung ourselves into each other's arms. Jacobo [the Mexican artist], who didn't know of Hart's proclivities and who merely saw me making a terrific fuss over an extremely good looking man, snubbed me and acted sulky during most of the meeting.

### September 12.
. . . Last night Hart came all the way in town to get me to go out to Mixcoac [the suburb where Hart had rented a house] with him for supper. We do enjoy each other so much. I am on the water wagon and Hart says I am taking it like some religious enthusiast.

### October 1.
. . . I too may have trouble with Hart, perhaps in more ways than one. He is drinking again all too heavily, acting all right but talking very erratically. . . . He is more than a little in love with me and almost fiendishly jealous of you. He spent all yesterday afternoon trying to make me promise not to write you and looked over the letters on my table to see if I had. By being in love with me I don't mean he wants my body, but he does want to marry me, all of course because he is more than a bit lonely and desires a close companionship that he has never found in sex.

### Undated, early in November.
. . . Z——'s party was all right as such things go. After it was over one of the men took me to the Broadway, where we sat until five in the morning talking art. Found out from him that Z—— was spreading the report that Hart was my lover and that it was a shame that a nice girl like myself was being led astray by a degenerate. He also seemed to think it was a shame and did his damnedest to make me change my status. Like all such fool rumors, I see no use in denying it. . . . Hart took me to dinner last night and I told him, at which he said: "You'd better marry me and make me a decent woman."

*November 15.*

. . . As for Hart, we are more or less all right now [he had sent her an insulting telegram]. He will not be allowed in the house when he is drunk, I told the porter and also told him. God, I hate to see that boy simply making a wreck of himself, how pitiful with his really great power.

About this time the Mexican artist disappeared from the story. Peggy had been ill, and she decided to seek relief at a lower altitude. Having rented a house in Taxco, she invited guests to a Christmas party. Her letters continued:

*December 21.*

. . . Just as I was starting dinner yesterday a little boy appeared carrying a suitcase, who said my señor was down in the place and would be right up. For a spinster like myself this was highly mystifying. It turned out to be Hart, who had decided that either I needed to be taken care of or he did.

*December 26.*

. . . Hart intends staying with me until after New Years. We are very close and companionable, strangely so, with him very thoughtful and sort of the head of the house. I just let him do everything and the more I put on his shoulders in the way of responsibilities the more he accepts. He carved chickens for dinner, moved tables, ordered servants [all this at the Christmas party], made guests feel at home, squeezed lemons for the rum punch, stayed sober and filled other glasses before his own, and this morning with the help of the maid replaced the whole household. I shall take all I can get of this mood while it lasts.

They were really lovers now, and Hart had begun to write an epithalamium, his first new poem in more than a year. Peggy copied out for me the first stanza in its original form:

*The bell-cord that gathers God at dawn*
*Dispatches me—as though I climbed the knell*
*Of a clear morn—I could walk the cathedral lawn*
*Clear to the meridian—and back from hell.*

Soon after New Year's, Hart went back to Mixcoac. "I presume he will wait," Peggy said on January 12, 1932, "until the house and the servants have become an albatross around his neck, go out on a binge and then rush to me for salvation." On January 16, "Hart arrived just as I expected." On January 25, "Hart has been with me ever since he wrote the letter to you. He is so lovely and thoughtful of me that I shall miss him terribly when he does leave." The story continued in rapid installments:

> *January 27.*
> . . . Hart finished the first draft of a poem yesterday [it was the same poem, later to be called "The Broken Tower"]. All prophecies to the contrary, he is by no means finished. It is a magnificent piece of lyric poetry that is built with the rhetorical splendor of a Dante in Hell. I'll send you a copy as soon as I'm sure he's finished working on it. The boy can commit any fool flamboyant act he wishes, or rot in jail, if he only gets something like this out of his system once in a while.
>
> We went on a jag last night all by ourselves, drinking a terrific amount, but so excited about the poem that neither one of us got drunk.
>
> *January 31.*
> . . . Hart left day before yesterday after getting in a huff with Clinton King. Since that time I have been receiving two telegrams a day for the simple reason that he is lonesome for me. . . . The boy has a gay time with his histrionics. Strange to relate I don't really mind them.
>
> *February 3.*
> . . . It was impossible to stay in Taxco after Hart's last telegram. I wired him to meet me at the Broadway at

seven-thirty and for five hours in the bus wondered
what in hell was in store for me on my arrival. But Hart
can always give you a surprise.

After this hot dusty ride I arrived at the Broadway
to find cocktails on the table, with Hart not having
touched his—a corsage of violets and sweet peas, a mag-
nificent meal ordered and two new records for me. We
dashed out here immediately after dinner and played the
records. . . . The servants had spent the whole day fixing wreaths all over the place for my reception and the
whole thing was very touching and sweet.

I too was touched, and delighted for both of them, especially
since the next letter reported that Hart was sober and back at
work on his poem. It was hard to believe, however, that his new
life was anything more than a respite from his private hell. And
I was slow to answer Peggy, engrossed as I was in preparations
for another mission to Kentucky.

One day in January, Charles Rumford Walker had come to
see me at *The New Republic* and had stayed all afternoon. He
told me that, from the standpoint of the National Miners Union,
Dreiser's visit to Kentucky had been a grand success. It had directed attention to Harlan County, it had forced "the law" to
be a little more legal, and it had encouraged the union to call a
strike in the Eastern Kentucky coalfields on January 1. According to Charlie, most of the miners had come out, and they would
stay out as long as their families had "maybe not enough to eat,"
so they said, "but just enough to breathe." Food was the central
problem and the hardest one for the union to solve, because its
relief kitchens were being burned or dynamited and its relief
trucks ambushed and looted by deputies. Having served as a
member of Dreiser's committee, Charlie thought that another
such mission might "open up the situation"—that was his phrase
—help in raising money for relief, and keep "the law" from interfering with the distribution of food.

Charlie had large, soft, bright eyes like a squirrel's, and his enthusiasm was infectious as he talked about the miners, their mountain speech, their ballads, and their courage. He wanted me to join a committee that would go, not to Harlan this time, but to Pineville, which was said to be less embattled. He didn't think the trip would be dangerous, but I could guess that the authorities would be better prepared to receive a second group of visitors. I told him I would go along if *The New Republic* would give me time off to write an article. As I started for the train I was humming under my breath a miner's song that someone had been playing on the phonograph:

> *Oh, Daddy, don't go to the mine today,*
> *For dreams have been known to come true.*
> *Oh, Daddy, dear Daddy, don't go to the mine,*
> *I never could live without you.*

The strike was being directed from Knoxville, Tennessee, the nearest city to the mines that was safe for union organizers. When our committee assembled there, it included among other writers Edmund Wilson, Waldo Frank, Quincy Howe (then editor of *The Living Age*), and Mary Heaton Vorse. Except for Mrs. Vorse, a novelist with radical sympathies who had been reporting strikes for thirty years, we had no experience in labor disputes. Waldo Frank had published more books than the rest of us, and we made him our chairman. We decided to keep out of trouble, if we could, and follow our own policies instead of being guided by the Communist union, which we felt would be delighted if we were all thrown into jail: think of the national publicity.

Just before starting for Pineville on the morning of February 10, we heard that Harry Sims, a Young Communist serving as a union organizer, had been shot by a sheriff's deputy and was dying in a Knox County, Kentucky, hospital. We drove north in hired cars through the lovely Powell River valley, afterward flooded by the Norris Dam, and then past the monument to Daniel Boone in Cumberland Gap. Beyond the Gap I remembered driving north from a French railhead in 1917 toward the front lines; the fact was that I hadn't seen so many guns since the Great War. A crowd of thirty men with rifles and shotguns was standing outside a filling station at a junction where one road led to Harlan. "They're fixing to keep you out of Harlan County," the driver said. "It's a tough county and Harlan is a tough town. I went there once, but I didn't stay long. A man came up to me in the street and said, 'I'll give you ten dollars for your gun.' I said, 'But you've got a gun already.' He said, 'A man ain't safe here withouten he has two guns.' So I took his ten dollars and got out of town."

There was another armed force of deputies waiting to meet us at the Pineville city line. There were deputies mingled with the crowd of miners that had gathered in the courthouse square. We stopped outside the office of W. J. Stone, the only local attorney who would plead for the miners, and went upstairs to consult with him. A miner was telling Stone the story of how he had been beaten, while only his lips moved in a grotesquely swollen face. "Don't stand near the window," someone said. "They've got needle guns pointed this way." I looked across the street. In the third-story windows of the courthouse I could see machine-gun muzzles commanding the crowd of miners below.

We did not know then that the union was scheming to make the most of our visit. Since calling the strike six weeks before, it had not been permitted to hold a meeting. Now, without warning us, it had summoned the miners into Pineville for a distribution of food and a "free-speech speaking," in order to raise their spirits. Revolution was in the air that year. When news of the union summons reached the respectable citizens, they decided that the miners intended to seize the town, loot the stores, and burn down the churches. They believed that they were fighting now to save their property, their God, and their daughters from the Red menace, and that any measure of defense was justified, even shooting men in cold blood. That explained the machine guns in the courthouse and the general air of tense waiting. Our committee, arriving innocently on the scene, was like a party of civilians wandering into no man's land to gather flowers.

Later that morning we were summoned to a meeting in the Pineville hotel, where Mayor Brooks had assembled some twenty-five of the leading merchants, professional men, and coal operators. Waldo Frank presented our requests, speaking reasonably (but his voice was high and he lacked Dreiser's imposing presence). We wished to take three truckloads of food to the relief warehouse established by the union (not knowing that it had been closed); we wished to distribute the food to the miners who had come into town to meet us; we wished to consult with the miners, hear their grievances, if any, and learn whether relief supplies had been prevented from reaching them. We had been advised that these requests were within our constitutional rights. . . . The mayor refused all of them.

Frank said that we were determined to obey not only the laws of Kentucky but also the commands of local officials, even though we knew them to be illegal. A coal operator delivered a speech on bolshevism. Another operator asked *Mr.* Frank if he had registered for the draft in 1917. A third operator, his mouth set like a steel trap, said that the meeting was no good anyway, and everybody started to leave. At the door Mayor Brooks stopped us to announce that if we attempted to distribute any food in Pineville, we would all be arrested. He walked out into the lobby of the hotel, then hurried back to tell us that if we held any sort of meeting in Pineville, whether on the public highways or in a vacant lot rented by ourselves, we would be arrested. He continued his series of prohibitions, stepping out into the lobby after each of them, like an actor who has forgotten his lines and must be prompted in the wings. We must not talk with the miners or we would be arrested. We must not print or distribute any handbills or we would be arrested. We must not invite any miners to our rooms in the hotel or we would be arrested for holding a meeting. If we wished to distribute our food outside of town, we must first get the permission of the county attorney, and he, Mayor Brooks, doubted whether it would be granted.

The coal operator with a steel-trap mouth walked up to us. "This is another war," he said. "I admire your nerve in coming here where you don't know anything about conditions or the feeling of the people. If you don't watch out, you'll find out how ugly we can be, and I don't care if your stenographer takes that down." "That goes for me too," some of the others said.

I learned afterward, by talking to witnesses at a Senate hearing, that the leading citizens held another meeting that continued through the afternoon. Some of the coal operators, I heard, had suggested shooting us all, as a means of proving to the outside world that nobody could interfere with their affairs, but they were voted down. Meanwhile our committee had been kept busy. We had visited the county attorney and had received his permission to distribute the truckloads of food on a county road, provided there was no speaking. We had handed out the food to miners—except for the last two hundred pounds of salt pork, which was stolen at gunpoint by one of the sheriff's men. A young miner who tried to speak had been chased by Deputy Sheriff John Wilson with two drawn guns, but had escaped into the crowd. Another deputy had beaten a miner whom we later saw in Stone's law office, his arms blue-black and swollen like toy balloons.

Early in the evening, our baggage was searched in the police station. The most incriminating document discovered in anyone's possession was a bulletin of the Foreign Policy Association, over which four men puzzled a long time before filing it away as evidence of criminal syndicalism. We went back to the hotel and some of us went to bed. At ten-thirty we were all arrested, in my case by two rather considerate deputies. "You'd better take along your toothbrush and razor," one of them told me while I was dressing. "You might be in jail for a spell." But after waiting half an hour in a locked police court, and breaking into nervous laughter when a deputy's gun slipped out of his pocket and clattered to the floor, we were informed by the judge that the charge against us, whatever it was, had been dismissed "for lack of prosecution." We began to be uneasy now, and demanded protection, but the judge ordered us to go back to the hotel. There, in the lobby, we found an armed crowd of deputies, coal operators, and merchants—"night riders and citizens," as they called themselves. They told us that we were to be carried out of the state and that, if we ever returned, it would be at our own risk.

Two by two we were placed in the back seats of automobiles. I noticed that Waldo Frank and Allan Taub, a lawyer for the International Labor Defense, were ordered into the same car. As the procession moved off I felt like a patient being wheeled into the operating room. I was thinking,"If they beat me I'll scream. It's the only hope of stopping them." The line of headlights undulated with the road, sometimes revealing a leafless patch of mountainside.

"This is some motorcade," said the young coal operator at the wheel. "Motorcade" was a new word then, and he repeated it lovingly: "I wouldn't have missed this motorcade for ten years of my life."

Quincy Howe sat beside me, sometimes answering a question politely in his flat Boston voice. Deputy John Wilson guarded us, and there were two men and a girl in the front seat. The driver talked like a college boy coming home from the big game. "You sure would have plugged that miner today, John, if you got a fair shot at him," he said. "It's a pity he got away into the crowd."—"I'll fix him," John Wilson said, "next time I see him. I'll take him to jail or I'll kill him." In Washington one of the witnesses would tell me that Wilson had killed several men for "resisting arrest" or "trying to escape." Still later I heard that he had been found in the woods with a bullet in his back.

We stopped at a filling station and John Wilson bought us each a bottle of Coke, then finished his own bottle at a gulp and wiped the last drops from the drooping ends of his mustache. The car speeded up to rejoin the procession. "They shot one of those Bolsheviks up in Knox County this morning, Harry Sims his name was," the driver said. "That deputy knew his business. He didn't give the redneck a chance to talk, he just plugged him in the stomach. We need some shooting like that down here. Say," he burst out, "they're striking down at my place. They talk about having a picket line. Let me tell you, I've got eight men with rifles waiting on the hill, and if any redneck tries to picket my mine, he's going to be dead before he knows it." The cars ahead of us had begun to climb out of the Cumberland River valley. "Listen," the driver said, "I want to ask you a question. Do you two fellows believe in a Supreme Being?"

"Yes," I said truthfully, but after a pause; I didn't like to placate an enemy. The "yes" was more confusing to the young coal operator than a "no" would have been, and he fell silent as the procession wound into Cumberland Gap. At the Tennessee line, there was a broad paved semicircle where motorists could stop to enjoy the daytime view of three states, and here the procession halted. We sat there for a while, then John Wilson nudged Quincy and me and told us to get out of the car. As we stood beside our bags in the headlights I thought to myself, "This is the operating room." Somebody ordered, "Lights out." Ten yards away in the darkness I heard a piercing and continued scream. Then the lights were turned on again and somebody shouted in a Kentucky-mountain voice, "Frank and Taub they've been having a fight."

Frank as our spokesman and Allan Taub as an argumentative lawyer were the two men against whom the coal operators were most incensed. Several deputies, one of whom was armed with a jack handle, had attacked them both in the darkness. Taub had escaped serious injuries by shielding his head with his arms, but Frank had some deep head wounds. "Now let lawyer Taub make a speech on constitutional liberties," one of the Pineville businessmen said.

They searched our luggage once more, this time for motion-picture films, and confiscated an unexposed reel from the camera-man, who had managed to get his pictures out of town before we were arrested. (His name was Ben Leider, and five years later he would be killed in Spain, flying a plane for the Loyalists.) Then they let us go and we stumbled down the highway into Ten-nessee. One of us turned a flashlight on the monument to Daniel Boone, dead a long time ago with all his world. When we reached the hotel in the town of Cumberland Gap, a mile below, we found that a newspaperman had notified the proprietor some hours before that he could expect a party of New York writers. But instead of stopping there, we managed to hire three cars and reached Knoxville in time for a few hours of sleep.

Next day we found that our real tasks were in front of us: publicity and money-raising. We had been helped with both by the "night riders and citizens." Waldo Frank was photographed time and again, his head swathed in bandages, and the pictures were printed all over the country. The rest of us were busy being interviewed and writing newspaper stories. We took the night train to Washington, a city which had suffered less than others from the depression, but which, it seemed to me, had a curious air of emptiness and waiting. On Capitol Hill we talked at length to Senator Bronson Cutting of New Mexico, an honest liberal and a great gentleman; I think the meeting had been arranged by Cutting's volunteer secretary, the poet Phelps Putnam. Cutting had heard about the hardships of the miners and promised that he would do his best to arrange a formal Senate hearing (which in fact was held three months later). Phelps Putnam kept rushing into and out of the conference room, always wearing a broad-brimmed black slouch hat which, with his clean, Yalie-from-a-good-prep-school face, made him look like a Bones man dis-guised as a decadent artist of the 1890s. I thought that his poems had the same double aspect, incongruous and appealing.

In New York there was of course a protest meeting, to raise funds and spirits. It was held in a big drafty auditorium near the Harlem River, and there must have been four thousand people in the audience. I spoke in public for the first time since dropping out of the Harvard freshman debating team. Coming first on the program, I started in a loud voice, but apprehensively, "We went into Kentucky because we were told that local authorities were interfering with relief to the striking miners." I paused, wondering if I could go on—and was the loudspeaker working? "We can't hear you," somebody called from the back rows. Others took up the cry. Much louder I repeated, "We went into Kentucky. Can you hear me?"—"We can't hear you," more of the audience chanted. So I roared as if through a megaphone, "WE WENT INTO KENTUCKY NOW CAN YOU HEAR ME?"—"Yes," the audience roared back, and my stage fright was gone. It wasn't a very good speech, in the end, but radical audiences were satisfied with hearing a stentorian voice and the proper sentiments. I was asked to make the speech again, in Philadelphia, and then to make other speeches, so that for me, as for some others, the trip to Kentucky had a long sequel.

That second mission to Kentucky was one of many that writers undertook during the 1930s. There had been or would be others to North Carolina, Alabama, Cuba, the Imperial Valley of California, and even to Vermont during a strike in the marble quarries. At some point in a hopeless struggle the Communist leaders would say, "Let's organize a writers' committee." The missions were widely reported and, though they did not win strikes in Kentucky or elsewhere, they helped to raise funds for the strikers (and for the party). Another series of effects was on the writers themselves. Some of these drew back when they found they were being used by the Communists, as Edmund Wilson did for one, but others resigned themselves to being used, since they thought it was for the common good. They committed themselves to a new life not merely by accepting opinions, which can change in a day, but more lastingly by their own actions. That was the effect on me of the Kentucky mission and its aftermath. I found myself committed to "the movement" by working and speaking for it (and in some measure, I suppose, by the sense of importance that comes from working and speaking). I was also committed by the hungry, ragged, but clear-eyed look of the miners' wives, by the talk of shooting men in cold blood, and by the machine guns pointing at me from the Pineville courthouse. This was another war, as the steel-mouthed coal operator had said, and I knew which side I was on.

# 8.
# The Broken Tower

The Hart Crane story continued in Peggy's letters, though I was too busy now to answer most of them. Peggy had moved to Mixcoac and was presiding over Hart's household, which included a drunken *mozo*, his wife, his babies, and a beautiful Communist girl seeking refuge from the police while she worked as second cook and housemaid. Peggy tried to keep her from attending meetings at which she might be arrested, and tried with some success to keep Hart and the *mozo* sober. Her letters seemed to be written in an Indian-summer haze of good feeling.

> *February 22.*
> Arrived here the other night and a delightful home-coming Hart achieved. There was good white Spanish wine, which we sat over after dinner until all hours of the night, our tongues going at both ends and scarcely listening to each other. . . .
> P.S. By the way I want to congratulate you on making the trip to Kentucky, both Hart and I feel that it is one of the most important definite acts you have ever

made. Too, I feel that one of the greatest compliments you have ever paid me was in saying I would have enjoyed the trip. . . . Hart wishes to include his love.

*March 21.*

. . . Bob Haberman made me sign the final papers [for the divorce], though they don't go through until your power of attorney comes. . . . I can't understand why I ever think of coming north. I am really happy here and Hart outside of everything else, is the grandest companion any human being could ask for. . . . Frankly it's a real joy to see Hart so happy, contented, and really in love for the first time in his life.

From Hart came a carbon copy of "The Broken Tower," the poem on which he had been working for the last three months. It ended with a triumphant invocation to love (and to Peggy, I thought):

> *The steep encroachments of my blood left me*
> *No answer (could blood hold such a lofty tower*
> *As flings the question true?)—or is it she*
> *Whose sweet mortality stirs latent power?—*
> . . . . . . . . . . . . . . . . .
> *The commodious, tall decorum of that sky*
> *Unseals her earth, and lifts love in its shower.*

Beneath the last stanza Hart had typed in a message to me. It was dated "Easter," which that year fell on March 27.

Peggy and I think and talk a great deal about you. That means in a very fond way, or it wouldn't be mentioned. I'm wondering whether or not you'll like the above poem—about the 1st I've written in two years. . . I'm getting too damned self-critical to write at all any more. More than ever, however, I do implore your honest appraisal of this verse, prose or nonsense—whatever it may seem. Please let me know.

And because I congratulate you most vehemently on your recent account of the Kentucky expedition—please don't tell me anything you don't honestly mean. This has already been submitted to POETRY—so don't worry about that angle.

I miss seeing you a great deal. Peggy is writing you some sort of account of the Easter celebrations here. We're very happy together—and send lots of love!

Happy, happy . . . the word was repeated in all the March letters, but then it disappeared from the correspondence. Hart drank at the Easter celebrations and again was violently drunk a few days later. On April 7 Peggy wrote me:

. . . To keep me here he has promised to give up tequila. I didn't ask him to, but I am frankly admitting to you that should he start drinking heavily again I shall wire immediately for money home. I don't want you to let him know I wrote this, and as you knew it already, it doesn't seem very disloyal. All in all, with my own disillusions I have probably been a great deal harder on him, than the other way around. Drinking only beer, the poor child is steadily losing his waist-line and gaining the healthy color of a Burgundian friar. I am so pampered that I feel at times I am done up in some superior kind of cotton wool. . . .

Though Hart was red-faced as a Burgundian friar, he had fallen into a black mood. He had been excited by the Kentucky mission and by the news that his friends were going left, but then he became resentful. "Waldo and Malcolm are just cutting paper dollies," he said. Hart's money was running out, and he had recently learned that he could expect nothing for years from his father's estate, which had been whittled away by the depression. He no longer felt capable of finding a job or of keeping it if found. Still worse, he was appalled by a suspicion that his talent—which he seemed to regard as a personality apart from his ordinary self—was leaving him and might never return. That was why he asked humbly for reassurance that "The Broken Tower" was not prose or nonsense, but a great poem. Unfortunately the copy he submitted to Morton Zabel, then editor of *Poetry*, went astray in the mail. I thought the poem was splendid, but I was so taken up with *The New Republic* and my after-hours work for the NCDPP that I put off writing Hart from day to day. It seems that he waited in Mixcoac for news while bewailing the state of the world. "What good are poets today!" he exclaimed more than once, by Peggy's report. "The world needs men of action."

One morning in the middle of April, full of tequila, he stared angrily at the fine portrait that Siqueiros had painted of him, then slashed it to pieces with an old-fashioned razor. Having killed himself symbolically, he tried to die in the flesh by swallowing a bottle of iodine, but he spilled most of it. Later in the day he seized and drained another bottle from the medicine cabinet, but that one contained Mercurochrome. Though it harmed nothing else, I suspect that it fatally wounded his self-respect: if he tried to die again, he must not fail. Peggy was terrified and wired me for money to come north. Hart, now sober most of the time, decided to take the same boat, the *Orizaba*, and they sailed from Veracruz on April 24. Three days later I received a telegram from Palm Beach:

MALCALM COWLEY, CARE NEW REPUBLIC
HART COMMITTED SUICIDE MEET ME
PEGGY

Next morning I read a brief account of the suicide in the morning papers, from which I also learned that the *Orizaba* would reach New York on the afternoon of Friday the twenty-ninth. After some official hesitation—for *The New Republic* had never before shown an interest in ship-news reporting—I obtained a newspaperman's pass on the Coast Guard cutter that met arriving vessels at Quarantine. The cutter was full of reporters that day; there must have been sixty on board. With horror I pictured them swarming over Peggy, asking her intimate questions, and I pictured the headlines over their stories: "Says Poet Died for Love," or, "Despaired of Fame, Courted Death." Then the cutter stopped beside another liner, the *Berengaria*, and all but two of the reporters went on board. One of them told me that they had all come down the Bay to meet Mrs. Reginald A. Hargreaves, then eighty years old, who was said to be the original Alice of *Alice's Adventures in Wonderland*.

Having struck up a conversation with the two reporters left on the cutter, I remarked that a poet named Hart Crane had committed suicide by jumping from the stern of the *Orizaba*. They didn't think the story was news any longer, and neither of them spoke to Peggy when we went on board. I saw that her left hand was deep in bandages. After a while she told me that the injured hand might have had something to do with Hart's death. Drunk in Havana, he had invaded the crew's quarters, where he had been beaten and robbed; then an officer had locked him in his cabin. Meanwhile a box of wax matches had exploded in Peggy's hand as she was lighting a cigarette. At twelve o'clock noon, after the wound had been dressed for a second time, a stewardess was helping Peggy into her clothes. Hart burst into the room wearing a topcoat over his pajamas. "Good-bye, dear," he said, and rushed out again. There was something in his tone that frightened her. If it hadn't been for the painfully burned hand, she would have jumped up, and perhaps she could have stopped him.

"Perhaps for that one time," I said.

At the dock I helped Peggy through customs with her collection of Mexican baskets and serapes. She was staying with friends whom I didn't want to see at the time, so I put her into a taxi and kissed her good-bye. Having mourned for Hart a year before he died, I now felt that his suicide and Peggy's decree of divorce were echoes of an era that had ended. It had been a good era in its fashion, full of high spirits and grand parties, but also, it seemed to me now, inexcusably wasteful of time and emotions. We had lived on the reckless margins of society and had spent our energies on our private lives, which had gone to pieces. Now I wanted to get married again and stay married, I knew to whom. I wanted to live as simply as possible and turn my energies toward the world outside. I wanted to write honestly, I wanted to do my share in building a just society, and it did not occur to me that those last two aims, both admirable in themselves, might come into conflict.

# 9.
# The Rout of the
# Bonus Army

On May 1, 1932, which was the Sunday after my trip down the Bay, I made a public confession of faith by marching in the May Day parade. It was a big parade that year, with thirty-five thousand marchers by the lowest estimate and a hundred thousand by the highest, which of course was *The Daily Worker*'s. Arriving early I ran into John Herrmann, one of the Paris crowd; he now looked pale, shabby, and, I thought, exalted. He invited me to join a delegation of writers from *The New Masses* and the John Reed Club.

After an interminable but high-humored wait in a side street, under a threatening sky, we formed eight abreast with our slogans red-lettered on cardboard and marched around Union Square, which was crowded with friendly spectators. Somewhere near us was a larger delegation of students from local universities. When the band stopped playing "The International," we could hear them chanting a sort of college yell: "We confess communism." The parade moved down Broadway toward Rutgers Square, its destination on the Lower East Side. At some point the rain began falling, gently at first, then in heavy gusts. The sidewalks were empty now, except for policemen in black-rubber raincoats, and the red paint dripped from our wilted placards. There was, however, one last outburst of high spirits. Far down on East Broadway, as the marchers passed the offices of *The Jewish Daily Forward*, a Socialist newspaper, each contingent in turn booed and shouted, "Down with the yellow press." It seemed that the Socialists, more than the capitalists, were the enemy to be defied.

Hundreds of policemen were waiting as we plodded into Rutgers Square. "It's all over," they said in businesslike voices, pushing into the crowd but not using their clubs. "Break it up. Go home." The policemen didn't want trouble that day, and neither did the marchers. "Cossacks," a few of them shouted back, but not belligerently. A May Day parade was intended to be a peaceful show of strength and of beliefs held in common, almost like a saint's-day procession in Naples, and besides it was raining too hard for a riot.

John Herrmann came home with me by subway. While his cracked shoes dried on the radiator, we were busy talking, but not about writing or Paris or what Hemingway might be doing next. We talked about John's trip to Russia two years before, when he had been fired with enthusiasm by attending a writers' congress in Kharkov. Also we must have talked about the prospects of revolution in the United States, as everyone seemed to be doing in that year of wild fears and wilder dreams of tomorrow.

A few weeks later there was more talk of revolution when the Bonus Expeditionary Force descended on Washington. The BEF was a tattered army consisting of veterans from every state in the Union; most of them were old-stock Americans from smaller industrial cities where relief had broken down. All unemployed in 1932, all living on the edge of hunger, they remembered that the government had made them a promise for the future. It was embodied in a law that Congress had passed some years before, providing "adjusted compensation certificates" for those who had served in the Great War; the certificates were to be redeemed in dollars, but not until 1945. Now the veterans were hitchhiking and stealing rides on freight cars to Washington, for the sole purpose, they declared, of petitioning Congress for immediate payment of the soldiers' bonus. They arrived by hundreds or thousands every day in June. Ten thousand were camped on marshy ground across the Anacostia River, and ten thousand others occupied a number of half-demolished buildings between the Capitol and the White House. They organized themselves by states and companies and chose a commander named Walter W. Waters, an ex-sergeant from Portland, Oregon, who promptly acquired an aide-de-camp and a pair of highly polished leather puttees. Meanwhile the veterans were listening to speakers of all political complexions, as the Russian soldiers had done in 1917. Many radicals and some conservatives thought that the Bonus Army was creating a revolutionary situation of an almost classical type.

Although the Communists had no share in starting the Bonus March—in fact it took them by surprise—they tried hard to seize control of it. Members of the Workers Ex-Servicemen's League, one of their so-called "mass" organizations, were urged to enroll in the BEF, and at one time there were more than two hundred Communist veterans in Washington. They lived by themselves in a dismantled building, having been jim-crowed by the other veterans, who were patriots to a man. Commander Waters had begun to nurse political ambitions, which would be frustrated if the Reds got into his army. He was known to have organized an intelligence force that was charged with keeping them under surveillance. Any Communist who ventured into the camp on Anacostia Flats was likely to be denounced and given fifteen lashes with an army belt. Still the Communists kept trying to make converts. They hoped that the veterans would yield to the logic of events, which must end by persuading them all that there was no hope for the unemployed under capitalism. Left-wing journalists by the score had been visiting Washington to report "the situation." When they got back to New York, some of them told me jubilantly that the Bonus Army newspaper was becoming more "militant," a friendly word in the Communists' vocabulary (their enemies were not militant but "ruthless" or "demagogic"). The journalists also said that although the rank-and-file (another friendly term) wouldn't listen to Communists, they were beginning to talk like Communists themselves.

But the marchers still put their hopes in medals worn on ragged shirts, in discharge papers carried in their wallets, and in making congressmen believe that they controlled thousands of votes. To many people over the country, the marchers seemed to be speaking in behalf of all the unemployed. Congress was not yet disposed to help the unemployed, though the Patman Bonus Bill squeaked through the House of Representatives on June 15. Two days later it was debated in the Senate. While eight thousand veterans picketed the Capitol, massing their American flags on the steps of the Senate wing, the bill went down to a crushing defeat. The veterans, however, were still in Washington, where they proposed to stay till they got their money. "If we have to," they said, "we can wait here till 1945." Many of them had nowhere else to go. In Washington they at least had shelter of a sort, and they were fed by public and private charity, even if they could never be sure what next would go into their big kettles of mulligan. Some of the veterans had been joined by their wives and children. The Bonus Army was beginning to develop its own style of life, its legends, its loyalties, and its defiant folksongs:

> *Mellon pulled the whistle,*
> *Hoover rang the bell,*
> *Wall Street gave the signal,*
> *And the country went to hell.*

The veterans liked to believe that Andrew Mellon was the engineer of the all-American business express, that Wall Street was the train dispatcher who had put it on the wrong track, and that Mr. Hoover was only the fireman. They did not intend to wreck the train, as they thought the Communists were trying to do. "Hell, we're not against the government," they said. "We're just against the guys that are running it." All sorts of amateur and professional politicians were scheming to make use of their mild rebellion. There was Father Cox of Pittsburgh, who had organized a Jobless Party and named himself as its candidate for president; he made a trip to Washington and pleaded with the veterans to endorse him. There was Father Coughlin, the radio priest of Royal Oak, Michigan, who also wanted their support and gave $5000 to their treasury. Jacob S. Coxey of Massillon, Ohio, had led his own army of protest in 1894. Now he was the presidential candidate of a new Farmer-Labor Party—not allied with the more practical Farmer-Laborites of Minnesota—and he asked Commander Waters to be his running mate. Waters had what he thought was a better scheme; he wanted to lead a national movement of the unemployed that would be organized on military lines. He must have been thinking of Hitler and Mussolini when he decided to call it the Khaki Shirts.

There is some evidence that high officials of the administration had their own scheme for profiting from the Bonus March. First they would try to persuade the public that most of the marchers were Reds bent on overthrowing the government. Then, at the first excuse, they would use military force to disperse the BEF, with the result, so they hoped, that the country would rally to Mr. Hoover as its saviour. Some but not all of the higher military officers were eager to prove that they knew exactly how to deal with civil commotions. At military posts near Washington all leaves were canceled and men were being drilled in the use of bayonets and tear gas against civilians. One difficulty had appeared in carrying out the scheme. As Secretary of War Patrick J. Hurley, famous for his indiscretions, complained in a private discussion with Waters, the BEF had been too law-abiding. There had been no "incident" that would offer an excuse for declaring martial law. After Congress adjourned on July 16, the Bonus Army had begun to melt away, with eight thousand men leaving in a week, and it now looked as though the episode would end peaceably, to the disappointment of many radical and conservative politicians.

Late in July I went to visit my father and mother at their country house near the village of Belsano, Pennsylvania. I wanted them to meet my new wife, and I wanted Muriel to see the house where I was born. In Belsano, on Friday the twenty-eighth, I read about the battle of Washington and the rout of the remaining veterans. While some of them were being evicted from an abandoned government building on Pennsylvania Avenue, there had been just enough of a fracas to serve as the incident for which Hurley and others were waiting. Mr. Hoover had called in the soldiers, and they had appeared in an imposing column: four troops of cavalry, all in gas masks and with drawn sabers, then a mounted machine-gun squadron, six tanks, a battalion of infantry with fixed bayonets, and a convoy of trucks. In command of the column was General Douglas MacArthur, then the highest-ranking officer in the Army of the United States.

I read about the march up Pennsylvania Avenue and the tear-gas bombs lobbed into the crowd of spectators. In the afternoon papers I read about the battle of Anacostia Flats, where the soldiers set fire to the miserable shacks and the veterans with their families scuttled through the smoke and the tear-gas fumes like dry leaves in a bonfire. I read a proclamation by Mr. Hoover, who announced that "after months of patient indulgence, the government met overt lawlessness as it always must be met if the cherished processes of self-government are to be preserved." I read more news about the veterans: outlaws now, they were being herded into trucks, which would carry them north into Pennsylvania, then westward along the Lincoln Highway. Mayor McCloskey of Johnstown, a red-haired ex-pugilist, had invited them to his city, and thousands of them were planning to establish a new camp there, if they could escape from the trucks that were rushing them toward the Middle West. That brought the story close to home. Belsano is only eighteen miles northwest of Johnstown, and the Lincoln Highway is about the same distance south of the city. On Saturday morning we set out in the family Hupmobile to see what was happening.

Johnstown, which had been one of the grimiest small cities in the world, looked unexpectedly bright and clean with the steel mills closed down. I had heard that half the working force of the city was unemployed and that a fifth or a sixth of the population was in need of charity. At such a time the arrival of several thousand hungry strangers was a threat in itself, but the editor of *The Johnstown Tribune* had conjured up new terrors. He wrote in an editorial published that morning:

> Johnstown faces a crisis. It must prepare to protect itself from the Bonus Army concentrating here at the invitation of Mayor Eddie McCloskey. . . .
>
> In any group the size of the Bonus Army, made up of men gathered from all parts of the country, without effective leadership in a crisis, without any attempt on the part of those leaders to check up the previous records of the individuals who compose it, there is certain to be a mixture of undesirables—thieves, plug-uglies, degenerates. . . . The community must protect itself from the criminal fringe of the invaders.
>
> Booster clubs, community organizations of every sort, volunteer organizations if no sectional group is available, should get together in extraordinary sessions and organize to protect property, women and possibly life.
>
> It is no time for halfway measures. . . .

The heroes of 1918, now metamorphosed into "thieves, plug-uglies, degenerates," were about to gather in the southern outskirts of the city, at a campsite that someone had offered them. Meanwhile the leading citizens, aided by state troopers, were planning to use "extraordinary measures" to keep them from reaching it. I thought as we drove southward that Mr. Hoover's proclamation had done its work.

At the village of Jennerstown, on the Lincoln Highway, we found a barracks of the Pennsylvania State Police that looked for all the world like a prosperous roadhouse. There was a traffic light in front of the barracks, and that was where the veterans would have to turn north if they went to Johnstown. It was the task of the state troopers to keep them moving west over the mountains, toward Ligonier and the Ohio border. In half an hour on Saturday morning I saw more than a thousand veterans pass through Jennerstown—that is, more than fifty open trucks bearing an average of twenty men each. Later I was told that the convoys kept passing at longer intervals until Sunday evening. The troopers waited at the intersection, twenty men on their motorcycles, like a school of gray sharks, till they heard that a convoy was approaching; then they darted off to meet it in a foam of dust and blue gasoline smoke, with their stiff-brimmed hats cutting the air like fins. One of the troopers stayed behind to manipulate the traffic light. As the trucks came nearer, he would throw a switch that changed it to a yellow blinker, so they could all shoot past without slackening speed.

The men in the trucks were kneeling, standing with their hands on each other's shoulders, or clinging unsteadily to the sideboards; they had no room to sit down. Behind each truck rode a trooper, and there were half a dozen others mingled with the crowd of farmers in overalls that watched from the front of a filling station. We stood not far away while my mother, a simple woman of strong feelings, kept clenching and unclenching her big hands. She was moved by the contrast between the hatless, coatless, unshaven veterans, all looking half-starved—most of them hadn't eaten or slept for thirty-six hours—and the sleekly uniformed, well-nourished troopers who were herding them past their destination. "I hate those troopers," she said loudly enough for some of the troopers to hear. The farmers looked down, and one of them gave a ruminative nod.

"Hey, buddies," the farmers began to shout as the trucks racketed past. "You turn right. Turn right. Johnstown"—swinging their arms northward—"Johnstown."

The hungry men smiled and waved at them uncomprehendingly. A few, however, had seen that they were being carried beyond their meeting place, and they tried to pass the word from truck to truck, above the roar of the motors. As they bowled through the level village street, there was no way to escape, but just beyond Jennerstown the road climbs steeply up Laurel Hill; the drivers shifted into second gear and promptly lost half their passengers. The others, those who received no warning or let themselves be cowed by the troopers, were carried westward. The following week I met a New York veteran who hadn't escaped from a convoy until it passed the Ohio line. A Negro from Washington, a resident of the city for thirty years—he wasn't a bonus marcher, but had made the mistake of walking through Anacostia in his shirt sleeves—was arrested, piled into a truck, and carried to Indianapolis before he managed to tell his story to a reporter.

As for the veterans who escaped at Jennerstown, they lay by the roadside utterly exhausted. Their leaders had been arrested or dispersed; their strength had been gnawed away by hunger and lack of sleep; they hoped to reunite and recuperate in a new camp, but how to reach it they did not know. For perhaps twenty minutes they dozed there helplessly. Then—I saw this happening—a new leader would stand out from the ranks. He would stop a motorist, ask for the road to Johnstown, call the men together, give them instructions—and the whole group would suddenly obey a self-imposed discipline. As they turned northward at the Jennerstown traffic light, one of them would shout, "We're going back!" and perhaps a half dozen would mumble in lower voices, "We're gonna get guns and go back to Washington."

Mile after mile we passed the ragged line as we drove toward the camp at Ideal Park. We were carrying two of the veterans, chosen from a group of three hundred by a quick informal vote. One was a man gassed in the Argonne and tear-gassed at Anacostia; he breathed with a noisy gasp. The other was a man with family troubles; he had lost his wife and six children when the camp was burned and he hoped to find them in Johnstown. He talked about his wartime service, his three medals, which he refused to wear, his wounds, and his five years in a government hospital. "If they gave me a job," he said, "I wouldn't care about the bonus."

The sick man, as we passed one group of veterans after another, some empty-handed, others stumbling under the weight of suitcases and blanket rolls, kept pointing north and calling in an almost inaudible voice, "This way, comrades, this way. Comrades, this way," till his head drooped forward and he lapsed into a wheezing sleep.

At Ideal Park, an abandoned picnic ground, the new camp was being pitched in an atmosphere of fatigue and hysteria. A tall man with a tear-streaked face marched back and forth. "I used to be a hundred-percenter," he said, "but now I'm a Red radical. I had an American flag, but the damn tin soldiers burned it. Now I don't ever want to see a flag again. Give me a gun and I'll go back to Washington."—"That's right, buddy," a woman said looking up from her two babies, who lay on a dirty quilt in the sun, under a cloud of flies. Two men sat at a picnic table reading the editorial page of *The Johnstown Tribune*. One of them shouted, "Let them come here and mow us down with machine guns. We won't move this time." The woman with the babies said, "That's right, buddy." A haggard face—eyes bloodshot, skin pasty white under a three days' beard—looked in through the car window like a halloween spook. "Hoover must die," the face said ominously. "You know what this means?" a man shouted from the other side. "This means revolution."—"You're damn right it means revolution, buddy," the woman said.

"But a thousand homeless veterans, or fifty thousand, don't make a revolution," was what I said in an article written the following week. "This threat would pass and be forgotten, like the other threat that was only half concealed in the *Tribune*'s editorial. Next day the bonus leaders would come, the slick guys in leather puttees; they would make a few speeches and everything would be smoothed over. They would talk of founding a new fascist order of Khaki Shirts, but this threat, too, can be disregarded; a fascist movement, to succeed in this country, must come from the middle classes and be respectable. No," I said, "if any revolution results from the flight of the Bonus Army, it will come from a different source, from the government itself. The Army in time of peace, at the national capital, has been used against unarmed citizens—and this, with all it threatens for the future, is a revolution in itself."

Rereading those words more than forty years later, I seem to find in them an undertone of something close to hysteria. Its presence does not surprise me. Not only the bonus marchers but millions of other Americans, rich and poor, were beginning to be hysterical in that summer of 1932.

# 10.
# Grass Grew in
# the Streets

In July 1932 the *New York Times* index of business activity went down to 52, or scarcely more than half of what it had been in the 1920s. Industrial stocks were selling in Wall Street for less than one-tenth, on the average, of their prices during the boom. The whole economy was afflicted with a slow paralysis that had started in the extremities and was creeping in toward the heart. Employment in manufacturing had fallen to an index of 55.2, while the wages of those factory workers lucky enough to keep their jobs had been reduced by an average of almost exactly one-third. And other indices of misfortune: the marriage rate had fallen over the country, and the divorce rate too; divorces cost money, but one kept hearing of more and more families in which the husband, no longer the breadwinner, had simply disappeared. Physicians reported that impotence, apparently caused by discouragement, was becoming a common symptom in men under forty. Though probably not for that reason, the birth rate was also falling; in the preceding year it had been 14 percent lower than in 1926, as if people were hesitating to bring life into an uncertain world.

At last the administration was trying to restore prosperity

by another means than making optimistic statements or calling out the troops. With the happy assent of Congress, voted in January, it had created the Reconstruction Finance Corporation (RFC) and had given it $2 billion of government credit, from which it could make loans to corporations in distress. The public soon learned, however, that most of the RFC money was going to a few of the larger banks, railroads, and trust companies, with the result that some of the greatest American fortunes were being preserved intact. Comparatively little of it went to the banks where poor people kept their savings, since few of those neighborhood institutions could offer the right sort of collateral; it was the Arkansas drought-relief policy of no help for the neediest, here repeated on a vaster scale. None of the loans went to American municipalities, which were struggling under the double burden of decreased revenue from taxation and greatly increased expenditures to keep the unemployed from starving.

Chicago was a famous example. On June 2, while the Bonus Army was pouring into Washington, Mr. Hoover was informed that Chicago was bankrupt, that municipal employees had not been paid for five months, that the city could obtain no more loans from the bankers, and that all forms of relief would cease in two days unless the federal government came to its aid. Mr. Hoover took no action, and none was taken by the Reconstruction Finance Corporation. General Charles G. Dawes, then president of the RFC, was a steadfast and voluble opponent of doles for the unemployed. On June 6 Dawes resigned his government post and went back to Chicago to resume direction of the Central Republic Bank; everybody wondered why. On June 22 Mayor Anton Cermak flew to Washington and testified that there were stirrings of revolt among the Chicago unemployed, then numbering seven hundred thousand, or nearly half of the local working force. He demanded a loan of $152 million from the RFC on the ground, among others, that it would be cheaper to send federal money in June than federal troops the following winter. Money was sent to Chicago that month, but not to Mayor

Cermak's administration, which would have used some of it to feed the hungry; instead the RFC made a loan of $90 million to its former president's Chicago bank. The Central Republic had by then lost half of its deposits, including many of the largest accounts. The loan arrived in time to protect the remaining depositors, but not in time to save the bank, which was soon forced into reorganization.

Many of us were incensed by such "doles to the rich," as *The New Republic* often called them, and it is hard for me not to feel indignant today as I think back on those unbelievable times. Nothing in the economy seemed to make sense, and nothing done by the government produced the desired effect. It was said that the RFC loans would revive the whole system of credit, would make it easier to find capital for new industries, and hence would create hundreds of thousands of new jobs. It was said that benefits conferred on the top layer of American business would "trickle down"—that was the phrase—through other layers, until everyone had been reemployed. In those days, however, nothing trickled down from the top but fear. As fast as the government printed money and sent it out to banks, the new bills disappeared from circulation, with gold certificates the first to go. The rich were frightened that year, and instead of building new factories, which would have been almost certain to operate at a loss, they were putting their capital into gold and hoarding it in vaults. There was a national campaign against hoarding, but it was no more effective than the other campaigns that the administration had sponsored; perhaps it created new hoarders by calling attention to what the rich were doing. In those days everyone was learning to interpret official statements of optimism "in the Pickwickian sense," to use another *New Republic* phrase. Mr. Hoover continued to make them, but every time he said Thumbs Up, the stock market turned down. For an official to state that a bank was in sound condition was sometimes enough to start a run on it.

Where were the great captains of business who had claimed, or encouraged their public-relations counselors to claim, that they had been responsible for making the nation prosperous during the boom years? Could they now disclaim responsibility for a national disaster? In August 1930, only two summers before, James W. Gerard, a former ambassador to Germany, had given the newspapers a list of "fifty-nine men who rule the United States." The list, which omitted Mr. Hoover and every other elected official, was composed of financiers and industrialists, beginning with John D. Rockefeller, Jr., Andrew Mellon, J. P. Morgan, and seven Du Ponts. "These men rule," Gerard said, "by virtue of their ability. They themselves are too busy to hold public office, but they determine who shall hold such office." By changing their nationality, he added, "They could make England the financial giant that America now is."

But America was already a sick giant when Gerard published his list—and what had the rulers been doing since then to cure its illness? A few of them had tried seriously to maintain employment in the industries they controlled. Others had cut wages as much as they dared and as soon as they dared, while making statements designed to restore other people's confidence. By the summer of 1932 most of the rulers were reduced to defending their personal fortunes, often at the expense of other rulers and sometimes without success. The Van Sweringen brothers of Cleveland, both on Gerard's list, had struggled vainly to prevent their railroad empire from crumbling away. Samuel Insull of Chicago, who stood higher on the list, had left suddenly for Europe after resigning eighty-five directorships, sixty-five chairmanships, and eleven presidencies, mostly of public-utility corporations which he had grandly mismanaged and left in or close to bankruptcy. Already there was talk of demanding his extradition. Many of the remaining rulers—including even Charles M. Schwab of Bethlehem Steel, a persistent optimist—were ready at last to confess their bewilderment. "I'm afraid," Schwab said at a luncheon, "every man is afraid. I don't know, we don't know, whether the values we have are going to be real next month or not." Said Andrew Mellon, the overlord of Pittsburgh, "None of us has any means of knowing when and how we shall emerge from the valley of depression in which the world is traveling." And Sewell Avery of Montgomery Ward, not on Gerard's list though he probably should have been: "To describe the causes of this situation is rather beyond my capacity. I am unfortunate in having no friends that seem able to explain it clearly to me."

The fifty-nine men who ruled the United States had resigned from their posts as national regents and had returned—except for the exiles and bankrupts—to their own beleaguered principalities. The unemployed were left to find such answers as they could to the always more pressing questions, "But why?" and "How much longer?" and "What can be done?" Sometimes they asked, "What can each of us do, now, to save himself and the others?"

That was the summer when the unemployed were trying to feed and house themselves by all possible methods, including some very old ones. Married sons and daughters moved back with their parents, huddling together for shelter like the members of a food-gathering tribe. All the tribes in a city block would sometimes unite against local authorities. It happened regularly in Chicago, and elsewhere sporadically, that when city marshals evicted a family for not paying its rent, a crowd would gather in the street, drive off the marshals, break down the padlocked door, and move back the furniture. Food was cheap that year, and many unemployed families lived on stale bread at five cents a loaf, while others raised their own vegetables if land was available. Even on Manhattan Island, with its poisoned soil, there were backyard vegetable plots—I could see them from my window— and a much-praised committee managed to find enough vacant lots for a thousand "family gardens," where potato vines yellowed among the broken bricks. Twenty or thirty miles away on the Long Island truck farms, there was a huge crop of potatoes that summer, but half of them rotted in the ground because the prevailing price of twenty-four cents a bushel was not enough to pay for digging and shipping them.

Subsistence gardens were more successful in the smaller industrial cities of the Middle West, where there was more and better land within walking distance of the unemployed. Relief bureaus divided the land, distributed free seeds, and sometimes furnished experienced truck farmers to supervise the planting and cultivation. In Gary, Indiana, there were twenty thousand gardens on land borrowed from its owners by the municipal government. Part of the crop, there and elsewhere, was canned or dried for winter use, thus simplifying the problem of public relief, but creating a new problem for the farmers of the nation, who found a shrinking market for everything they had to sell.

We followed "the situation" in *The New Republic*. The farmers, besides complaining to Washington, were trying to solve their problems at home. With no money to buy industrial products, they either did without them or used home-grown substitutes. Some of the products that many did without were new clothes first of all—they patched the old ones—then in succession newspapers, movies, new parts for the farm machinery, electric lights when the bills went unpaid, toilet paper, gasoline, and finally coffee and sugar. They laid up the tractor and plowed with mules, for which there was a new demand that year—and not for young ones, which still cost money, but for any broken-down mule that was strong enough to work in harness. When a family car wore out, the owner removed the engine and attached a wagon pole to the chassis; that made a "Hoover wagon," and there were thousands of them on the back roads, especially in the South. The farm wives cooked with wood instead of coal or kerosene; on the prairies, where wood was scarce, abandoned houses disappeared into the neighbors' kitchen stoves. Honey or sorghum syrup from a home plot served for sweetening. The old shoemaker's last came down from the attic, and farmers cobbled their own shoes, while the children went barefoot. Many farmers managed to lead good lives without money, if they owned rich land free from mortgages, but others back in the hills lived like East European peasants, and the sharecroppers lived like serfs.

In broad sections of the countryside time stood still, or rather the calendar turned back toward earlier years. Millions of farmers—as Jonathan Norton Leonard said in his angry book *Three Years Down* (1939)—and other millions of former industrial workers had seceded, or had been expelled, from the modern American system of production and exchange. The system itself had been weakened by losing all those producers and consumers; in fact there were many communities where it had ceased to operate: the local factories were idle, the stores did no business, the banks had closed, and little money remained in circulation. Local systems of exchange began to develop in the wreckage of the national system. Often they started in the simplest possible fashion, with a farmer swapping a pound of honey for a dozen eggs or a barrel of potatoes for half a cord of firewood. Soon there were accepted times and places for barter—Saturday morning, for example, at the schoolhouse or Friday afternoon at the local grange—and some of the transactions would be on credit. An unemployed mechanic would appear from the county seat and offer to repair farm machinery in return for tomatoes or beans that his wife might can for the winter. Sometimes the owner of an idle cannery would let his equipment be used free of charge for preserving a crop that could not be sold.

By the summer of 1932 there were more complicated systems of barter and "production for use" in many parts of the country, as notably in Ohio, in the region around Minneapolis, and in southern California. The Minneapolis system, started by a Methodist minister, included skilled workers in almost every trade, machines loaned out by the owners of closed factories, gangs of men cutting firewood, warehouses full of canned goods, a large restaurant, and a store with fifteen hundred customers each day; it was an enterprise supporting thousands, and it had been undertaken without the help of currency issued by the U.S. government. The system as a whole had its own unchartered "bank," which issued its own money, redeemable in merchandise, in denominations up to ten theoretical dollars.

Lack of currency was a serious problem in many counties where all the banks had closed. Factories that continued to operate in some of those counties had to pay their employees in small bills and silver, since paychecks couldn't be cashed. A general store in Yellow Springs, Ohio, had a local printer run off a thousand dollars in "money" of various denominations from ten cents to five dollars. It was supported only by the good name of the store, but farmers accepted it for their produce, and it helped to keep business going in the neighborhood. The town of Tenino, Washington, issued $5000 in "wooden money" printed on strips of veneer; it was supposed to be guaranteed by the assets of a closed bank. Later there would be magnesium money in Michigan, minted by the Dow Chemical Company, and the employees of many bankrupt municipalities would be paid in tax-anticipation certificates. These were often accepted by local storekeepers, who had to choose between selling their goods for "funny money" and not selling them at all.

Some old forms of enterprise were revived in that disastrous summer. One of them was panning for gold in the Sierra Nevadas, where some of the luckier miners earned as much as two dollars a day. Small-time bootlegging was a more remunerative occupation for scores of thousands among the unemployed, even though the beer barons and the syndicated whisky smugglers had entered a period of declining profits, like all the other lords of industry. While the barons warred among themselves, mowing down a business rival with machine guns or sinking him into a barrel of wet concrete and dumping it into the river, they were faced by myriads of new competitors, each too small to be worth the trouble of rubbing out, but impressive in the mass. There was even a new industry that supplied the needs of home brewers, vintners, and distillers. Hundreds of shops on modest streets kept a stock of malt syrup and ten-gallon crocks for making beer, of raisins and dried Dalmatian cherries for heavy wines, and of copper stills just the right size for a tenement kitchen. Most of the homemade beer was consumed by the brewers and their cronies, but the wines and the white mule were peddled in mason jars to thirsty neighbors. Another flourishing industry, at least in the anthracite country of northeastern Pennsylvania, was the bootleg mining of coal. When a big colliery closed down, the unemployed miners would open their own pits on colliery land. The coal would be trucked to a big city, most often to Philadelphia, and would be sold for about two-thirds the price of legal anthracite. At one time it was being shipped from five thousand bootleg mines. The operation was open theft, but it provided a living for some thirty thousand families, and these included so many voters that the tough Pennsylvania state troopers did not interfere.

Young men all over the country who could find no jobs for themselves, and no opportunities for private enterprise in the new illegal industries, might simply take to the road. At first they would have the notion of finding work in another city, but all cities were the same that year, and they would continue wandering for the simple reason that they had nothing better to do. The number of migrants increased from season to season. In 1929 the Missouri Pacific Railroad had "taken official cognizance" of 13,745 migrants; that is, its brakemen and bulls had thrown them off the trains. In 1931 it took the same cognizance of 186,028. Jonathan Norton Leonard, who collected these figures, also found that the Southern Pacific ejected 416,915 migrants during the eight months from September 1931 through April 1932. By that time the other Western roads had stopped counting or interfering with the migrants; they found it cheaper to provide them with free transportation. Almost every through freight now included two or three empty boxcars, with open doors, so that the passengers wouldn't break open the loaded cars or hang in clusters all over the train.

During the summer more than a million unemployed Americans were traveling with no fixed destination. Nobody counted them, but none of the estimates was lower, and some were as high as two million. According to social agencies, most of the migrants were men or boys between the ages of fifteen and thirty. There were older men too, some of whom were aggressive homosexuals—"wolves," in the jargon of the road—but the boys were simply adventurous youngsters. Teenage girls disguised themselves as boys before hopping a freight, and some of the migrants were married women traveling respectably with their husbands. One saw whole families along the highway thumbing for rides, in addition to the "loners," but most of the migrants traveled by railroad, spending the night in empty boxcars or in hobo jungles beside the tracks and begging for food by day or snatching it from grocery stores. Usually they kept out of trouble with the police. Sometimes, though, a band of sturdy beggars a hundred strong would march into a little town and demand something to eat. It was cheaper to give them food, on condition of their leaving by the next train, than it would have been to put them all in jail and feed them from the public treasury.

A whole social world was growing up outside the accepted American system of earning and spending. Curiously the lowest members of that world—I am thinking of the derelicts used to living on Skid Row—were in some ways the luckiest. They could get plenty of food by standing in breadlines, of which there had never been so many, and even the problem of money for liquor was simpler than it had been in the 1920s. The police of most cities had stopped arresting panhandlers, and prosperous citizens, feeling guilty about being well fed, were more generous with their silver. The dimes and quarters collected by the derelicts went mostly for jellied cooking alcohol—they squeezed it through a rag and drank the liquid—or Jamaica ginger, called "jake," or bottles of Passover wine. The more self-respecting of the homeless men, especially those who were too old or not adventurous enough to wander over the country, settled down in their own urban colonies, the famous Hoovervilles. These were huddles of one-room shacks on vacant land, most of the shacks about eight feet square, with walls made of grocery cartons smoothed flat, with a door that sagged on hinges cut from worn-out tires, and with a roof of hammered-out tin cans. Building materials of the sort could be found on any city dump, and every city had at least one Hooverville; New York and Chicago each had dozens. The better ones were situated near a municipal comfort station. For sanitation and plumbing most of the others had a trench more or less concealed with burlap curtains and called a Hoover Villa. Many of the earlier colonies were destroyed by the police, on the ground of their being a menace to public health, but by 1932 they were almost all being tolerated as independent steps toward housing the unemployed. The colonists were usually law-abiding; in fact almost every cluster of huts had a so-called mayor who charged himself with maintaining order. If he failed to control noisy drunks and troublemakers, these were likely to be evicted by a general vote of the citizens.

More and more middle-class people were talking about revolution, but there was no sign of it in the streets. With almost all the riveting hammers stored away, American cities had become blessedly quiet, like country towns. People were also talking about a crime wave, especially after the kidnapping and murder of the Lindbergh baby, but that proved to be a single revolting incident. Although we read about more than the usual number of gangland killings, all as grotesque and seemingly aseptic as a Bugs Bunny animated cartoon, there was no statistical increase in crimes of violence. I can testify that the streets of New York were much safer than they would be half a century later. Young wives—mine, for example—would walk home alone at midnight after visiting friends in the Village, not even hurrying as they passed the new Hooverville that slept in the half-acre excavation for an unbuilt apartment house on Abingdon Square. The revolution, if it was coming, was being prepared in a curious atmosphere of peace and apathy.

Almost the only violence that summer—except for official violence against the bonus marchers—flamed up where it was least expected, among the conservative farmers of western Iowa. They had been prosperous ten years before, and they had gone into debt to raise more corn and make more money. Now corn was selling for next to nothing, like everything else they produced—milk, for example, brought them only two cents a quart from the dairies in Council Bluffs—and many of them were about to lose their rich land because they couldn't pay taxes or interest on mortgages. Under the leadership of an angry man named Milo A. Reno, they banded together into a Farmers' Holiday Association, with the aim of holding grain, meat, and milk off the market until prices rose sufficiently to cover the cost of production. At first they merely argued with other farmers who wouldn't observe the holiday. Soon, however, they barricaded the roads —either with logs or with nail-studded leather belts from threshing machines—stopped every truck bound for town, turned the cattle loose, and emptied milk into ditches. Young men wearing khaki shirts, as a token of membership in the new fascist movement founded by Commander Waters of the Bonus Army, came out from Sioux City and Omaha to join their picket lines.

On August 24 there was a battle near Council Bluffs. The sheriff arrested fifty-five of the pickets, but released them the following day after a thousand armed farmers threatened to storm the jail. The Communists, again taken by surprise, sent out Mother Bloor and her son Harold Ware, later active in Washington, to preach their doctrines among the farmers. By that time, however, everyone was becoming a little frightened, and Reno called off the strike on the promise of the Midwestern governors to hold a conference about farm prices. The country settled back to watch and listen to the election campaign.

# 11.
## The Writers' Crusade

It was the year when everyone with a scheme for saving the
country wanted to start his own party and run for president.
By midsummer there were twenty-six "third parties" in the field,
each claiming that it would receive a million votes—except the
Socialists, who were making a vigorous campaign and expected
two million. Some of the parties vanished in the early autumn
for want of support, but twenty-three minor-party names remained on the ballots of various states, as symbols of confused
discontent and simple confusion. Besides Socialist, Communist,
and Prohibition, each representing an organized movement with
a history and with plans for the future, the names included Labor,
Socialist-Labor, Farmer-Labor, Progressive, Liberty, Independent
Liberty, Independent, Independent Republican, Berks Independent, Independence, Law Preservation, Enforcement Allies, Citizens, Peoples, Populist, Security, American, National, Jacksonian,
and Jobless.

Almost all the new parties made their appeal to voters by
promising radical measures to combat unemployment. The Liberty Party, for example, nominated the aged "Coin" Harvey as
its candidate and advocated the unlimited coinage of silver, as

well as greenbacks enough for everybody. In the election it was the least unsuccessful of the new parties; it received 53,435 votes. The Populist Party broke the record for unpopularity by receiving—or being credited with—exactly four votes over the nation. The National Party was credited with 1615. Father Cox of Pittsburgh, the self-nominated candidate of the Jobless Party, set out on a national speaking tour, but he was stranded for want of funds in Tucumcari, New Mexico, and withdrew from the race. Nevertheless he was credited with 740 votes, mostly from Pittsburgh, and perhaps he actually received a few hundred more. Election boards, even the honest ones, were not scrupulous in reporting the vote for minor parties: "What does it matter?" they said among themselves. It mattered little to the nation at large, but a great deal to the minor-party candidates, all of whom were eager to learn that they had not been disgraced.

They were not so much disgraced, on election day, as simply abandoned by their supporters, for the old reason that Americans hate to waste their votes. After one makes the greatest possible allowance for failures to count the minor-party ballots, the fact remains that at least nineteen voters out of twenty chose one or the other of the two parties that had a chance to win. The Republicans had been the majority party since 1896, with their slogans of sound money, high tariffs, and the full dinner pail. Before the depression they showed every sign of remaining a majority. It seemed to their leaders that the strongest Republican argument in 1932 would be expressed not in words but in figures on ticker tape; it would be a vigorous advance in the prices of stocks and commodities that could be taken as a sign that the depression was ending. Providentially there were means of obtaining an advance of the sort. The Farm Board could withhold its great stocks of wheat and cotton from the market; the Reconstruction Finance Corporation could transfuse new capital into sick corporations; and most—not all—of the big financiers were Republicans eager to help the party at a profit to themselves. The operation got under way in the middle of July, while the

Bonus Army was still in Washington. Stocks had already been rising when *The Annalist*, a financial weekly published by *The New York Times*, said in its issue of July 29:

> Many Wall Street observers believe that a vigorous attempt will be made to advance the security markets and to bring about some measure of business recovery before the election. Such a movement would fit rather well into the usual pattern of stock market cyclical movements. But an advance of this character would, of course, contain a large manipulative element and regardless of the outcome of the election, would probably be followed by a severe relapse beginning in November and December.

The manipulators were busy that summer. Stocks rose all during August, and early in September their average price was twice as high, or half as low, as it had been on July 8. Commodities also rose, with the help of a new Commodities Finance Corporation supported with federal money. Wheat was bringing 56½ cents a bushel, a high price for the depression years, and cotton was nearly ten cents a pound. On the other hand, the general level of business had risen hardly at all. Only a few workers were rehired, hourly wages continued to decline, and the public displayed a vast indifference to what was happening on the stock exchange. Soon the manipulators became uneasy. For all their loyalty to the Republican Party, they were still more attached to their private fortunes, and they were ready to transform themselves from bulls into bears at the least excuse. It came that month with the first election news: Maine, which still held its state election in September, had chosen a Democratic governor, and it now seemed that the Republicans had no chance in November. At once the market turned down. Cotton went back to six cents a pound, and before election day wheat was quoted at 41⅞, or less than its price in the days of Queen Elizabeth I. For the last six weeks of their campaign, the Republicans had to seek other arguments than rising prices; they had to depend on the natural conservatism of American voters and appeal to their fears of what the Democrats might do.

Roosevelt was a vastly better politician than Hoover, and also he had easier problems in 1932. He was convinced that Hoover had defeated himself by his failure to end the depression. Therefore he thought that the Democrats should confine themselves to the safe policy of keeping old friends, encouraging the disaffected Republicans, and not making any serious blunders. Actually he did a little more in his major speeches, of which there were twenty-seven. They more or less suggested every measure that would be adopted during the early days of the New Deal, but the suggestions were expressed vaguely, so as to hearten the radicals without frightening the conservatives. There were issues on which he preferred not to take a stand. Thus, he was presented with two contradictory drafts of a speech on the tariff, one written by a protectionist and the other by a free trader. Instead of choosing between them, he simply turned them over to Raymond Moley, the leader of his Brains Trust. "Weave them together," he said.

Many of his speeches seemed "woven together" in this fashion, but of course they had another purpose than that of explaining what the candidate proposed to do. There had been gossip that Roosevelt's illness had left him too feeble to be president, and his best way to answer it was by presenting himself tirelessly to voters in every part of the country. Another of the practical questions in the campaign, also raised by rumor and answered by indirection, was that of Al Smith's hold on the Irish Catholics. Would his millions of admirers stay away from the polls? Would they even go over to Hoover as revenge for Smith's failure to win the Democratic nomination? Roosevelt met that issue by appearing on one platform after another with a retinue of Irish Catholic politicians, until it seemed that the campaign was becoming a series of communion breakfasts.

Many other groups received special attention from the candidate or his lieutenants. Among them were farmers, women, organized labor, small businessmen, big financiers—some of whom contributed to the Democratic treasury—Italians, Czechs (through Mayor Anton Cermak of Chicago), unreconstructed Confederates, and Negroes. Strangely the party showed little concern with one minority that would play more than its part in the New Deal: I mean the intellectuals. Of course there was Roosevelt's Brains Trust, which included three professors from Columbia, but it did not direct its arguments to other professors. The fact is that intellectuals had too little voting power at the time for any candidate—except Norman Thomas—to bother about winning them over.

The intellectuals as a class supported Thomas and the Socialists. I am thinking now of political reformers like Paul Douglas and Paul Blanshard, of politically minded philosophers like John Dewey, of independent journalists like Elmer Davis and Heywood Broun, of liberal college professors—then mostly in the departments of economics and government—of social workers in general, and of the liberal wing of the Protestant clergy. Thomas, who was himself an intellectual and a former clergyman, used the sort of idealistic and uncompromising language they liked to hear. When they listened to Roosevelt, on the other hand, they found him evasive. After reading over his address to the New York state legislature, Heywood Broun said that he offered "a meal of parsnips and fine words. To be sure, there is a little chestnut stuffing." *The New Republic*—that meant Bruce Bliven and George Soule, who made the political decisions—supported Thomas in a mild fashion and said that Roosevelt was "an untried jockey on a very lame horse." Walter Lippmann, a former Socialist who was preparing to vote Republican, called him "a pleasant man who, without any important qualification for the office, would very much like to be President." In an open letter to voters, Elmer Davis urged them to support Norman Thomas "when Roosevelt fails."

Most of the writers I knew agreed with the unfavorable

judgment of Roosevelt that prevailed in the intellectual world. But they were not intellectuals themselves, in any strict sense of the term, since they hadn't much interest or skill in abstract thinking—"God, it was difficult," Scott Fitzgerald said. He compared his effort at thinking to "The moving about of great secret trunks. In the first exhausted halt, I wondered whether I had ever thought . . . save within the problems of my craft." Those problems had less connection with ideas than with images, structures, persons, feelings, judgments of moral value, and the use of language. In 1928 the writers had voted for Al Smith, if they voted at all, chiefly because they liked his language and because he expressed their feelings about Prohibition. In 1932 their feelings were centered on the depression, and most of them judged that Roosevelt, though he was more engaging personally than Hoover, would follow the same economic policies. Both men were defenders of American capitalism, which was certain to collapse—in the opinion of many writers—and which would quite possibly lead to fascism before the old system was replaced by a workers' republic. This notion that Roosevelt was "just the same as Hoover, only with meringue on top" persisted much longer among writers than it did among intellectuals properly speaking. It helps to explain why, somewhat later, many writers did not share the wide enthusiasm that was aroused by the early New Deal and why they suspected it of being a step toward fascism. Once again they were losing touch with what Communists called "the proletariat" or "the broad masses."

They were isolated even from the body of liberal opinion represented by Norman Thomas. Some writers supported him, but usually they were older men like Van Wyck Brooks, whose Socialist loyalties went back to the days before the Great War. Most of the younger writers I knew thought that Thomas was entirely too moderate. They had been formed by the tradition of the 1920s, which was to despise the moderates and admire the authors who went to extremes: Flaubert, Dostoevsky, James Joyce. Now the standard of judgment was being extended to the political world, so that some of their favorite words acquired new meanings. "Bourgeois" was one of the bad words, applied first to the enemies of art and now to the enemies of the workers. Of course the Socialists were "petty bourgeois," as the phrase was spelled—almost nobody wrote *petits bourgeois*—and that was a still more contemptuous term. "Revolution" had been a good word for writers in the 1920s; there had been *la révolution sur-réaliste* and the Revolution of the Word; now there would be a total revolution. Norman Thomas and his party were not in the least revolutionary. Dos Passos said, "I should think that becoming a Socialist right now would have about the same effect on anybody as drinking a bottle of near beer."—"I don't know," Sherwood Anderson said when asked the difference between a Socialist and a Communist. "I guess the Communists mean it."

That year the Communist candidates were William Z. Foster, the head of the party, and James W. Ford of Alabama, who was the first Negro to be nominated for a national office. Foster had been meeting with groups of writers and had impressed some of them—Dreiser, for example—as "a man of sweet disposition" and a kind of saint. On September 12 some of the metropolitan newspapers carried a statement issued by fifty-three writers, artists, and composers, but with writers in the majority. "We believe," it said, "that the only effective way to protest against the chaos, the appalling wastefulness, and the indescribable misery inherent in the present economic system is to vote for the Communist candidates." The fifty-three were forming a League of Professional Groups for Foster and Ford. Among the writers who signed the statement there were admired novelists like Dreiser, Anderson, Dos Passos, and Waldo Frank; there were several of the younger "proletarian" novelists, including Erskine Caldwell and Robert Cantwell, then regarded as the most promising; there were a dozen rebel poets, each of whom had published at least one book; there were critics—Newton Arvin, Granville Hicks, Edmund Wilson, Malcolm Cowley—and there were authors in assorted fields like Sidney Howard the dramatist, Matthew Josephson the biographer, Sidney Hook the philosopher, Kyle Crichton the humorist, and Lincoln Steffens, whose *Autobiography* had been the most influential book of the preceding year—in all, a pretty imposing parade of names. The question was how many voters would listen to their plea and also—though nobody thought of it then—how many of the signers would continue to support the Communists, and for how long.

For the only time in my life I took part in a political campaign. A strange campaign it was, considering that the party I supported had little chance of carrying so much as a single precinct, that it did not believe in elections except as an opportunity to preach its doctrines, and that its candidate for president was no longer in the field. Foster had started out on a speaking tour, but it was interrupted by his arrest in California, and then on September 15 he withdrew from campaigning because of illness—some said a heart attack, while others said that the illness was strategic and that Foster had simply been displaced as party leader. But he remained on the ballot, and the party remained there too as a symbol of the dream we had come to share. It was the great dream that men would cease to be slaves of history; that instead they would study its laws, as Marx had already done, and would shape the history of the future by their joint efforts. We had the feeling in those days that history and the future and the Russian Revolution were all on our side, and that the little assignments we carried out were bathed, as it were, in a supernal light.

Our first assignment was to write a campaign pamphlet addressed "to the writers, artists, teachers, physicians, engineers, scientists, and other professional workers of America." A committee was chosen, I don't remember how, and it held two or three meetings in the back parlor of somebody's brownstone house; by that time the party had acquired a number of prosperous sympathizers. Although the committee was composed chiefly of writers, all recent converts, it also included two or three men who had once been party members and were eager, so it seemed, to be taken back. Regarding themselves as professional revolutionists, they did not propose to let the pamphlet fall into the hands of amateurs. One of them was Lewis Corey, who, under his earlier name of Louis C. Fraina, had helped to found the Communist Party in this country, but then had been accused of high crimes and deviations. Much later—in Theodore Draper's book *The Roots of American Communism* (1957)—I read the whole story of this South Italian who had grown up on the Lower East Side, where he helped to support his parents by selling papers on the Bowery. He showed an indomitable spirit that afterward sustained him through persecutions by Communists and anti-Communists alike, and the story revealed him as a tragic figure. But he was not tragic or even appealing when we first saw him pacing up and down that back parlor in Greenwich Village, a short lopsided man with his thin nose high in the air, who gestured with one hand and fixed us with one dark eye, while the other flashed around the room as he enlarged on our absolute ignorance of Marxian economics.

Corey wrote much of the pamphlet, but I seem to remember that a Communist pundit "from the ninth floor" (of the Communist headquarters at 50 East Thirteenth Street) insisted on contributing the section about the party platform. What he offered was a collection, gritty as crushed limestone, of all the party slogans, including the crazy one of "self-determination for the black belt." Corey wrote a little better than the pundit, and he was regarded as a brilliant economist, but he was not a man of letters. He had the Marxian bad habit of transforming complicated patterns of behavior into words ending with "ism" and then of using the words as if they were mathematical symbols. The result was a series of almost algebraic equations that might or might not describe what was happening in the world. "American capitalism has plunged into imperialism, and imperialism marks the decay and decline of capitalism"—in other words, the two can be equated at a given stage. "The Democratic Party . . . is the demagogic face of Republicanism." That was another equation: Republicanism plus demagogy equals Democratism. I also noted, "Fascism . . . is the death rattle of decaying capitalism"; "The Socialists are the third party of capitalism"; and "National economic planning strengthens state capitalism, which constitutes the economic aspect of the Fascist dictatorship."

We argued a little, not so much about the ideas presented in the pamphlet as about the algebraic language. It didn't sound like the work of professional writers, we said. As a concession to our belletristic fancies, I was allowed to contribute an exordium of a page and a half, and Matthew Josephson was given the task of writing a peroration. I was rather proud of introducing a figure of speech. "The United States under capitalism," I said, "is like a house that is rotting away; the roof leaks, the sills and rafters are crumbling. The Democrats want to paint it pink. The Republicans don't want to paint it; instead they want to raise the rent." Josephson in his peroration made an emotional appeal to writers and artists. "We too, the intellectual workers," he said, "are of the oppressed, and until we shake off the servile habit of that oppression we shall build blindly and badly, to the lunatic specifications of ignorance and greed. If we are capable of building a civilization, surely it is time for us to begin; time for us to assert our function, our responsibility; time for us to renew the pact of comradeship with the struggling masses, trapped by the failure of leadership in the blind miseries of a crumbling madhouse."

With these embellishments, about which the Marxists grumbled, and with a few changes in style to soften our own objections to the rest of the text, we accepted the pamphlet, and we liked the suggested title, which was *Culture and the Crisis*. It was printed in October, and more than fifty thousand copies were swiftly distributed through the Workers Bookshops. Then we went on to our next assignment, which was to organize and address a meeting at Cooper Union, in the old-fashioned auditorium where Lincoln had given a famous speech on excluding slavery from the territories. The meeting was our own responsibility, and this time the party didn't bother to suggest what we should say. It did, however, give us publicity, and the hall was crowded mostly with party workers come to inspect their new literary allies, in much the same spirit in which they might have stared at a band of aborigines converted to the true faith. The speeches by writers were innocent and fervid, with many allusions to the Great Emancipator and some personal confessions. I remember one speaker, James Rorty, who testified that since he had become a revolutionist he had started to write poetry again. He exhorted everyone to join the revolution and write poems, whereupon, as a sample, he recited two of his own. They were pretty good poems; I would not say that they were good enough for an ideal audience in the future, but neither were they bad enough for a political audience that had come to have its beliefs confirmed through the mouths, as it were, of sucklings. Other speakers, though, were a little more faithful in playing their expected parts, and the new-fledged orators went home in a glow of elation.

The question often strikes me why I didn't join the party, since I believed at the time in its ideals for the future. "I had too much sense" would be an easy answer, but it wouldn't be accurate; what I had at the most was reservations. Of these the party had even more. It was still very small—more like a preaching order, as I said, than like a political organization—and it was rigorous about accepting novices. After testing them in a variety of humble tasks, such as selling *The Daily Worker* on street corners and getting up at five in the morning to push leaflets under tenement doors, it wanted them to take vows, not of chastity, but of poverty and utter obedience. The proselytes for whom it yearned were men employed—or unemployed—in the mass industries, true proletarians who were ready to go on strike when the party thought best. Intellectuals as a class it distrusted, partly because they had ideas of their own, partly because they had displayed a weakness for Trotskyist or Bukharinist heresies, and partly because they expected to become party leaders. As for writers, the party regarded them in 1932 as a bohemian and wholly undependable element. Sherwood Anderson said, on hearing that Dreiser was accused of being a Communist, "He isn't, any more than I am. He couldn't be if he wanted to be. They wouldn't have him."

They wouldn't have had me either, except in return for a greater sacrifice of freedom than I was prepared to make. I was a writer primarily and not a revolutionist or a politician. I thought and said that the revolutionary movement could do a great deal for writers, by carrying them outside their personal affairs, by enlarging their perspectives, and by giving them a sense of comradeship in struggle. I thought this notion was confirmed by the lives of many great poets, including Blake, Wordsworth, and Baudelaire, all of whom had been full of revolutionary enthusiasm in their early days. But I was dubious about the effect of the movement on the comparatively few writers who had joined the Communist Party of the United States. All of them—even Mike Gold with his natural warmth and anger—seemed to be declining into party hacks, and the level of writing in the party press was abysmally low. It was these literary reservations, more than caution or good sense, that kept me from applying for membership in 1932. Three years later the party would change its policy to the extent of beseeching writers and almost anyone else with radical sentiments to join it on their own terms. By that time, however, I had developed other than literary doubts about what the party was doing in America and in Russia too.

I would never be more than a fellow traveler, and yet I was an ardent one at the time, full of humility, the desire to serve, and immense hopes for the future. Because any disaster seemed possible in that strange year, so did any triumph. Suddenly the range of possibilities had widened and deepened, as had the picture of our relation to history. It was as if we had been walking for years in a mist, on what seemed to be level ground, but with nothing visible beyond a few yards, so that we became preoccupied with the design of things close at hand—friendships, careers, love affairs—and then as if the mist had blown away to reveal that the level ground was only a terrace, that chasms lay on all sides of us, and that beyond them were mountains rising into the golden sunlight. We could not reach the mountains alone, but perhaps we could merge ouselves in the working class and thereby help to build a bridge for ourselves and for humanity.

The working class was part of the dream, and there were writers who pictured it as endowed with spiritual as well as physical power. Waldo Frank was one of the believers. He set to work on an exalted novel, *The Death and Birth of David Markand* (1934), partly based on our expedition to Cumberland Gap. The hero, a middle-class intellectual, has his moment of transfiguration when he stands at the grave of two friends murdered for having led a strike of Kentucky miners. In spirit he says to them, "I envied you, knowing how different I am. I will no more envy you. I will be like you. I will do like you. . . . I embrace your class. All men who want to live today must embrace it to live. I have only the dead body of a class that dies. I need, that I may live, the living body of the class which now is life."

The casting out of old identities; communion with the workers; life in a future world that the workers would build in America as they were building it in Russia: all those religious elements were present in the dream of those years. It made everything else seem unimportant, including one's pride, one's comfort, one's personal success or failure, and one's private relations. There wasn't much time for any of these. Everything personal except marriage—and even marriage for many—was allowed to remain provisional until the glorious day when the bridge had been built and crossed. All one's energies turned outward, and they seemed to be vastly increased by being directed toward purposes shared with others. One borrowed strength from the others and gave it back twofold. There was no time for reflection, but there was time for going to meetings, making speeches, writing in terms of "We demand" or "We protest," walking on picket lines, and sitting through the night in smoky rooms while one argued about the program and personnel of a new committee. A voice: "There should be a woman on it." Another voice: "Of course there must be a Negro." Still another voice, brightly: "Shouldn't we have someone to represent the labor unions?" It was a sort of liturgy, and hearing it once again I lost my patience. "What we need," I said, "is just one person, a Negro woman trade-union organizer. She can serve on every committee. Let's try to find her at an employment agency."

I remember that remark, but not much else of what I said or did in those busy months; it has faded out as if it were the plot of an adventure story read late at night. Searching back I can find only a few pictures. For example, I am sitting at a pine table in a big, hot, dimly lighted room somewhere on upper Broadway while I look at rows of strangers on folding chairs. It must be summer, for the windows are open. The strangers seem to be wondering what I will say, and I am wondering too. We are there to found a national peace movement, a project that doesn't interest me much at the time, and suddenly I have been asked to preside. Sitting beside me is a crop-haired Russian named Yurevich who looks as if he were playing a character bit in a musical comedy.[1] He is giving me stagewhispered directions in bad German that I would have understood no better if it had been good German. What I chiefly gather is a sense of urgency as he mutters, "*Schnell, ein Präsident. . . . Schnell, ein Sekretär.*" A fire truck rumbles past with a screeching siren. Not even smiling, I produce a president as if from space and a secretary as if from my sleeve. There is one other picture, a street scene. I have been asked to climb on a portable rostrum, of the sort often called soapboxes, and I lean forward on the railing while addressing a crowd of unemployed longshoremen. They listen, having nothing

1. Later I learned that Yurevich had been sent to this country by a famous German Communist, Willi Muenzenberg, who was promoting a World Congress Against War.

else to do. Between my shouted phrases I have time to wonder what I am doing there and why the phrases seem to be robbed of meaning by the act of speaking them. I catch the eye of a scarfaced man, who looks down and spits. A cold wind blows from the North River, bearing the dockside smell of dead fish and raw sewage.

That must have been during the first week of November, at the end of the presidential campaign. By that time Roosevelt had become even more cautious, and he was chiefly adjuring the voters to be courageous and have faith in God. Mr. Hoover, as I said, was appealing to their fear of what the Democrats might do, and the appeal was made with utter sincerity. Timid as Roosevelt's speeches seemed to those of us who dreamed of the golden mountains, Hoover saw in them the promise of changes "which," he said, "would destroy the very foundations of our American system." The phrase is from the speech he delivered on the last night of October, in Madison Square Garden, where he also said that if the Democrats lowered the tariff, "The grass will grow in the streets of a hundred cities, a thousand towns." A few days later he addressed his last big audience, in St. Paul. He said that the Democrats had "the same philosophy of government which has poisoned all Europe [with] the fumes of the witch's caldron which boiled in Russia." Then he called them "the party of the mob" and said that "Thank God, we still have a government in Washington that knows how to deal with the mob." Many people wondered, quite unjustly, whether Hoover was implying that there would be a military coup d'état if Roosevelt won the election.

Such fears were typical of the period, and so too were the heavy-handed efforts of some manufacturers to make their employees "vote the right way." Henry Ford, for example, posted a notice in his plants: "To prevent times from getting worse and to help them get better, President Hoover must be elected." Ford's private police, called the "Service Department," tried hard to learn how each man was voting. From many industries in different parts of the country came reports of men discharged for wearing Roosevelt buttons. The office where my wife worked —and doubtless many other offices as well—tried a form of reverse bribery. It had been a friendly place where people planned to stay until they retired, but the atmosphere had changed in the second year of the depression, when it became a question whether the enterprise could survive. Everyone bickered and worried, beginning with the president, who had to surrender a million-dollar life-insurance policy only a few weeks before he died of a heart attack. All the employees had their salaries cut in successive stages by a total of close to 50 percent. Then, on the first Friday in November, the general manager called a staff meeting and announced an additional reduction of 10 percent for everyone. "But," he said, "we hope to restore this cut after the election, if it *goes the right way*—as I'm sure everyone here will help to make it go."

It would be unrealistic to hold that such economic threats and promises had no effect on the election. They did win votes for Hoover, and there were reports in the last week that his position had improved in some of the industrial states. But they also won votes for Roosevelt, not only from employees who didn't like to be bullied—they remembered that there were curtains on voting booths—but also from liberals who had intended to vote for Norman Thomas and then, in that last week, began to fear that Hoover might win after all. The wonder afterward, when one considered the mood of the country, was that Hoover had received nearly 16 million votes and had lost by only 7 million. As for Thomas, his vote was 885,458, or less than half of what the pollsters had predicted it would be.

The Communist vote was slow to be reported and was probably counted even less scrupulously than that of the other minor parties. It was clear from the partial returns, however, that there had been no upsurge of faith in the proletarian revolution and that few recruits had joined the writers' crusade. After a month or so we learned that the Communist vote had been

103,152, which put the party a little ahead of the Prohibitionists and which, incidentally, was the largest vote it would ever receive in a national campaign. The party had one local success: it elected the mayor of Crosby, Minnesota, an iron-mining village on the Cuyuna Range. So far as I can ascertain, that was the only occasion on which the American Party won even a local election.

# 12.
# Hunger March

The League of Professional Groups did not disband after election day. During the chaotic winter of 1932–33 it met frequently over Chaffard's French restaurant on Seventh Avenue, in a big, bare room no longer in demand for banquets. Meeting-places were easy to find and cheap to rent all through the depression years. That was a great convenience for the radical movement, which sustained itself on meetings and could scarcely breathe except in a thick atmosphere of spoken or printed words. Its symbol, if you looked for one, was the folding chair, brought out of a storage space and arranged with other chairs in rows on a bare floor. Facing the rows was always a big pine table, behind which I often sat as chairman or speaker or member of the executive committee.

The movement was, in turn, a source of income for small landlords and job printers, who were losing other clients. Radicalism was one of the few industries—with bootlegging, placer mining, and social work—that were creating a new demand for services. Most of the radical organizations had grown, and the League seemed likely to grow with the others. It accepted a good many new members, and the early winter meetings were occupied with plans for creating branches in all the professions, beginning for some reason with chemists and architectural draftsmen. Then I noticed a change. There were fewer writers at meetings; the established ones had seldom appeared, being too busy, but now the younger novelists and the critics were vanishing in their turn. Most of the new members seemed to regard themselves as revolutionary intellectuals. There were no longer many of the ironical remarks that writers make when they mean to be amusing or impudent or self-deprecating; instead there were speeches from the floor, full of solemn words and intellectual assurance.

There was bitterness too, for the League was dividing into factions. Groups of half a dozen or more members would gather in corners to consult in low voices while glancing suspiciously at the rest of us; then they would scatter to different rows of folding chairs, from which they would rise one after another to interrupt a speaker or criticize the chairman or demand the floor. After the meeting adjourned, they would gather again to leave in a body.

I was told that the largest group consisted of Trotskyites and that a smaller, less vehement group was of right-wing Lovestoneites, two names that meant little to me then. In my innocence of radical politics I did not realize that the groups were acting precisely as orthodox Communists did at meetings organized by Socialists or liberals. Chiefly I felt disheartened by the acrimony that many displayed, though I tried to be amused by the way in which those identified as Trotskyites fell into the roles of the conspirators in *Julius Caesar:* here was Cassius with his hungry look, here was smooth-tongued Decius, here the resentful Ligarius, and I wondered which Caesar they were plotting to overthrow. I also wondered what was the real background of those disputes, since they led to outbursts of contempt and hatred out of all proportion with their ostensible causes.

Partly—so I concluded later—the disputes belonged to an old tradition in the movement, one that Marx himself had authorized by his vendetta against Bakunin and every other revolutionist who refused to accept his leadership. Partly they reflected at a distance the struggles for power in Russia, where the Trotskyites on the left had already been purged and the right-wing Bukharin-ists would soon follow them—this well before the purges had become an organized slaughter. But also, I am now convinced, those disputes in the big room above Chaffard's restaurant re-sulted from the fondness of all revolutionary theorists for living in a dream of tomorrow. Consider—

Each of the theorists, in every sect, believed that history itself was on his side. The future must have existed in the minds of some as a screen on which their present struggles were pro-jected as enormous shadows. The leader of ten in the good cause appeared on that screen as the leader of ten million. The little group in a corner, by its proper use of revolutionary tactics, might become the Central Executive Committee of a party that controlled the destiny of nations. Just as the result of any cor-rect decision would be magnified in the future, so too would be the consequence of errors made by some other revolutionary theorist. His mistaken notion of the tactics to be adopted in the present situation might lead to years of suffering and delay in achieving the workers' state. Therefore the notion must be exposed in all its falsity, and therefore the man who propounded the notion must be shamed and annihilated, to keep him from ever again misleading the workers.

By then I had already observed that no revolutionary theo-rist would admit to making errors of his own. The need to be al-ways right was part of his revolutionary pride, another tradition in the movement that, as I learned, went back to Marx himself. I had little of that pride—too little pride of any sort, I sometimes thought, though I acknowledged my share of vanity—and no de-sire to impose my will on the future. I did not regard myself as a theorist except in the one field of literature, and even there my theories were offered in a tentative fashion, always with the suspicion that the best of them might be contravened by some new work of art. I had a pragmatic mind, full of the American admiration for things that worked and successful organizations that owed their growth to the loyalty and goodwill of their members. At one meeting I made a speech. I said, as I remember, that the League had started by working hard in its proper field. I said that some of its members had suddenly turned from practice to theory, so that recent meetings had been given over to such questions as whether a correct theoretical approach might have prevented the defeat of the Chinese revolution in 1927. I said that we had no competence in questions of the sort and that arguments about them had paralyzed the League. I pleaded for putting the differences aside and resuming the activities on which we were all agreed.

It was a hot speech, applauded by most of the members, but it did not save the League of Professional Groups. The disputes continued, no work got done, and pretty soon no meetings were being scheduled. In some ways the brief history of the League foreshadowed what would happen to many other radical organizations and to the movement as a whole. But my speech, though completely ineffective for its purpose, had one result that might have been foreseen: it got me involved in the factional quarrels I detested and wanted to avoid. The Trotsky faction didn't like it at all, and from that moment many of them regarded me as a dangerous misleader to be exposed and annihilated.

The Communists had organized a National Hunger March that was to start from various parts of the country, converge on Washington December 4, and present a petition for unemployment relief to the lame-duck session of Congress. Washington had a new chief of police, Major Ernest W. Brown, who thought that his predecessor had been too gentle and long-suffering with the Bonus Army; he wanted to show what his force could do to discourage the new band of intruders. There promised to be trouble, and I drove to Washington with Robert Cantwell to write a report for *The New Republic*.

Cantwell was a young man from the Northwest who had left college at seventeen to work in a plywood mill on Grays Harbor. He had taught himself to write fiction, so he said, by reading the prefaces of Henry James while out of a job, and at twenty-three he had published a brilliant first novel, *Laugh and Lie Down* (1931). Now he was a year older, married, still out of a job, and still reading Henry James, though he was also reading Marx, with particular attention to the historical essays. What he admired in them and hoped to reproduce in his own writing was their fashion of presenting characters as dominated by great movements that operated under the surface of events. He was a slight, sallow, hungry-looking young man who dressed neatly in dark suits that were always too large, as if he had shrunk since buying them, and who stuttered with excitement—which he passed on to others—as he explained the dramatic value of a strike or imagined the secret maneuvers that went on in a crisis. For him the hunger march was a pageant that revealed the conflicts in a decaying society.

We joined the western column of the march as it passed through a Virginia town thirty miles southwest of Washington. The column was a convoy of wheezing old trucks with banners tacked to their sides, but it was interspersed with the passenger cars of government employees who had been taking a Sunday drive in the country. At the Key Bridge, then on the outskirts of the city, all traffic was halted and divided into two lines—just as the righteous, I thought, would be divided from sinners before God's judgment seat. The left-hand line was composed of cars belonging to "citizens," as the word was used in those days—that is, to persons still having jobs or property and paying taxes to maintain the police. They would be allowed freely to enter the city. In the right-hand line were unemployed hunger marchers, who had ceased to be called citizens when they asked the government for relief. These too would be allowed to enter the city, but under police escort, to make sure—I thought at the time—that they would not contaminate the citizens with their discontent.

A few citizens made the mistake of driving very old cars or of wearing caps instead of hats and sweaters instead of overcoats. Some of them were jockeyed into the line of hunger marchers and had a hard time getting out of it. Cantwell and I had a different experience, one that revealed the ambiguous position of all the left-wing writers. The car I had borrowed from a friend was only moderately old, and both of us wore overcoats and hats. We looked like citizens, and the Virginia highway police couldn't understand why we insisted on joining the right-hand line. But they let us stay there, in the end, possibly on the assumption that we were undercover agents with a job to do.

After the line had waited half an hour, the Virginia police let the hunger marchers go. The Washington police took charge of the column, and motorcycles herded it across the city from southwest to northeast, by a route kept secret until the last moment. There was hardly anyone on the sidewalks, for the police had closed them to all except the residents of each block. The column wheezed and grumbled past red and green traffic lights without distinction, past lines of traffic halted in the streets on either side, past barricades of double-parked cars with just enough space left in the middle of the avenue for trucks to get through in single file, till it reached an empty and desolate mile of concrete highway—the New York Avenue extension, we afterward learned, as it ran along the slope of a ravine to reach Bladensburg Road. Here the trucks and jalopies were halted under guard.

The western column of the hunger march had joined the other columns in the sort of trap that staff officers might devise for confining prisoners of war until a stockade had been built for them. The ends of the trap were closed by city police with machine guns, and there was no escape through the sides. At the bottom of the ravine was the Washington Terminal Railroad, which was guarded by scores of railroad police, some patrolling the tracks, others hidden in passenger cars on a siding. At the top of a steep clay bank on the other side of the highway were roving squads of city police armed with tear-gas rifles and also—I was to read in the Washington papers—with the new "D.M.," or nauseating gas, in the use of which two squads had been given special training. Behind the squads a field-telephone line had been strung from tree to tree, and, still farther in the rear, United States park policemen were waiting to arrest stragglers. Police sidecars went chugging up and down among the marchers; plainclothesmen circulated from group to group, listening for scraps of the conversations that died away as they approached; and three army planes were circling overhead.

I suppose this deployment of forces must have been caused by the nightmare that hungry mobs would take over the streets, when the revolution came that everybody talked about and nobody got round to starting. Salesmen had been peddling riot insurance up and down Bladensburg Road, leaving terror behind them. Washington was full of rumors: for example, that the blue van third from the front in the eastern column was loaded with machine guns, that these would be distributed among the local unemployed, and that the mob would then loot the downtown stores and seize the White House. All leaves had been canceled for the four thousand Regulars at Fort Meyer, and they were ready to take over the city on an hour's notice. Meanwhile the target of those fearful preparations—as it were, the mob incarnate—was an unimposing collection of twenty-five hundred persons representing the Unemployed Councils. They were unarmed by their own strict orders, about a third of them were women, the men looked underfed and shabby, and they were all deathly tired after being jolted across the country.

On that December night we watched them gathering in little groups at the tailgates of trucks to share out the last stale sandwiches. A truck had come out from Washington with hot soup and coffee, but the police had turned it back. Nobody was allowed to light a fire. Soon there were larger meetings, addressed by the leaders of the various columns. "Comrades!" I could hear them shouting. "We must maintain proletarian discipline. Comrades, we must defend ourselves against provocation by closing our ranks." The cold was striking in through the soles of my shoes. After the meetings broke up, the comrades got ready to sleep, some in trucks or passenger cars and others on quilts spread out on the bare concrete. Once more Cantwell and I took advantage of our ambiguous position. We drove slowly up to the western line of police, halted on command, passed over our credentials from *The New Republic* to be studied in the headlights, then drove downtown to sleep in a hotel.

We missed a good deal of what happened next day on the New York extension. The vanguard of another protest march was beginning to arrive in battered trucks, and we watched it with fascination. This second march was composed of farmers from Iowa and the Dakotas, come to demand higher prices for corn and hogs and a law against the foreclosure of farm mortgages. Farmers had a special status in Washington, and the police let them alone. They were all, it seemed to me, huge men in overalls with bright red faces and yellow hair. I talked with some of them in the office of Workers International Relief, which was the Communist Red Cross. They were ready to work with the Communists for the time being, but without hiding their contempt for the mild ways of the urban unemployed. "We'll go to see our congressmen and tell them what's what," the farmers said. "Hell, aren't they our hired men?"

When at last I got back to the detention camp on New York Avenue, I heard what the police had been doing all day. Briefly, they had been trying to create an "incident" that would give them an excuse for using their $10,000 worth of tear gas and vomit gas, for clubbing the intruders into their trucks, and for rushing them out of the city. They bullied and cursed the marchers in the hope of meeting resistance. They built a little bonfire beside the highway, to windward, and one policeman dropped a vomit-gas capsule into it. Some of the fumes drifted along the line of trucks. That morning the Washington truck with soup and coffee had been permitted to enter the camp, so the marchers had food, but there was neither running water nor any sort of latrine. If a woman went alone into the bushes, she would be surrounded by jeering policemen. I heard many stories of the sort, and then I witnessed still another provocation. The comrades, besides holding their inevitable meetings, had been forming into columns and marching back and forth to keep warm. One of the columns was then approaching a police barricade. "Come on, you yellow bastards," a policeman shouted, putting his right hand to his hip. "Try and break through."

"Column left!" said the file leader, and that was all. The marchers wheeled and went back in silence. It was one of the dramatic contrasts that Cantwell liked to describe, this time between a disciplined column of suspected rioters and what was practically an armed mob of police. But I wondered even at the time why the discipline of the Communists, admirable in itself, kept leading them into hopeless situations where there was nothing to do but turn and march back. And why—to ask another question—did they keep boasting of their revolutionary militance when they were, in reality, much less militant than the Iowa farmers? They talked about the ruthless seizure of power, which they had indeed seized in another country, and had exercised ruthlessly against their enemies; but such little victories as they had gained in the United States—always moral ones—had been due to tactics of nonviolent noncooperation much like those practiced by Mahatma Gandhi.

It was so in Washington that December. The Communists had put the police in the wrong simply by obeying laws while the police were breaking them. There were angry stories in the Washington papers; congressmen asked questions about what the police were doing; and on Tuesday the hunger marchers, released from detention, were permitted to march on foot up Capitol Hill. Many of them were too exhausted to join the procession. It was a ragged little parade without music, and with more policemen on the sidewalks than marchers in the street, but there were spectators too, silent but curious and not unfriendly. Once more the

Communists had gained a small victory that was chiefly a moral one. Nobody thought that winter relief for the unemployed might conceivably be granted by that lame-duck session of Congress, which was unable to agree on positive measures of any sort.

Having marched in the parade as another token of our ambiguous position, Cantwell and I drove back to New York on Tuesday night. We took along a Communist for company, a curly-haired young poet whose father, from whom he was estranged, owned a department store in a middle-size Midwestern city. When I first heard of Leftwich—that wasn't his name—he had just been graduated from the state university and had founded a defunctive little magazine that recorded the excursions into pure art of himself, his friends, and some of the lesser-known expatriates; it wasn't a bad job of editing. Next I heard that he had lost interest in aesthetics and was working at little or no pay as reporter for a left-wing news service. He was wounded in Harlan County by coal-company gunmen and was lucky to get out of Kentucky alive. In the autumn, after joining the party, he had been arrested in Memphis and sent to the chain gang for trying to organize the unemployed. Now he talked amusingly about the hunger march, as if it were a vacation from his more serious assignments.

I was driving fast, for U.S. 1 was empty of traffic at midnight in that depression year. There were no lighted windows except in an occasional service station. After a while I asked Leftwich a question that bothered me: with all those meetings and marches and party assignments, when did the Communists get time for making love? He laughed and said, "I guess they slip it in between meetings." Then he told us that a girl had lost her cherry on Monday night in one of the touring cars parked on the New York Avenue extension—"Of course they had the side curtains on," he said. I thought of love on that bleak highway: the rite of lost innocence performed while cold seeped in through the curtains and police sidecars chugged up and down the column looking for trouble. Then, as we drove past factories that had not been opened for months or years, I wondered about the habit that Communists had of devoting little time or thought or kindness to their personal relations: was it the right foundation for a new society? In those days, however, doubts like that were always adjourned for want of leisure to consider them.

# 13.

# From a Coffee Pot

The week after my article on the hunger march appeared in *The New Republic*, I received a rather imperious summons from the national headquarters of the John Reed Club. Some representatives of the club wanted to discuss the article, and they asked me to appear at a given time. Curious about what they would say, I made a first and last visit to their clubroom at nine o'clock one evening shortly before Christmas.

The clubroom, full of smoke and voices, was the second story of a loft building on Sixth Avenue, in the Village. I picked my way to a corner office where four young men were waiting at a table. Two of them, I remember, were Philip Rahv and William Phillips, soon to be founding editors of *Partisan Review*. They had before them a thick manuscript which, as they read it aloud, turned out to be a line-by-line criticism of the article. Not many of their comments were eulogistic. Roughly, they had concluded that the article failed to emphasize the correct leadership of the Communist Party in the struggle for bread, that it did not suggest the growing militance of the broad masses, that it did not mention the part in the struggle played by Negroes and other minority groups, that it did not explain how the Washington police were acting as agents of a capitalist conspiracy, and, in general, that it revealed my petty-bourgeois illusions and my insufficient grounding in the Marxian dialectic.

On hearing those by-now familiar comments, all based on party slogans, I was amused and polite. It seemed to me that young writers who hadn't been published, except perhaps in the party press, were turning the tables on one of the editors who had rejected their work. I told them I was sorry not to have produced the sort of article they wanted, especially as I could have written it simply by reading *The Daily Worker* and thus might have saved myself the trouble of making a trip to Washington. Unfortunately, I said, such an article wouldn't have been printed in *The New Republic*.

We shook hands all round. After leaving the dimly lighted office, I stopped for a moment in the clubroom that stretched out between its high walls of tenement-house green. My first impression was of hot yellow light, noise, excitement, and clutter. Coats lay in heaps on kitchen chairs. Young men, mostly in cotton-flannel shirts, stood arguing in groups, or leaned over chessboards, or sat in corners reading *The New Masses*. There were a few older men, a few Negroes, but no women—and where, I wondered, were the representatives of that oppressed majority? If women had been there, they might have insisted on sweeping the floor, which was deep in dust and calico-spattered with cigarette stubs and scraps of paper. As I stood watching, still more young men came tramping up the stairs, some of them looking like Russian workers—or like Mike Gold—with caps perched back over shocks of hair. Many of them wore leather jackets. They glanced around for friends, and either found them or tramped down again. Though nobody was drinking anything stronger than coffee, always in paper cups, I could not help thinking of the Café du Dôme in 1923. For men of a new generation, the John Reed Club had become "the place."

The club had been founded in October 1929, the month of the Wall Street crash, by a group of contributors to *The New Masses*. Its aim, they announced, was to "clarify the principles and purposes of revolutionary art and literature, to propagate them, to practice them." That was why it had been named for John Reed, author of *Ten Days That Shook the World,* the only American, and almost the only poet, to be buried with the heroes of the Russian Revolution, under the Kremlin wall. Soon there were John Reed Clubs in other American cities. It was in November 1930 that the parent organization sent half a dozen delegates, including my friend John Herrmann, to the congress (or "plenum") of revolutionary writers then assembling in Kharkov. The Russians scolded them for "insufficient political development," for "remnants of petty-bourgeois ideology," for not being truly proletarian in their work, and for neglecting "cultural activity among the Negro masses." Nevertheless, the John Reed Club was accepted as the American section of the International Union of Revolutionary Writers.

When the delegates came home, they carried with them a special Program of Action for the United States, which, as they boasted in *The New Masses,* was "intended to guide every phase of our work." They solemnly resolved that it should be "realized in life." In many respects this program imposed on them by Russian literary bureaucrats was grotesquely unsuited to American life, as it was to our language, but still the John Reed Club continued to grow in spite of Russian misdirection and its own abundant errors. It grew because writers and artists had been rebelling against the illogic of capitalism, and because the club was the only haven to which the younger ones could turn.

The younger ones were those who had been graduated from college, or forced by poverty to drop out of college, in the period from 1927 to 1932. Perhaps they were the least fortunate of all the "generations," or age groups, that had been succeeding each other every ten or a dozen years. The artists among them had almost no hope of selling or even exhibiting their pictures. Some of the writers were able to publish their work in little magazines, of which there were even more at the time than during the 1920s, but—with a few exceptions like *The New Republic*—the magazines that paid their contributors had stopped looking for new ones. Book publishers, whose volume of business had been reduced by 60 percent in three years, no longer offered advances against royalties to unknown authors. The younger men could see no way of supporting themselves by their chosen profession, and neither could they go to Paris and live cheaply while waiting to be famous, as men of the twenties had done. That sort of life, cheap as it was, largely depended on checks from home, and these had stopped coming. The young men of the early thirties had to stay close to home—often with their parents, who could at least give them shelter—and had to support themselves by whatever unskilled and miserably paid work they could find. In the evening they went to a public library or sat alone in a coffee pot—as neighborhood lunchrooms were called in those days—brooding over a single mug of coffee until it turned as cold as fate. It was the life that Alfred Hayes recorded in one of the more impressive poems of the period, "In a Coffee Pot."

> I brood upon myself. I rot
> Night after night in this cheap coffee pot.
> I am twenty-two I shave each day
> I was educated at a public school
> They taught me what to read and what to say
> The nobility of man my country's pride
>
> .   .   .   .   .   .   .   .   .   .   .
>
> The men the names the dates have worn away
> The classes words the books commencement prize
> Here bitter with myself I sit
> Holding the ashes of their prompted lies.

Hayes, who might stand for all the younger poets in the John Reed Club—though he had an ironic wit and a stronger feeling for language than many others—was born in the London ghetto and was brought to New York in 1914, when he was three years old. He went to a public school in Harlem, which was not yet the black metropolis, and was graduated from the High School of

Commerce. His mother wanted him to become a certified public accountant, but he spent only six months at City College of New York, chosen because it did not charge for tuition. Already he was working at night as copyboy for a Hearst paper, *The New York American*. He left college, so he told me, when he found that he could write better compositions than anyone else in his class. That was in 1930, a year when a million young Americans finished their schooling, such as it was, and when nearly half a million employed men and women were losing their jobs each month. In spite of competition, Hayes managed to find several jobs in succession, since he was a firm-jawed and confident young man. First he worked as reporter for another Hearst paper, *The Daily Mirror*, until he was fired; then he was a waiter, a process server, a delivery boy, a bootlegger; he saved enough money to go to Pittsburgh, but couldn't find work there; he took to the road for I don't know how long; he pitched hay on a Connecticut farm; and finally he spent a year in New York haunting the Sixth Avenue employment agencies, with his confidence worn away. It was the black year described in the poem from which I have quoted.

> *You'll find us there before the office opens*
> *Crowding the vestibule before the day begins*
> *The secretary yawns from last night's date*
> *The elevator boy's black face looks out and grins.*
> *We push we crack our bitter jokes we wait*
> *These mornings always find us waiting there*
> *Each one of us has shined his broken shoes*
> *Has brushed his coat and combed his careful hair*
> *Dance hall boys pool parlor kids wise guys*
> *The earnest son the college grad all, all*
> *Each hides the question twitching in his eyes*
> *And smokes and spits and leans against the wall.*

For many writers only a little older than Hayes, who was born in 1911, the early depression years were not such a grim period. They had not yet established themselves in their calling, but at least they had made friends, and they had learned the lesson that they could not write their first books while living like respectable taxpayers. As John Steinbeck says in an article, "I Remember the Thirties," they "had been practicing for the depression a long time." Steinbeck, born in 1902, had already published two books, but they had not repaid his investment in them of cigarettes, typewriter ribbons, and postage. While working on a third book, which was to be no more successful, he was living happily with his wife in a rent-free cottage in Pacific Grove, next door to Monterey, California, on a total income of twenty-five dollars a month.

> . . . there was a fairly large group of us poor kids [he says], all living alike. We pooled our troubles, our money when we had some, our inventiveness and our pleasures. I remember it as a warm and friendly time. Only illness frightened us. You have to have money to be sick —or did then. And dentistry was out of the question, with the result that my teeth went badly to pieces. Without dough you couldn't have a tooth filled. . . .
>
> Given the sea and the gardens, we did pretty well with a minimum of theft. We didn't have to steal much. Farmers and orchardists in the nearby countryside couldn't sell their crops. They gave us all the fruit and truck we could carry home. We used to go on walking trips carrying our gunny sacks. If we had a dollar, we could buy a live sheep, for two dollars a pig, but we had to slaughter them and carry them home on our backs, or camp beside them and eat them there. We even did that. . . .
>
> For entertainment we had the public library, endless talk, long walks, any number of games. We played music, sang and made love. Enormous invention went into our pleasures. Anything at all was an excuse for a party: all holidays, birthdays called for celebration. When we felt the need to celebrate and the calendar was blank, we simply proclaimed a Jacks-Are-Wild Day.

It's not easy to go on writing constantly with little hope that anything will come of it. But I do remember it as a time of warmth and mutual caring. If one of us got hurt or ill or in trouble, the others rallied with what they had. Everyone shared bad fortune as well as good.

Young writers in the Eastern cities had few of Steinbeck's advantages. They couldn't catch fish when they were hungry, or gather vegetables from their gardens, or wander into the country with gunny sacks to beg for whatever the farmers couldn't sell. If they were younger than Steinbeck, they probably hadn't met "a fairly large group of us poor kids," all living alike for art; and this was especially true of those who came from working-class neighborhoods where there was not much talk about writing or painting. These last were the young men who brooded alone in coffee pots and for whom, if they joined the John Reed Club, it became not only a meeting place but a career. It gave them warmth, excitement, friends, and a forum in which to express their opinions about art and revolution. It gave them a chance to hear about cheap places to live, and possible ways of earning money, and parties to which girls would be coming—"We're having a party on Saturday night to raise money for the magazine. Why don't you come and bring your own bottle?"

Much more than that, the club gave them self-respect by giving them work—unpaid, to be sure, but still the sort of work they were training themselves to do. The painters were invited, almost commanded, to make posters for mass meetings and for the May Day parade. The fledgling politicians learned to address workers' clubs. The writers edited or contributed to little magazines, of which almost every branch of the club published one of its own. Among them were *Partisan Review* and *Dynamo* in New York, one devoted chiefly to criticism and the other to proletarian poetry; *Leftward* in Boston, *The Hammer* in Hartford, *Left Review* and *Red Pen* in Philadelphia, *New Forces* in Detroit, *Cauldron* in Grand Rapids, *Left Front* in Chicago, *Left* in Davenport,

Iowa (it died after two issues), and *Partisan* in Hollywood, besides a number of allied magazines like *Blast* in New York, *Kosmos* in Philadelphia, and *Anvil* in Moberly, Missouri, all three of which specialized in the proletarian short story. To unknown writers, especially those with a working-class background, such magazines provided almost the only opportunity to see their work in print, to have it criticized in the helpful spirit reserved for beginners, and to prove themselves as soldiers in a revolutionary crusade.

There were some like Richard Wright, to mention one name, for whom a first visit to the club was the beginning of a totally new life. Wright was a handsome and gentle-voiced young Negro from Mississippi with only a grade-school education, but with a hunger for books. He had dreamed of becoming a writer after reading H. L. Mencken's *A Book of Prefaces*. At twenty-five he was unemployed and was living on the South Side of Chicago with his crippled mother. He had made some white friends while working in the Chicago post office, and one of them begged him to attend the meetings of the John Reed Club. Wright hesitated, feeling as he did that white Communists could not possibly have a sincere interest in Negroes.

> One Saturday night [he says in a chapter contributed to *The God That Failed*], bored with reading, I decided to appear . . . in the capacity of an amused spectator. I rode to the Loop and found the number. A dark stairway led upward; it did not look welcoming. What on earth of importance could happen in so dingy a place? Through the windows above me I saw vague murals along the walls. I mounted the stairs to a door that was lettered: The Chicago John Reed Club.
>
> I opened it and stepped into the strangest room I had ever seen. Paper and cigarette butts lay on the floor. A few benches ran along the walls, above which were vivid colors depicting colossal figures of workers carrying

streaming banners. The mouths of the workers gaped in wild cries; their legs were sprawled over cities.

"Hello."

I turned and saw a white man smiling at me.

"A friend of mine, who's a member of this club, asked me to visit here. His name is Sol—" I told him.

"You're welcome here," the white man said. "We're not having an affair tonight. We're holding an editorial meeting. Do you paint?" He was slightly gray and he had a mustache.

"No," I said, "I try to write."

"Then sit in on the editorial meeting of our magazine, *Left Front*," he suggested.

"I know nothing of editing," I said.

"You can learn," he said.

Wright sat in a corner listening to the editorial meeting; then his new friend, whose name was Grimm, sent him home with an armful of revolutionary magazines, after inviting him to contribute something to *Left Front*. Instead of going to bed, Wright spent most of the night reading the magazines, in which he found "a passionate call for the experiences of the disinherited." Toward dawn he wrote what appears to have been his first poem, "a wild, crude poem in free verse, coining images of black hands playing, working, holding bayonets, stiffening finally in death. I felt that in a clumsy way it linked white life with black, merged two streams of common experience." He wrote four more poems during the week and carried them all to his friend at the John Reed Club. Grimm accepted two of them for *Left Front*, sent two others to *Anvil*, and reserved the last and best of them for *The New Masses*. That must have been the one in which Wright imagined himself at the mercy of a white mob:

*My voice was drowned in the roar of their voices, and my black wet body slipped and rolled in their hands as they bound me to the sapling.*

*And my skin clung to the bubbling hot tar, falling from me in
   limp patches.
And the down and quills of the white feathers sank into my raw
   flesh, and I moaned in my agony.*

"Your poems are crude, but good for us," Grimm told him
that day. "You see, we're all new in this. We write articles about
Negroes, but we never see any Negroes. We need your stuff."

A few months later there was a factional struggle in the
Chicago club, and Wright became its new head, or executive secretary. (The president of a Communist organization was usually
no more than a name on its letterhead.) Wright was elected partly
because members of the opposing faction were afraid that they
would be accused of prejudice if they voted against a Negro, but
of course he had other qualifications for the office besides his
color; he was friendly, unassuming, immensely gifted, and willing
to learn. Nevertheless, he ran into troubles, which were on a
grander scale than those of a young man on the South Side dreaming about the world of books. The Chicago club, besides having
its quota of hard-working young writers and artists, was infested
with amateur politicians and professional nuts. One of the nuts
accused other members of being police spies, and his charges
were taken seriously until the police escorted him back to the
insane asylum from which he had escaped. The Communist Party,
of which Wright had become a member, regarded the club as a
source of unpaid labor. It kept the John Reeders so busy raising
funds, making posters, and addressing meetings that they had no
time to write or paint. Soon it decided that *Left Front* was using
up time and money that should have been devoted to political
activities. The magazine was suppressed by a party order, against
which Wright protested, thereby committing a breach of party
discipline. Eventually he was expelled from the party as a Trotskyist (which he wasn't) and an incurable individualist, but he
never forgot that the John Reed Club had started him on his
literary career.

Meanwhile the party had its own troubles with amateur politicians in every local branch of the club. Some of the members wanted to be young Robespierres intriguing for power and consigning their opponents to the scaffold. It was the politicians who did most of the talking in May 1932, when the John Reed Club held its first national convention in Chicago, with delegates representing ten of the local clubs. The hottest argument was about the attitude to be adopted toward established writers such as Theodore Dreiser, Edmund Wilson, and Waldo Frank, who had revealed their sympathy for the revolution. Two delegates who spoke for the editorial board of *The New Masses*, Joseph Freeman and Mike Gold, thought that such writers should be treated as honored guests. One of the principal functions of the John Reed Club, they said, was winning their firm support. But the young Robespierres didn't agree. "We must not cringe in our approach to these intellectuals," one of them said. Another dismissed all professional writers as "part and parcel of the middle class," soon to be liquidated by the revolutionary workers.

Joe Freeman was ten years older than most of the other John Reeders. He had written books, he had helped to found *The New Masses*, and he tried to serve as a mediator between the two worlds of professional writing and radical politics. Appalled by the intrigues within the John Reed Club and by the sectarianism of its members, he composed a memorandum to himself and filed it among his papers. Many years later he showed it to Daniel Aaron, author of *Writers on the Left* (1961).

Most of the people in the writers' group do not write and cannot write [he said]; they do not read; they do not know what is going on in the intellectual field and it is impossible to struggle with them on the basis of ideas. This is one of the reasons for the continual turmoil. The moment the struggle is settled on paper, it crops up again; not being Party members, these elements cannot be disciplined by the needs of the economic struggle; not

> being intellectuals, they cannot be reasoned with. . . .
> Unable to express their indecision in *art forms*—as do
> writers for the liberal journals—they express it in politics.

Freeman's memorandum to himself, though no more scathing
than it had a right to be, left out two features of the situation.
One of them was that the John Reed Club did not consist merely
of writers and painters who couldn't write or paint. It also included a fair proportion of talented beginners eager to do their
best. Richard Wright tells us that during his first visits to the
Chicago clubroom he was introduced "to a Jewish boy who was
to become one of the nation's leading painters, to a chap who was
to become one of the eminent composers of his day, to a writer
who was to create some of the best novels of his generation. . . ."
The Chicago club was remarkable for the number of soon-to-be-
published novelists among its members. If Wright had gone
instead to the New York clubroom, he would have found more
of the semiliterate politicians with whom Freeman was exasper-
ated, but he would also have found more poets, critics, and future
playwrights.

The second circumstance not mentioned by Freeman is that
the battles in the John Reed Club, besides having a political aspect—like everything else at the time—were part of the old war
between literary age groups. Writers in their twenties are always
tempted to regard writers in their thirties or forties as natural
enemies. I suppose that the great sin of the older men is simply
to be there, standing as apparent obstacles in the path of younger
men who are trying to enter an overcrowded and highly com-
petitive profession. In the course of becoming established in the
profession, the older men will probably have made concessions
and compromises. The younger ones will make them later, but
they haven't been tempted as yet, and hence they indulge in a
feeling of moral superiority that makes them still angrier at their
want of success. One must add that each new age group has been
shaped by a different sort of childhood. The work of the older

men does not express what the younger ones feel to be their particular sense of life—so down, they say (always choosing the current epithet), with those lost leaders, those philistines, those uptown smugs, those middlebrows, or those squares, and hurrah for our own truths, however crudely or violently expressed.

Not a few of the twenty-year-olds in the John Reed Club were the sort of artists, or hangers-on of the arts, who begin by adopting extreme principles to affirm their own identities. If they had been born sooner or later, the principles would have been different. Coming of age in 1920, they would have been Dadaists; in 1927, they would have been Surrealists; in the late 1940s, Existentialists; in the 1950s, Beats or Zen Buddhists or Action Painters. In 1932 those who pictured themselves as forming an avant-garde were almost all proletarian writers (or painters or politicians). The new doctrine called Proletcult, which is the telescoped Russian term for proletarian culture, gave them a new vocabulary for attacking established writers. If these lived as respectable citizens, they were "rotten with bourgeois hypocrisy." If they flirted at cocktail parties, it was because they "aped the moral decay of the owning classes." If they wrote for magazines that tried to earn a profit, they became "the lackeys and running dogs of capitalism." If they remained liberals, they were beneath a revolutionist's contempt. Even if they joined the Communists, but still counseled tact and moderation—as Gold and Freeman had done at the Chicago convention—they could be charged with "clinging to petty-bourgeois illusions." It was hard for anyone who had started publishing in the 1920s to escape the guilt, in the young men's eyes, of being ten years too old.

This war of age groups helps to explain the continuing small battles between the John Reeders and the literary pundits of the Communist Party. After 1935 the battles would lead to a wide secession of younger writers from Communist leadership. In 1932, however, almost all the self-consciously young—or at least their vanguard in the arts—were trying to be proletarians and revolutionists after the Russian pattern. It was a situation that flattered the Communists, who boasted about it in the party press and tried to conceal their distrust of these new allies. Meanwhile they used the converts as best they could, partly as errand boys, but chiefly in the large effort to create a sense of common purpose in the working class. "Art is a class weapon," the Communists kept saying, and it seemed at the time that the weapon might become more effective in the United States than it had been in western Europe.

In the very trough of the depression there was an amazing burst of cultural activity, all on the proletarian front. Mostly it took the form of groups assembled for self-improvement and for spreading revolutionary ideals. The list of groups is endless. Besides the John Reed Clubs and their dozens of little magazines, there were the Pen and Hammer Groups (I never learned exactly what they did), the Workers Film and Photo League, the Workers Dance League, Red Dancers, Rebel Dancers, American Revolutionary Dancers, the Theatre Union, the Theatre Collective, the Theatre of Action, the Workers Laboratory Theatre, the Harlem Prolets, the Pierre Degeyter Club (named for the composer of "The International"), the Music Vanguard, the Workers Music League, and, for a group of groups, the League of Workers Theatres. All these were connected by a common purpose and formed an audience for one another's work. A young playwright, for example, might be invited to write "agitprop" plays (another telescoped Russian term, in this case meaning agitation and propaganda) for production on a bare stage, with audience participation; eventually the best of these would be Clifford Odets's *Waiting for Lefty*. A young poet might have his work interpreted by a dance group, then given an accompaniment of revolutionary music and recited to workers' clubs. All the new proletarian writers seemed to gather strength by thinking in terms of "we," not "I," and by merging themselves first with other workers in the arts—provided they were true proletarians under thirty—then with an audience of workers drawn from all the crafts and professions, and finally with the entire working class in its just anger, as it marched by millions with fists held high in the Red Front salute toward the dawn of a workers' republic. It was the sense of destiny implied by Alfred Hayes at the end of his monody in a coffee pot:

> *We shall not sit forever here and wait.*
> *We shall not sit forever here and rot.*
> *The agencies are filing cards of hate.*
> *And I have seen how men lift up their hands*
> *And turn them so and pause—*
> *And so the slow brain moves and understands—*
> *And so with million hands.*

# 14.
# Comes the
# Revolution

The winter of 1932–33 was the last and worst time in American history when four months intervened between the election and the inauguration of a new president. Hoover was still in the White House, but he no longer had enough moral authority to carry through new measures against the depression; the fact was that he hadn't any measures to offer, except an international conference and a federal sales tax that would have made things worse. Roosevelt had many new measures in mind and a vast willingness to try others if they suggested themselves—anything to get industry moving again—but he was still a private citizen. In happier times the solution might have been for the two presidents to collaborate by issuing joint statements of purpose. Hoover approved the notion, but he had a fixed belief in the rightness of his own policies and such wild apprehensions of what the new president might do that the joint statements he suggested were of a sort that Roosevelt could not sign.

On one critical occasion Hoover urged him to assure the country of three things: "that there will be no tampering or inflation of the currency; that the budget will be unquestionably balanced, even if further taxation is necessary; that the government credit will be maintained by refusal to exhaust it in the issue of securities." The third of those provisos meant that there would be no public-works program, no support of farm prices, and no federal relief for the unemployed. Hoover then wrote to a conservative senator, David A. Reed of Pennsylvania, "I realize that if these declarations be made by the President-elect, he will have ratified the whole major program of the Republican Administration; that is, it means the abandonment of 90% of the so-called new deal." Of course Roosevelt refused to make the declarations, whereupon Hoover accused him privately of acting like "a madman." They could not collaborate; they could scarcely speak to each other.

In other days Congress might have supplied the leadership that failed to come from the presidency, but this was a Congress full of defeated members waiting to go home and protect their private fortunes. It was also full of would-be leaders, including Huey Long, each of whom revolved in his own orbit like a satellite in space; what the Congress chiefly lacked was followership. It argued in cloakrooms, filibustered, and summoned men of affairs to explain the cause and cure of the depression. During a widely reported investigation one senator asked Jackson Reynolds of the First National Bank of New York whether he had a solution. "I have not," Reynolds answered, "and I do not believe anybody else has." Other financiers declared in lugubrious succession that nothing could be done but balance the budget and wait till we hit bottom. There was half of a revolutionary situation, in that the governing class had confessed its inability to govern. With nobody in command, the country drifted like a dismasted ship in the wake of a hurricane. It was a time, now forgotten, that we have repressed into the national subconscious as if it were an agonizing wound to our self-respect, a collective trauma.

Halfway through the interregnum Calvin Coolidge died peacefully on January 5, 1933, at his home in Northampton, Massachusetts. Mayor Bliss of Northampton announced that the merchants of the city would draw their shades during the funeral, but would keep their doors open. "I'm not going to ask them to close them," the mayor said, "because I don't think Calvin Coolidge would want that. He knew what they've been through. Every nickel counts with them. He wouldn't want them to lose a sale." The merchants of Northampton and of the nation were in straits that month. Their Christmas volume had declined by 18 percent since 1931, by more than 40 percent since 1929, and now they were slashing prices to get rid of unwanted merchandise. On Monday, January 2, Macy's advertised the "Greatest January White Sale"; Bonwit Teller, "Extraordinary Reductions"; Bergdorf Goodman, "Final Clearance Sale. *Prices cut to less than half,*" with gowns, not simply dresses, for $15. The price of full-length fur coats at Russek's was $495 for mink, $188 for leopard, $150 for Alaska seal (all government-stamped skins), and $59.75 for muskrat, leopard cat, or pony.

In the same issue of *The New York Times* that carried these extraordinary offers, the Classified section was small and was mostly devoted to apartments for rent. There were only seven items under the rubric of Help Wanted, Male. One of them read, "COLLECTORS—Want several men, thoroughly experienced installment collection work; must have car," and pay for its maintenance, apparently; "salary $100 per month to start." Curiously there were almost as few items under the other rubric of Situations Wanted. Jobs had become so scarce that the unemployed would no longer spend money to advertise for what they couldn't hope to find. They moped and brooded, nursed their lukewarm cups of coffee, and thought that sometime, in some fashion, everything must be changed.

Prophecies of revolution were heard in broader circles of society. Communists had started the talk long ago, but then it had been taken up by all sorts of public figures, including some who had been famous for their conservatism. Arthur Schlesinger, Jr., amused himself by collecting their remarks when he wrote *The Crisis of the Old Order.* Thus, Senator Bilbo of Mississippi said late in 1931, "Folks are getting restless. Communism is gaining a foothold. Right here in Mississippi some people are about ready to lead a mob. In fact, I'm getting a little pink myself." Edward F. McGrady, a right-wing official of the American Federation of Labor—in Communist terminology, a labor skate—told a Senate committee in the spring of 1932, "I say to you gentlemen, advisedly, that if something is not done and starvation is going to continue, the doors of revolt in this country are going to be thrown open." About the same time Congressman Hamilton Fish, Jr., of New York declared to the House of Representatives, "I am trying to provide security for human beings which they are not getting. If we don't give it under the existing system, the people will change the system. Make no mistake about that." Ham Fish was a bitter enemy of the Communists, as he would soon be of the New Deal, but for the moment, like Senator Bilbo, he was feeling a little pink.

In the intellectual world, where the coming revolution had long been a subject for argument, it became an article of faith and then a fascinating parlor game. The first object of the game was to designate an American Lenin and an American Trotsky. About the American Kerensky there was not much debate, since everyone knew that Roosevelt would play the part. But who would serve in the Council of People's Commissars? I found one list of candidates in Louis Adamic's book, *My America*, in which he quotes a high-spirited letter from his friend Benjamin Stolberg, a labor journalist. Stolberg wrote on August 7, 1932:

> From Union Square to Park Avenue, New York is full of crazy talk about the "coming revolution." The other night some of us made out our own revolutionary cabinets. Here is mine—at the moment:
> *Chairman of the Soviet Commissars:* B. Stolberg (no maybe).
> *Chairman, Supreme Economic Council:* Abe Harris.
> *Commissar of War, Navy and Kites:* L. Adamic.

*Foreign Affairs:* Kyle Crichton.
*Sex and Public Hygiene:* V. F. Calverton.
Etc., etc. . . . Some of the names you don't know.
But then you'll meet them at the first cabinet meeting
when you get back. I haven't yet decided who'll have the
OGPU job. I guess we can advertise in the *Times* for
somebody. Maybe Red Lewis will do.[1]

It was the time when people said as they waved good-bye,
"Meet me on the barricades." Of course they were being bright,
but with an undertone of speculation: perhaps there *would* be
barricades before the winter ended. A new series of jokes appeared with the tag line "Comes the revolution." The most popular of the series used to be shouted in chorus at the Players Club:
"Comes the revolution and you'll *eat* stromberries wit cream." A

1. Stolberg was an independent Marxist with a genius—it isn't too
strong a word—for finding stupidity and venality almost everywhere; I
called him Pejorative Ben. Among his epigrams at everybody's expense, the
one most often repeated was his judgment of the New Deal: "There is
nothing [it] has so far done that could not have been done better by an
earthquake." Having mortally offended the radicals of almost every faction, Stolberg later carried his Marxism to *The Saturday Evening Post.*
As for the other members of his cabinet, Abram L. Harris, not a revolutionary, was the distinguished Negro economist. Louis Adamic, born in
Croatia, was a diarist essentially, recording his conversations and his yearly
changes of opinion in a long series of books. He was anti-Communist all
during the 1930s, then in wartime he became a Titoist. He committed suicide (or was murdered by political opponents) in 1951. Kyle S. Crichton,
big and chuckling, was a humorist on the staff of *Collier's,* but he also
wrote a column for *The New Masses* under the pseudonym of Robert
Forsythe. The commissar of sex and public hygiene, V. F. Calverton, was a
prolific writer who applied a mixture of Marx and Freud to the criticism
of American literature and institutions. He had his own magazine, *The
Modern Monthly,* later *The Modern Quarterly,* which for a time published everyone on the left. Soon, however, Calverton was furiously attacked by *The New Masses,* and all his fellow-traveling contributors
dropped away, with Crichton among the first to go. Almost everyone
quarreled. By the end of the decade most of these writers, far from making
jokes about serving in the same revolutionary cabinet, would hardly have
entered the same room.

more elaborate story began with a speaker in Union Square. "Comes the revolution," he says, "and everybody will go to Harvard." His ragged audience applauds. "Comes the revolution"—the speaker pauses—"and everybody here will sleep with Peggy Hopkins Joyce," an actress then famous for her persistent habit of getting married to millionaires. More cheers from the audience, but there is one man who growls, "I doan *wanna* sleep with Peggy Hopkins Joyce." "Comes the revolution," the speaker says, wagging his finger, "you'll sleep with Peggy Hopkins Joyce *and* like it."

In the financial world, the prospects of revolution were discussed more somberly, as a rule, though one heard of toasts at cocktail parties: "To the last hour of capitalism. Let's make the most of it." Not smiling, Archibald MacLeish had written an open letter "To the Young Men of Wall Street," in which he addressed them collectively as "the heirs of Caesar." He adjured them to "create an idea of capitalism which men will support with their hope rather than their despair. . . . If you cannot, you and your children and ourselves with you will vanish from the West." Some of the younger Wall Street men were impressed by his warning and tried to learn more about their enemies. I can remember being invited (and refusing with dismay) to give a talk on communism to the Downtown Harvard Club. But the mood that seemed to prevail was one of dreamlike helplessness. Henry F. Pringle, a level-headed political historian who had just come back by train from Los Angeles, told me about sitting next to a banker in the smoking car. "There'll be a revolution, sure," the banker said in an indifferent voice, as if he were saying, "There'll be rain tomorrow."

Seeing hardly more prospect of saving the country than of changing the weather, most financiers confined themselves to the urgent task of saving their fortunes. Lloyd's of London was used to insuring almost anybody against almost anything, but in 1930 it became involved in what, even for Lloyd's, was an unfamiliar field, that of insuring wealthy Americans against "riot and civil commotion"; the business increased from year to year. More of the rich were insuring themselves in another fashion, by turning their wealth into gold bullion and shipping it abroad; in the first two months of 1933 the flight of gold by every transatlantic liner was putting an intolerable strain on the banking system. The panic spread to older men of letters; for example, Theodore Dreiser put his money into postal savings or changed it into gold notes, while Helen Richardson, later his wife, rushed to his country place in Westchester to stock up on canned goods. Richer men laid in a supply of firearms, while wondering whether the servants could be trusted to use them in the right way; or they bought farms in Vermont or ranches in Wyoming, two states thought to be safe against revolutionary mobs; or they looked farther afield and thought of living in Italy or in New Zealand. One prominent stockbroker gave a luncheon for Joe Freeman and Mike Gold of *The New Masses*. Comes the revolution and he wanted to have friends on both sides of the barricades.

Conservative statesmen were beginning to doubt whether the republic could survive under the Constitution. There was a good deal of talk about the advantages of a corporate state on the Italian pattern. "I do not often envy other people their governments," Senator Reed of Pennsylvania had already declared, "but I say that if this country ever needed a Mussolini, it needs one now." Others called for a presidential dictatorship under martial law. Al Smith did not use those terms, but he said in February 1933 that the depression was a greater crisis than the World War had been. "And what does a democracy do in war?" he asked. "It becomes a tyrant, a despot, a real monarch. In the World War we took our Constitution, wrapped it up and laid it on the shelf and left it there until it was over." At *The New Republic* we heard—but did not publish—persistent rumors of conferences between army officers and financiers about what to do in an emergency. "There is no doubt in my mind," Rexford Tugwell of the Brains Trust says in one of his memoirs, "that during the spring of 1933 the Army felt that the time was approaching when it might have to 'take over.' " Meanwhile Roosevelt was waiting at Hyde Park, where all the rumors reached him promptly, but where he said almost nothing for publication. A visitor told him that if he succeeded he would go down in history as the greatest American president, and that if he failed he would live on as the worst. He answered, according to the visitor's report, "If I fail I shall be the last one."

The question that strikes us after all these years is whether there might or could have been a new American revolution. "If Hoover had been re-elected . . ." people used to say with a speculative air. They were venturing into the highly improbable. One virtue of the American system is that every four years an administration is approved or rejected by what amounts to a national plebiscite. Hoover's administration was almost certain to be rejected because of its failure to end the depression. If it *had* been returned to office, against every political likelihood, the lesson would have been that most Americans approved of what he was doing. One might have expected a series of local revolts during the next four years, but they would have been suppressed for want of national support. There is, however, another possibility. Roosevelt came close to being defeated at the Democratic convention by a coalition of his rivals. Some of these had taken a stand that, except on the one issue of Prohibition, was hard to distinguish from Hoover's. If one of the conservatives had been nominated and had won the election, as almost any Democrat was sure to do; if he had followed Hoover's policies of retrenchment, deflation, and giving doles to the bankers, but none to the unemployed; and if he had also proved himself to be tactless and either stubborn or vacillating, then I think the government would have been overthrown in some fashion, by popular revolt or simple coup d'état—but not by a Communist revolution.

It seems likely that any popular revolt would have been led by some organization that could count on its share of middle-class support. Soon there would be dozens of these, including Khaki Shirts, Silver Shirts (with a larger membership), Blue Shirts, Black Shirts, White Shirts, Minute Men, American Nationalists, Coughlinites (with their powerful radio station), and Huey Longites (with their control of Louisiana), all in general sympathy with one another and all hoping to seize power. Together they had more sympathizers—and active members, probably—than the Communists would ever have. The social composition of the country did not favor the success of a revolution based chiefly on the proletariat, a class that was not quite certain of its own existence. The Communist Party had to start by persuading millions of Americans that they were truly proletarians, like workers in foreign countries, before convincing them, if it could, that they should unite under Communist leadership and cast off their other chains.

For this double task of propaganda the party had the wrong sort of language, bristling with abstractions, and usually the wrong sort of tactics, based on what had happened in Russia or what it still hoped would happen in Germany. The tactics might change overnight, for better or worse, but at any given moment they were the same for every industrialized country in the world. Any Communist who argued that the American situation was different or demanded special tactics was accused of "exceptionalism" and threatened with expulsion from the party. It is not surprising that the Communists with whom I talked at the time all defended the party line. "Mistakes have been made," they said with the air of conceding a point to my rotten liberalism, but they insisted that the mistakes would be corrected in the future. Communism would triumph here and everywhere, they said and believed sincerely; it was the new synthesis ordained by the dialectics of history. In confidence they were willing to admit, however, that it would not triumph in the United States by the unaided efforts of the party. First there might have to be a capitalist dictatorship, which would be so tyrannical and so riddled with contradictions that the masses would be driven to revolt, inevitably. Or else—this was the hope of the more sophisticated—the American fascists might try to seize the government, and the Communists would then have the advantage of fighting on the side of legality; they might even be supported by part of the army.

Meanwhile the industrial workers, for whom they claimed to speak, had shown a distressing lack of revolutionary fervor. There were very few strikes that winter; it was a time when any job—even if it paid only ten cents an hour, as did unskilled work at the Briggs Body plant in Detroit—was too precious to be surrendered. The unemployed, who had nothing to lose, held demonstrations in one city after another. Often thousands of them joined in a march to the city hall, under Communist leadership, and sometimes they frightened the mayor and his council into finding a little more food for their families, but the protests remained strictly legal. There were no riots unless the police started them, as they were doing less often in that fourth winter of the depression. The atmosphere of working-class neighborhoods was still one of despair, apathy, bewilderment, and waiting for something to turn up.

Once again the only mobs that defied the law were composed of solid Midwestern farmers, that is, of landed proprietors, independent enterprisers, kulaks, in a word, who would have been dispossessed and deported or sent to labor camps if they lived in Russia. Many of them, now, were about to be dispossessed in Iowa and all the neighboring states. They had gone into debt to buy land during the war years, when a bushel of wheat was worth more than two dollars. The mortgages were overdue, and the farmers could not pay them off in terms of wheat at forty or fifty cents a bushel; in effect their debt had quadrupled or quintupled. They could not find money even for taxes, but they were banding together to keep their land. On January 3 *The New York Times* printed a brief dispatch: "Passive resistance blocked efforts of three County Treasurers in Iowa to sell property on which taxes are overdue. Crowds attended the tax sales but there were no bids." Two days later there was a longer dispatch from the town of Le Mars in the northwestern corner of the state. It began, "Eight hundred Plymouth County farmers today forcibly prevented the sale of a foreclosed farm after overpowering Sheriff R. E. Ripley and Judge C. W. Pitts of the District Court and threatening to lynch an agent of the mortgage holder."

The farm—320 acres of rich land—was owned by an old farmer named John A. Johnson, well-liked in the neighborhood. It was mortgaged for $33,000, or less than one-third of what its value had been before the crash. The mortgage had been foreclosed by Herbert Morton, a local attorney, acting as agent for the New York Life Insurance Company. On the morning of the sale, which was to be held on the steps of the courthouse, farmers from the whole county drove into town over the frozen roads. They had told their wives to stay at home. One of them cut a length of rope from a swing in the courthouse square and knotted it into a hangman's noose. The sheriff appeared in the doorway, shivering, and announced the sale in due form. Nobody spoke but Morton, who followed instructions from the home office by making a bid of $30,000—more than anyone else in the county could have offered, but less than the face of the mortgage. The next legal step would be for New York Life to obtain a deficiency judgment of $3000, to be satisfied by the forced sale of Johnson's movable property. Those deficiency judgments, which had come to be expected in foreclosures, were what infuriated the Midwestern farmers. They meant that the victim and his family lost everything, including the tools they might have used in making a fresh start.

This time, before the sale of the farm could be completed, the crowd pummeled the sheriff, took Morton by the back of his collar, and dragged him down the stone steps of the courthouse. He was told that he could either raise his bid or be hanged from the highest tree in Le Mars. When he gasped out that he couldn't bid more without permission from the home office, he was marched to the telegraph office, where he sent off a desperate wire. Permission to raise the bid came back from New York within the hour. Morton saved his neck, and Johnson saved his equipment, his feed, and his cattle. At least he could rent another farm and keep his family alive.

Two days later the Plymouth County farmers stopped another forced sale; then they set out for the state capital in a motorcade. News of their victory had spread everywhere through the farming country. In Doylestown, Pennsylvania, that same week a farm with all its equipment was auctioned off for $1.18 to angry neighbors, everyone else having been warned not to make a bid. The neighbors promptly gave it back to the farmer. That was probably the first of the "five-and-ten-cent sales"; very soon they were being reported daily from county seats as far west as Texas and north to the Canadian border. Five cents would be the first and only bid for a hog, ten cents for a team of horses, twenty-five cents for a tractor. The farm itself might bring as much as five or ten dollars. After the Doylestown incident, which led to court proceedings, it wasn't given back to the farmer outright; instead the purchaser leased it to him for ninety-nine years, thus protecting it from a second foreclosure. The sight of several hundred farmers standing grimly round the sheriff as he offered a farm for sale—or perhaps of a noose dangling from the barn door —was usually enough to silence the mortgagee and his agents, but sometimes they were mauled and chased away. Near Pleasanton, Kansas, a man who had just foreclosed a mortgage on a 500-acre farm was found murdered in a ditch. His death was the first and I think the only one that resulted from the farmers' revolt.

But there would have been many more if the revolt had either been suppressed by force or allowed to continue. The farmers were desperate, and they had the sympathy of many state officials. On January 19 Governor Herring of Iowa issued a proclamation calling on all mortgage holders to avoid foreclosures until the state legislature had time to act. Says Jonathan Norton

Leonard, who describes the rebellion in *Three Years Down,* "Other governors followed his lead, often using force to back up persuasion. The federal government stopped selling farms which were mortgaged to national banks in process of liquidation." The government, incidentally, was among the harshest of creditors at the time. On January 30 the New York Life Insurance Company, which owned farm mortgages with a face value of more than $200 million, announced that it was halting foreclosures, and the other major insurance companies halted them a few days later. The farmers' little revolution ended at the same time, having gained its immediate objective in scarcely more than a month.

But the farmers' victory put a new strain on the whole crazily unbalanced structure of debt, investment, and credit. As a beginning it threatened the safety of life insurance. When debts secured by farm mortgages became uncollectable, several of the smaller companies were forced into liquidation (including the one that had insured my father). The biggest companies were insolvent at the time, in the sense that the cash value of their assets had become substantially lower than their liabilities. Of course the giants of life insurance could depend on the Reconstruction Finance Corporation not to let them go bankrupt. But little banks in county seats had also invested heavily in farm mortgages, and the RFC did almost nothing to keep them open. There had been more than five thousand bank failures during the three years since the crash. Early in February there was a new epidemic of failures that spread from small banks to larger ones and from city to city.

The banking system of Detroit was about to collapse. On the morning of February 14 Governor Comstock came to its help by closing every bank in the southern peninsula of Michigan for eight days. That was not the first of the "bank holidays." In 1932 some of the smaller Ohio cities had employed this euphemism to describe the temporary closing of banks by official proclamation when they were in danger of being permanently closed by their frightened depositors. One of the largest banks in New

Orleans was about to fail during the first week of February. It was granted a huge loan by the RFC, but the currency would not arrive until Sunday. Huey Long and his puppet governor of Louisiana, O.K. Allen, paged through almanacs trying to find some event that would give them an excuse for closing the banks of the state on Saturday. Finally Allen proclaimed a holiday "in commemoration of the sixteenth anniversary of the severance of diplomatic relations between the United States and Germany." That made a good story, and it seemed all the better when the banks reopened on Monday, but nobody laughed about the holiday in Michigan. After three years of depression it was the start of the real panic.

People who still had money waited in line to take it out of banks all over the country. Deposits were shrinking at the daily rate, by now, of $37 million withdrawn in gold coins and $122 million in banknotes. A great deal depended on what would happen next in Michigan: if the banks there reopened after eight days, the national credit structure might still be saved. There were desperate consultations in the White House and missions to plead with Henry Ford, who first refused to help—"Let the crash come," he said—then finally made an offer that nobody would accept. The holiday ended on February 21, but the Michigan banks did not reopen. Three days later Governor Ritchie had to close the banks of Maryland, locking up another billion dollars of deposits. As the panic spread from state to state it was like a windstorm in a grove of pine trees whose roots have been loosened by weeks of rain. Only the saplings are hurt by the early gusts, but then the first of the big trees crashes against a second, bringing it down, and the second brings down a third, till the wind is sweeping over a tangle of fallen trunks and roots high in the air.

In that calamitous winter there were other storms in Europe and Asia. The Japanese, having seized Manchuria under pretense of restoring order, were now invading the Chinese province of Jehol under the new pretense that it belonged to Manchuria.

When scolded by an international commission, they announced that they were resigning from the League of Nations. It was the end of the dream that wars might be prevented like cheating at cards, by the rules of a gentlemen's club. In the Ukraine and the North Caucasus, among the richest farmlands in Russia, there was a severe food shortage, or so we read in *The New York Times;* the word "famine" hadn't yet been used except in the Hearst press, which had told so many lies about Russia in the past that we didn't believe it when it told the truth. Later we learned that the famine resulted from Stalin's decision to seize all the peasant holdings and combine them into huge collective farms. The collectives were fantastically mismanaged by Communist officials most of whom knew little about agriculture. The peasants went on strike and refused to harvest the wheat. "Let them starve then," the Politburo said in effect; "it will teach them a lesson."

Nobody knows how many of them died of starvation, whether two, five, or seven million. The rest of the world had wheat that it couldn't sell and the Soviets had gold to pay for it, if they bought less machinery; lives might have been saved for a dollar or two apiece. Like the Great Hunger in Ireland, but on a vaster scale than in 1847, this was famine by administrative decision. One reason for the decision to let the peasants starve—besides the wish to teach them a lesson—was fear of the Japanese: if they heard about the discontent in Russia, they might invade the Far Eastern provinces. Another reason was Germany, where six million Communist votes had been cast at the recent election and there still seemed to be hope of a Communist revolution. The hope might vanish if the Russians acknowledged that there was a famine in the Ukraine provoked by their own mismanagement. More and more often the storms in one country were leading to disasters in another.

In Germany Hitler had taken office as chancellor on January 30. The event was reported by the *Times* as the second most important story of the day (the most important being a request by Governor Lehman of New York for $94 million in new taxes). "Herr Hitler," the *Times* said, "was maneuvered into heading a coalition government of National Socialists and Nationalists by Lieutenant-Colonel Franz von Papen, former Chancellor." Von Papen had indeed boasted that Hitler was hemmed in by a cabinet in which there were eight respectable Nationalists and only three Nazis. But Hitler outmaneuvered the Nationalists by immediately calling for new elections, to follow a campaign in which his party could employ all the resources of the federal radio network and of the Prussian state police, now commanded by his lieutenant Hermann Göring.

When it seemed that those resources, used to the utmost, would not be enough to win a majority for the Nazis, Göring, so it would seem, had his men set fire to the Reichstag building. That was on the evening of February 27. All night the German radio screamed that the Communists had burned the Reichstag as the first act in a bloody revolt. On the following day Hitler obtained from President von Hindenburg a decree suspending civil liberties throughout the German Reich. Four thousand Communist officials were arrested, beaten, and carried off to concentration camps. In defeat the Communists retained their faith in the historical process: the faster it moved in any direction, even toward fascism, the sooner their party of the workers would come to power.

The historical process was also moving faster in the United States, though nobody knew toward what new order. On February 28, the day after the Reichstag fire, bank holidays were proclaimed in Delaware, West Virginia, Tennessee, Arkansas, and Nevada. Governor Ruby Laffoon of Kentucky announced four "Days of Thanksgiving." On March 1 the states where the banking system collapsed were California, Oklahoma, and Louisiana. On the afternoon of Thursday, March 2, Roosevelt and his presidential party boarded a special train for Washington. They learned on reaching the Mayflower Hotel that the banks had been closed, or were about to be closed, in twenty-one states and the District of Columbia. The Federal Reserve reported that it had lost $226 million in gold during the last four days. On Friday, while Hoover and Roosevelt conferred with each other and separately with their advisers, the states were falling in clusters. Hoover said at midnight, "We are at the end of our string. There is nothing more we can do." When Roosevelt went to bed at one o'clock, closings had been authorized—at the plea of the bankers—in every state except New York and Illinois. In those two strongholds the bankers were holding out for a mixture of reasons: professional pride, obstinate hope, and—at least in some cases—political calculation. The hope was that with a new president taking office at noon on Saturday the mood of the country might change over the weekend; depositors might come streaming back. The political forethought was that if they stayed open for one more day—for a single morning—the collapse of the banking system might be blamed on the new radical administration.

But the banks of Chicago alone had lost $350 million in deposits during the last two weeks. Realizing that another morning would break them, they capitulated at 1:45 A.M., and Governor Horner of Illinois proclaimed the next-to-last holiday. In New York the bankers still refused to surrender, but both the old Republican and the new Democratic officials of the Treasury, working together in the crisis, were convinced that the bankers had to be protected from their own folly. Governor Lehman, a banker himself, proclaimed the final statewide moratorium at four in the morning. When Roosevelt took the oath of office, a few minutes after twelve, every bank in the country was closed.[2] There was not enough gold in the Federal Reserve to cover the currency then in circulation, let alone the huge new issue of paper money that would have to take the place of checks. In

2. The Mellon National Bank of Pittsburgh had defied the holiday proclaimed by Governor Pinchot of Pennsylvania and had stayed open on Saturday morning. It had closed at twelve o'clock, however, and it remained closed for the following week.

the Treasury there was not enough cash to meet the next government payroll, and an issue of $700 million in short-term notes, redeemable in gold, was falling due in less than two weeks. The United States of America had gone bankrupt. Bob Cantwell told me happily that March 4, 1933, would be celebrated in future years as the last day of capitalism all over the world.

# 15.
## Inaugural Parade

And what was the author doing in that month when the American economy was sliding faster toward the abyss? He was working hard for *The New Republic*, where he felt gratified at being an informed and somewhat privileged witness of great events. He was reading two or three newspapers a day, with special attention to brief reports on the inside pages that were more revealing than the stories with banner headlines. (Even the statewide bank holidays were quarantined on pages five, eight, or nine of the *Times*.) The author was also attending those last dreary meetings of the League of Professional Groups and listening impatiently to speeches about the betrayal of the Chinese revolution in 1927. With the inconsequence that people have always shown in the face of historical crises, he was having a good time at parties and was playing a lot of Ping-Pong.

Later I found myself thinly disguised in a novel about the intellectual turmoil of that year. (For the curious, it was Albert Halper's *Union Square*, 1933.) Looks, mannerisms, opinions were pretty faithfully described, and there was at least one incident from life: my first speech about the Kentucky miners. The novelist was a good observer of the *what*, but I thought he revealed a curious picture of the *why*. The notion was that I had prospered during the 1920s, that I had lost inherited money in the stock-market crash, and that faced with poverty for the first time I had then and therefore become a radical. It was the standard Communist explanation for the way that writers acted during the depression; in my own case it was the opposite of the truth. I had been poor all through the 1920s, not ever starving, but worried about whether the grocer would give me credit. I had never inherited money and had never owned a share of stock, even on a ten-point margin. It was after the crash that I paid off my debts, mostly consisting of loans from friends, and for the first time in my life felt at ease financially.

My case was not at all a special one. Even in the fourth winter of the slump, when most of the older magazines were cutting down their staffs and getting rid of once valued contributors, there were younger magazines that flourished. *The New Yorker*, then eight years old, had more readers than in the boom years. It was taking on new writers and editors, most of whom seemed to be shy, worried, talkative men in their thirties with newspaper experience. *Time* and *Fortune*—the latter founded in 1930—were hiring bright kids from the Ivy League colleges. Except in the weeks of actual panic, young novelists were being called to Hollywood or were coming back with reports of fabulous salaries to be had there for the asking. I kept meeting people who had money to spare for the first time. It seemed to me that the more they earned, in the midst of a general catastrophe, the more likely they were to be studying Marx and talking about the revolution that must come.

The same sort of talk, leading to similar disputes and agreements, was being heard in many other countries. I was impressed at the time by a letter from Louis Aragon that I received after delays in the mail. In Paris ten years before, Aragon had been my sponsor with the Dada group at a time when the group was breaking apart into quarreling fractions. One of these had created a new movement, Surrealism, with Aragon's friend from schooldays, André Breton, as its leader. The Surrealists had announced that they were Communists and had tried to form an alliance with the French Communist Party, but the party had rejected them. The Trotskyists had been more hospitable. Not attracted by Trotskyism, Aragon had gone to Russia in 1930, had accepted the Communist Party line, and had adjured Surrealism, at the cost of a lasting quarrel with Breton. He had written a long declamatory poem, *Red Front*, that was translated into English by E. E. Cummings (before Cummings went to Russia in turn and became violently anti-Soviet). In the poem Aragon denounced the French government, the army, and the police, and called upon the workers to rise in rebellion; for this he was accused of sedition and was placed on trial in Paris. He was convicted, too, but hundreds of public figures had signed an appeal to the court, which suspended his sentence. I had followed the story as best I could and had wondered what would happen next to my increasingly prominent friend. Now he was in Moscow again. In his schoolbook English he wrote me an unexpected letter:

Dear Malcolm,
    I wanted very much to write you for ages and ages. Being in Moscow since seven months now, I thought of you, and Slater Brown (and Matty also from whom I had good news when I saw his signature in New Masses, tell him) in a different way, in a different view than I used to have, when reminding the old days of Giverny and so on. We are people of the same kind, of the same time, and more or less what happens to one of us one day will happen to the others the day after. All this being not so Mallarmean as it sounds first. And coming to this point that we *must* write to each other (I know what you will say!), and know about each other.

The letter suggested an article on Russia that Louis might write for *The New Republic;* then it returned to personal matters.

Anyhow do write, dear Malcolm, and let us take this not very literary pretext as a first occasion to speak together after years. And how is Peggy? Tell her my love. What about a trip in this country?

Friendly yours,
Aragon

I had no intention of taking a trip to Russia, then or later. Its official prose made me uneasy, for all my revolutionary enthusiasm. What impressed me in Aragon's letter was the sentence that began, "We are people of the same kind, of the same time. . . ." Perhaps we were again following Aragon, if at a distance.

In the American literary world, almost everyone younger than James Branch Cabell was having qualms of social conscience. I remember debating with myself whether it wasn't my duty to go to work for *The New Masses* at the salary of $25 a week that all its editors were paid, when there was money enough in the till. The prospect of making a financial sacrifice was rather appealing, in a romantic fashion, but I suspected that I would have less freedom than at *The New Republic* and that the party might tell me which books to admire. Another duty might be to stay where I was, even if I was more comfortable in the old brownstone house than I felt that a man of my radical opinions had any right to be. *The New Republic* hadn't fired anybody or made a single reduction in salary, and the result, in that time of low prices, was what amounted to a substantial raise for everyone on the staff. There were rumors, though, that the paper might lose its subsidy and have to be discontinued. Muriel and I held a family conference and decided that we had no reason for worry about our personal affairs. We might both lose our jobs, but we were young, healthy, used to being poor, and we had skills for which there would be a demand in almost any sort of society. We could still survive even if the worst happened and we had to go into exile, I said, thinking of the German refugees who were beginning to crowd the cheap hotels of the Upper West Side. Meanwhile it was no use trying to save money, considering that the dollar might lose its value overnight. We might as well simply live from day to day.

From day to day we lived very well that winter. We had a studio apartment not far from *The New Republic;* there were two huge rooms, plus a tiny kitchen and a bathroom with a sliding freight-car door, and the rent had been reduced by negotiations to $65 a month. Our motherly Swedish maid did the shopping; she liked to buy very thick steaks and insisted on polishing the furniture with olive oil. There was always a five-gallon keg of applejack under the hinged lid of the window seat; we used to siphon off a pitcherful when guests dropped in for Ping-Pong. Over the applejack, while waiting for a turn at the Ping-Pong table, we used to talk about what? There was the usual gossip, but also we spent a lot of time discussing the German situation: what would Hitler do about the radicals in his own party? Would he be overthrown by them or by a Communist revolution? A little after ten, somebody would appear with the bulldog edition of *The Herald Tribune,* which came out an hour before the *Times,* and we skimmed through it for the latest disasters at home and abroad. I remember the contrast between our long public faces, as we read the news, and the sudden hilarity as we rushed back to the Ping-Pong table.

So the private face of that winter was a rather happy one for me and for many of the writers I knew. It was the Ping-Pong winter, the Jersey applejack winter, the winter of small parties and excited conversation. A larger party I didn't attend was in Dorothy Thompson's apartment on the night of January 20. "Dorothy looked very handsome in evening gown," Louis Adamic noted in his diary. He tried to make a list of the guests, but most of their names, he said, "did not register with me. One was a journalist from Berlin, who spoke English. Talk was about Hitler, Germany, Russia, 'revolution in the United States.' Some of the things said were pretty wild." That was typical, and so was a remark by the hostess. "Dorothy Thompson said that, having lived in Europe through most of the past decade, she did not know much about the United States, and was anxious to learn, to get a feeling about the country." Many other writers had tried to get that feeling, but they were laboring under a new handicap. Partly because they had fewer personal worries than the unemployed or the small businessmen, but also because they were more willing to adopt new beliefs, the more extreme the better, they were once again losing touch with popular feeling.

They had been closer to the masses a year before, when they were still puzzled and looking for answers to questions that everyone else was asking too. But now most of them had found some variation of the Marxian answer to all the questions, and it set them apart from the people they were trying to understand. They were not fellow seekers any longer; they were teachers standing on a platform and expounding doctrines that the masses were not ready to accept. It seemed to many writers at the time that their new doctrines not only explained the depression but enabled them to predict the course of events by achieving what Vincent Sheean, in his *Personal History* (1935), would soon be calling "the long view." In that view the capitalist system was falling apart so rapidly, here and everywhere, that there was no hope of patching it together. Any serious effort to preserve the system would lead to a fascist dictatorship, as in Germany. Socialism was the only alternative; there was no possible compromise, and the battle was raging all over the world. Quite possibly the future of America would be decided in Berlin or Shanghai or the Russian factories.

That was "the long view," and it was widely held in the literary community. Even John Chamberlain—conservative by instinct, honestly groping, always glancing up from a book with the air of a friendly young owl exposed to a strong light—had recently published a *Farewell to Reform* (1932). His thesis was that minor improvements in the social system were futile or even disastrous. One effect of the reforms achieved by the first Roosevelt, La Follette, and Wilson—as of those suggested by the second Roosevelt in his campaign speeches—had been and would be to "make the system which they are intended to patch up only the more unpatchable." In that negative sense, however—and in the long view—they might be regarded as a prelude to the revolution that must come. . . . When Chamberlain wrote the book, which was praised widely, he was still a reporter for *The New York Times*. Instead of being discharged for subversive opinions, he was soon promoted to the newly created post of daily book reviewer.

*The New Republic* was not a revolutionary magazine, except sometimes in the book department. Bruce Bliven and George Soule, who wrote the political editorials—we called these "leaders" in the English fashion—were both mild-spoken men and advocates of social and economic planning, to be achieved by strictly constitutional means. They were, however, sufficiently affected by "the long view" to regard the cataclysmic events of that season as merely steps in a continuing historical process. Why get excited about disasters that they had been predicting for years? It must have been Soule who said dispassionately in a leader on the banking crisis, "The dam finally broke, first in Michigan, then in Maryland, then throughout the country." His tone was that of a historian describing the panic of 1837. In the same issue, dated March 15—it went to press on Tuesday, March 7—Bliven must have written the frosty leader about the new president. "In none of this," he said after summarizing the inaugural address, "is there anything surprising to those who understand Mr. Roosevelt's character or followed closely his speeches in the campaign. He is, as we said at that time, an intelligent man and on the whole a progressive. He is also highly sensitive to the currents of public thought, and prepared to respond to them, when he believes it is right and wise to do so, rapidly and skillfully. Much of his inaugural address had an odd sound, as though it were not a statement by the President to the people, but a statement to a President by, let us say, an editorial writer or an expert press agent, telling him what line would be most popular just now."

The paper had sent Edmund Wilson to Washington for the inauguration, and his report appeared in the following issue. It was even frostier than Bliven's leader. Standing near the Capitol on that gray noonday of March 4, Wilson thought that the big building had the air of being "a replica of itself in white rubber." "The people seem dreary," he said, "and they are curiously apathetic. . . . They wait in the park in front of the Capitol. 'What are those things that look like little cages?' 'Machine guns,' says a woman with a giggle. They wait till they see Roosevelt's dim figure on the platform on the Capitol steps, hear dimly the accents of his voice—then the crowd rapidly thins."

> And even when you read them [Wilson's report continues], the phrases of the speech seem shadowy—the echoes of Woodrow Wilson's eloquence without Wilson's exaltation behind them. The old unctuousness, the old pulpit vagueness. . . . The old Wilsonian professions of plain-speaking followed by the old abstractions: "I am certain that on this day my fellow Americans expect that. . . . I will address them with a candor and a decision which the present situation of our people impels. This is pre-eminently the time to speak the truth, the whole truth, frankly and boldly," etc. So what? So in finance we must "restore to the ancient truths" the temple from which the money-changers have fled; so in the field of foreign affairs, he "would dedicate this nation to the policy of the good neighbor."
>
> There is a warning, itself rather vague, of a possible dictatorship.

Rereading Wilson's article after forty years, I feel that it lacks a quality that was admirably present in his first reports of the depression. Those reports of 1930 and 1931 had caught the new mood of the country and they had a prophetic value: in terms of local situations and personal misfortunes, freshly observed, they had predicted what scores of millions would soon be feeling. In Washington, however, he failed to perceive that the mood of the country was changing again or that Roosevelt's speech contained something more than "the old unctuousness, the old pulpit vagueness." Like many other writers at the time, he was misled by "the long view" and the notion it implied that there was no middle ground between capitalism in its agony and the new socialist order that was struggling to be born. Roosevelt was defending the old order, and hence he could offer nothing, in Wilson's view, but machine guns and "a warning, itself rather vague, of a possible dictatorship."

But Wilson's article, besides misjudging Roosevelt and the mood of the country, also contains a masterly report of the inaugural parade as it appeared to a jaundiced eye. The first part of the parade is dignified, he says, and "It is fun to hear 'The West Point Cadets' March' and 'The Stars and Stripes Forever'— they bring back the America of boyhood: the imperial Roosevelt, the Spanish War. And the airplanes against the dark sky, flying in groups of nine and moving as they reach the reviewing stand into exact little patterns like jackstones, awaken a moment's pride in American technical precision.

"But from this point on," he continues, "—and there are something like three hours of it yet—the procession crazily degenerates." Paragraph by paragraph, Wilson plots its course from idiocy into nightmare. Here are some of his observations:

> . . . as the weather grows darker and more ominous, the parade becomes more fantastic. . . . Comic lodges and marching clubs go by. Men appear in curled-up shoes and fezzes, dressed in hideous greens, purples and reds. Indians, terribly fat, with terribly made-up squaws. A very large loose old Negro in a purple fez and yellow-edged cloak, carrying the prong of an antler as if it were the Golden Bough. The airplanes overhead have been replaced

by an insect-like autogyro, which trails a big advertising banner: "Re-Tire with Lee's Tires." The Negro lady hussars wear gorgeous bright purple stockings. The Spirit of '76 have all the appearance of being cockeyed: one of the trio is always getting behind and running to catch up with the others. . . .

An uncanny music now tickles the ear, and ambiguous figures loom, out of Little Nemo's Adventures in Slumberland. Some seem half-Indian, half-angel, with feather headdresses that sweep to the ground; others (who get big applause) have hoods with spiky dorsal fins, like Martians in the barbershop weeklies; and all are clad in pale flowing female robes, tinted with celestial pinks and blues and making an effect of unpleasant iridescence such as sweat sometimes leaves on white shirts. As they move, they tease mosquito-buzzing dance music out of xylophones, banjos, guitars and violins. Interspersed are the Loew's Theaters Cadet Band; a drum-major who can juggle two batons; and a drunk with Leon Errol rubber legs, who ricochets back and forth and shakes hands with people on the sidelines.

Then come two final short paragraphs that might serve as a peroration to everything that Wilson wrote about the early depression years:

If the parade went on any longer, it would be too dark to see, too cold to stay out. And you are glad when it is over, anyway. The America it represented has burst, and as you watched the marchers, you realized that it had been getting sillier and sillier all the time.

The America of the boom definitely died today, and this is the ghost it just gave up.

# 16.

# Echoes of
# the Jazz Age

What followed the inauguration on March 4, 1933, was a curious week when retail business came to a halt, except in neighborhood stores that offered credit to anyone they knew. The big stores also offered credit—even Macy's, which then had no charge accounts—but customers stayed away. All the stock exchanges were closed. The midtown restaurants were empty at night, except for waiters, and box-office receipts for motion pictures fell by a countrywide average of 45 percent. Wage earners had not been able to cash their Saturday paychecks. Most families of the middle class had a few hoarded banknotes, but were cautious in doling them out. For many people with money in their wallets, the chief annoyance was that they had no silver and copper for bus rides or tips (after signing the check in a restaurant) or the afternoon paper. Merchants complained that strangers offered them twenty-dollar bills for small purchases and that they couldn't make change. It was the week when piggy banks were broken open.

On Monday we read that a sixteen-year-old boy in Elgin, Illinois, had saved 11,357 pennies toward his college education. Local merchants read the story too, and within an hour they had

the boy's house surrounded. On Wednesday John D. Rockefeller, Sr., who played a daily round of golf at the age of ninety-
three, ran out of dimes for the first time and gave his amazed
caddy a dollar. The papers were full of good-humored anecdotes
like these, and they appealed to the mood of the nation. Instead
of bringing hungry mobs into the streets, the emergency had produced a vast feeling of relief. "Now things can't get any worse,"
our corner grocer said happily. Another happy man was "Prince"
Michael Romanoff, whose personal checks, signed with a flourish,
had never been gladly accepted by nightclubs. "A great many
people's checks," he said grandly, "are now as good as a great
many others'." He was not the only one to feel cheered by the
calamities of the bankers. Almost everything that had happened
over the last four years had deepened the antagonism between the
frightened rich and the resentful poor, but now they were all
victims of the same crisis. The nation was united, for the moment,
in hoping for the "direct, vigorous action" that Roosevelt had
promised and was beginning to provide.

Even the new Congress, which he had already summoned
to meet in special session, was determined to act promptly for the
nation, instead of being divided and obstructed by a diversity
of local interests, as every other Congress had been. For once,
nobody asked of a bill, "Is it good for Crabb's Corners?" The
bank in Crabb's Corners had been closed with the others, and they
all had to be reopened by means provided in the same new law.
An Emergency Banking Bill, whipped together in three days
and nights, was read aloud to the House of Representatives on
Thursday afternoon, before there was time to have copies of
it printed and given to members. Among its other provisions was
one that ratified all measures with regard to the banking system
"heretofore *or hereinafter* taken" by the president and the
secretary of the treasury, an astonishing delegation of power.
The House discussed the bill for exactly thirty-eight minutes,
then "whooped it through," as one observer said, without a
roll call. The Senate, always more deliberate, spent three hours
over the bill before sending it to the president, who signed it at

8:36 in the evening. The whole legislative process had taken less than eight hours.

An hour later that Thursday evening, Roosevelt had a meeting with congressional leaders and proposed a bill that would reduce all government salaries, including those of congressmen, while authorizing the president to reduce all pensions paid to veterans. The leaders told him it couldn't pass, but he submitted the bill with a message the following day. At the White House supper on Sunday he said as if to himself, "I think this would be a good time for beer." Also on that Sunday evening, March 12, he gave the first of his effective "fireside chats" to the nation, explaining what had been done during the week, and he scribbled off a message to Congress calling for modification of the Volstead Act to permit the sale of beer. On Monday, Tuesday, and Wednesday all the banks that were ruled to be solvent reopened their doors. The stock exchange opened on Wednesday in a flurry of rising prices; the first message printed on the ticker tape was "Happy Days Are Here Again."

By the end of that second week Roosevelt had written still another message to Congress, this one to urge passage of an agricultural adjustment act, later known as Triple-A. It would be debated for nearly two months, since all sorts of regional and class interests were affected, but everything else kept moving fast. The Economy Act passed Congress, in spite of all prophecies, and was signed by the President on Monday of his third week in office. The bill for 3.2-percent beer was signed on Wednesday, March 22. By that time Congress was already considering the bill to establish a Civilian Conservation Corps, which would be signed on March 31.

The CCC—and later the Tennessee Valley project, TVA— were the only undertakings of the first New Deal that roused my enthusiasm. I was a conservationist by instinct, and I began to see then what everything later confirmed: that Roosevelt was making himself the hope and leader of the conservationists. He wanted to save the countryside with all its resources, and he wanted to make it yield a better life to Americans: that was a double purpose always close to his heart, which sometimes wavered in regard to other purposes, especially when he felt that the voters weren't ready to accept them. The Conservation Corps was designed to have a double effect in keeping with its purpose. It would rescue young men from unemployment—all its members were to come from families on relief—and would teach them to live outdoors, while the work they did would help to save the forests and improve the national parks. But the CCC was established for another reason too, though I didn't learn about it till forty years later when reading Rex Tugwell's memoirs. Roosevelt believed that young men standing hopelessly on street corners were the human material from which Hitler—and the German Communists, for a time—had recruited their political armies. He confided to Tugwell that putting the young men to work planting trees would be a grand way of preventing revolution in the United States.

Meanwhile—but in this case without conscious intention—his new laws were also helping young men of a different type, those who, if denied opportunities within a social order, have played a great part in fomenting revolutions all over the world: I mean the displaced intellectuals. The New Deal kept the ablest of them out of revolutionary movements by giving them employment. In 1933 the country was full of ambitious young lawyers without cases to plead, of young economists with plans that nobody would put into effect, of college instructors without hope of finding better places on faculties, of social workers eager to use their training in a wider field, and of newspapermen with more ideas than their editors would let them express. They invaded Washington that spring; the first to come were young lawyers with letters of recommendation from Felix Frankfurter, still at the Harvard Law School, and economic planners inspired by the projects of Rex Tugwell and Raymond Moley. Most of them found work to do, and they sent back word to their friends in the universities, who poured after them like the Bonus Army.

A few of the intellectual recruits were secretly Communists.

Though not all of those remained faithful to the party, a few others were enrolled by it after they went to work for the government. It does not appear, however, from all the volumes of testimony in the records—and here I can add nothing from personal knowledge—that the Communists had any effect on the first New Deal. They were opposed to every measure that Roosevelt brought forward except relief for the unemployed, which they were convinced would be inadequate. Everything else they regarded as a step toward fascism, especially the bill that would establish a Civilian Conservation Corps. Herbert Benjamin of the Unemployed Councils was speaking for the party when he testified against the proposal at a committee hearing. "This bill," he said, "undertakes to establish and legalize a system of forced labor."

So the Communists stood aside to protest and expostulate during those first hundred days, as indeed for a long time afterward. Washington was happy to get along without them. It was the spring when the new men—those *Filii Aurorae*, as Judge Learned Hand called them scathingly—worked hard in government offices drawing up bold memorandums to their superiors or helping to draft new laws. Often their luncheon was a sandwich munched abstractedly at a desk covered with papers and cigarette stubs. A conference that started in the afternoon might continue into the night, while their wives sat at home feeling neglected. On evenings free of government business there were gatherings in Georgetown houses, partly flirtatious or bibulous, partly devoted to games and singing, but mostly conversational, with arguments that continued till the first streaks of light over Capitol Hill. All the Sons of the Dawn loved to talk. All were excited by ideas, and still more excited by the prospect that some of the ideas they had been discussing since 1929 would at last be tested in action. For Rex Tugwell and many others it was "the renaissance spring . . . a time of rebirth after a dark age."

But it was a renaissance for intellectuals, not for writers by profession. The writers I knew, most of them "politically conscious," as they liked to say of themselves at the time, were skeptical of the first New Deal (which was that of the planners, as the second New Deal would be that of the spenders and social workers). Some of my friends might be attracted by one or two of the New Deal measures, as I was by CCC and TVA (not to mention beer), but in general they had adopted the "long view" that there was no middle ground between a fascist dictatorship and a workers' republic. Roosevelt's little reforms would fail, in the long view, so why get excited about them? The real battle between two systems was being fought in Russia and Germany.

I do not think that the first New Deal lost heavily by not engaging the interest of writers, except possibly in one respect. If a few writers had been part of it, they might have explained it better to the public. The New Dealers themselves were inspired talkers, but most of them didn't write English; they wrote in the different jargons of economists, sociologists, lawyers, or administrators, or in that mixture of all four to which Harold Ickes, I think it was, later gave the name of gobbledygook. Rex Tugwell sometimes threw off a brilliant phrase, but that was a weakness rather than a gift, since his phrases aroused the terror of conservatives. Roosevelt himself—who redictated in his own words the speeches that others wrote for him—was the only New Dealer whose language touched the common heart. Good writers in Washington might have helped the Brains Trust to project a less sinister image of itself; in that one respect the projects of those early days may have suffered from their absence. The writers suffered much more, I think, considering the value they then placed on political consciousness. Preoccupied as they were with the long view, which meant, in effect, the view across the Atlantic, they failed to understand or even pay close attention to the most exciting political struggles of the time, which were in their own country.

I was almost as indifferent as the others. When I tried digging into my mind, I unearthed very few memories of the March and April that were a heroic time for the planners. But I did find one memento among my papers: a message on the letterhead of the Communist Party, with an illegible signature ("Meb" somebody) and the message badly typed as if to show that it was authentic:

> PLEASE XXXXXX ADMIT MALCOLM COWLEY
> TO SPEAKERS' PLATFORM, MADISON SQUARE
> GARDEN, WEDNESDAY EVENING APRIL % 5

It was a huge mass meeting called "to protest," as the Communists always said transitively, the Hitler dictatorship. I must have been there to speak for "the leftward-moving writers," who in those days had their token representative on every committee and every panel of speakers, along with the inevitable woman to speak for women, the organizer to speak for the trade unions, and the Negro to be displayed like a trophy. But we token people weren't expected to talk for more than five minutes or ten at the most; the big speech was always reserved for a member of the Central Committee, usually Earl Browder himself. I can remember looking out from a folding chair on the speakers' platform over the immense cave, rendered misty by the smoke from ten thousand cigarettes, as if from fires where Nazis were being roasted, and I can remember thinking that it would be just as easy to speak in the biggest hall as in a smaller one: there was nothing to do but shout louder and confine oneself to even simpler ideas. I don't remember what I said, but it must have been honest in its simple way, for I was as deeply convinced as the other speakers that German fascism was a step toward fascism in this country and then to another world war.

About the same time I wrote a piece about Trotsky for *The New Republic*, based on *The History of the Russian Revolution*. I was vastly impressed by the narrative, but was less impressed by Trotsky's argument that "socialism in one country"—a Russian slogan of the time—could not be a success; also I was puzzled about the application of Trotsky's theories to the United States, where the middle classes were vastly more numerous and powerful than they had been in Russia. I said in a last paragraph:

> Yet I do not doubt that the United States will have its revolution. Alexander Hamilton saw to that when he contrived to fashion a Constitution difficult to change (except by will of the Supreme Court) and a national legislature slow to reflect the shifts in popular opinion. The Supreme Court prepared us for revolution by its decisions regarding the "due process" clause of the Fourteenth Amendment. But when the revolution comes, in five years or fifty, it is not likely to be a communist revolution. Germany, not Russia, has traced the path which we seem destined to follow if the crisis continues or recurs. Except for a disastrous war or the happy discovery of new markets, the only thing that can turn us aside from that steep path into the sea is the influence on the middle classes of the Russian experiment, the success of "socialism in one country."

That will never be offered as an example of political prescience. The American system has proved to be vastly more flexible than it seemed to me or others at the time (though we still can't tell what would happen if there was another crisis that set the poor against the rich, as in 1932, and if no branch of the government was able to take effective action). The Russian experiment, even when I wrote, was losing its brief glamour for the middle classes. But my paragraph is an indication of what many people—I was not original in my notions—were thinking in April 1933. Fascism on the German model already seemed to be the great danger for the United States. Germany under Hitler was becoming the bad country, and Russia, dramatically set against it, had to be the good country, on the side of freedom. That explains why many of us, later, would be slow to admit, especially to ourselves, that Stalin was making himself a tyrant as bloody as Hitler.

After the middle of April I paid still less attention to what was happening in Washington—except for one event, that is. On April 19 Roosevelt took the country off the gold standard by presidential proclamation, as he had been given the power to do. The dollar fell steeply on the money-exchange markets. That was a crisis for the Americans I had known in Paris and most of them came trooping home, even those who had thought of living in France for the rest of their lives. Among them was the gifted, self-questioning poet John Peale Bishop, who had bought a château at Orgeval, forty minutes from Paris; his three sons were born there. The crisis brought him back to the States, though his wife still had a small fortune. Even prosperous writers no longer felt at home in France; it was in 1933 that the novelist Louis Bromfield bought a thousand acres of farmland in his native Ohio. As for impecunious or unpublished writers, those who had clustered in the Montparnasse cafés, many of them had already been driven homeward when the flow of American tourists stopped in the depression years, and with it the supply of small jobs and borrowable money. Only a few stayed on like Henry Miller, always on the nether edge of destitution.

Harold Stearns was one of those who surrendered. Long before, at the beginning of the 1920s, he had become famous as the editor of *Civilization in the United States*, a big volume of essays on our cultural poverty. In another book, *America and the Young Intellectual*, he had asked the famous question "What Should a Young Man Do?" and had answered it on July 4, 1921, by taking ship to Europe as a refugee from Babbittry and Prohibition. He had soon become a tottering monument of the Quarter, famous for the piles of saucers that he accumulated night after night at café tables. Hemingway had depicted him in *The Sun Also Rises* under the name of Harvey Stone: "Harvey was just a little daunted. Hadn't eaten for three days. Doesn't eat any more. Just goes off like a cat." But he worked too, though he no longer wrote books or challenging essays. Almost every afternoon he went to the races, won or lost a few bets, and selected his favorites for the next day. His choices, signed "Peter Pickem," appeared in that zany newspaper, the European edition of *The Chicago Tribune*. Then suddenly he found that during eleven years in France he had lost everything: his job, his girl, his room, his clothes, his talent, and every tooth in his head. There were nights when he dozed on a bench beside the boulevard Montparnasse, waiting for a church to open at four in the morning. The American Aid Society bought him passage on a freighter bound for Hoboken. He arrived in February 1932 without money or luggage or a typewriter.[1]

So, there had been a little stream of returning exiles since 1931, but now it became a torrent. At the end of April 1933 all the westbound liners had full passenger lists in what had always been an empty season. Some of the repatriates came to see me at *The New Republic*. I remember Arthur Moss and Florence Gilliam, who together had founded *Gargoyle* in 1921; that had been the first of the little exiled magazines. Now Art complained, "We can't find a decent café." They and others impressed me as being fossils of Montparnasse, innocent of everything that had happened in New York since the crash.

Between visitors I was busy clearing my desk before taking a leave of absence. That was an opportunity I owed to Allen Tate and his wife, the novelist Caroline Gordon, who were then living near Clarksville, Tennessee. They had found me what proved to be exceptionally comfortable quarters on a farm owned by one of Caroline's many cousins in what she called the Meriwether connection. Rent and board had been set at a low figure (and in the end my kind hosts would not accept any payment whatever). For the first time in my life I would have ten

---

1. It is pleasant to record that he was sheltered for some weeks at the house of the poet and trotting-horse pundit Evan Shipman (though Evan was in Europe) and that the correspondent Walter Duranty paid a good dentist to make him a set of choppers. Stearns became a reformed character. In 1935 he published his candid memoirs, *The Street I Know*, and in 1938 he edited another big symposium, *America Now*, as a reaffirmation of American values. It lacked the freshness of his earlier work.

uninterrupted weeks to work on a book. My only sorrow was that Muriel was still tied to her job and couldn't come with me.

I stayed in New York for the May Day parade. It was so big in 1933 that it had to be divided into two sections, one starting from near the Battery and marching north, the other from midtown and marching south, with the two sections converging in Union Square. The John Reed contingent, with which I marched again—this time recognizing many more faces and singing "The International" as loudly as the others—was part of the southbound column. In all there were fifty thousand marchers, if you read the *Times;* of course *The Daily Worker* said more than a hundred thousand. The whole New York police force of nineteen thousand men was on duty to suppress a riot, if one occurred, and the crowd in Union Square was sprinkled with plainclothesmen. But the sun was bright, the crowd was good-humored, and nobody wanted a riot—not even the plainclothesmen, who were always suspected of trying to start one. I didn't stay for the speeches, since I had to pack before leaving early in the morning for Tennessee. The first night of my leisurely drive was to be spent with relatives near Philadelphia, and the second near Baltimore with Scott and Zelda Fitzgerald.

That spring the Fitzgeralds were established on a parklike estate, La Paix, belonging to Bayard Turnbull, who lived with his wife and children in the more comfortable of two houses. There were acres of lawn shaded by tall red-oak trees just coming into leaf, with a white shimmer of dogwoods in the background. The second house, which the Fitzgeralds rented, wasn't a small one; it was a high-peaked wooden structure built in the dark-brown hunting-lodge style of the 1890s, looking dingy but still pretentious. Scott, having saved a little money from his *Saturday Evening Post* stories, was at last making progress on the big novel on which he had worked intermittently for eight years. The book was still untitled—sometimes he called it "The Drunkard's Holiday"—but most of it was written and he knew how the story would end. Zelda was home from the sanitarium recovering or—Scott feared at times—relapsing after a second mental breakdown and also after two aborted careers: as a ballet dancer and as a writer. I had never met Zelda, but Scott told me she was working hard on a collection of drawings for an exhibition that she had been promised by a New York gallery.

On the afternoon of my arrival, the brown lodge seemed a cheerful place in which the Fitzgeralds had decided to camp for a week or two before moving into permanent quarters. There was not much furniture downstairs and all of it was shabby; there were no carpets, and the only pictures on the walls were two or three framed reproductions out of *The Dial Portfolio*, which, ten years before, had introduced modern art to the American middle classes. Still, the house was full of comfortable noises: four or five Negroes laughing in the kitchen, Zelda upstairs talking to her nurse or rustling about her studio as she painted furiously, and little Scottie, home from school, playing with the Turnbull children on the big front porch. She was a pretty and mischievous girl of eleven who looked younger than her age, but who sometimes talked like a grown-up European. Big Scott, still handsome, had a gray skin, a drinker's paunch, and his sandy hair was getting thin on top. He asked questions engagingly as he strode up and down the living room.

Zelda didn't come down for dinner, which was served in style, but afterward Scott took me upstairs to meet her and look at her drawings. They were mostly of ballet dancers and were better than I had expected; they had freshness, imagination, rhythm, and a rather grotesque vigor, but they were flawed, exactly as her writing had been, by the lack of proportion and craftsmanship. Zelda herself dismayed me. "She curled up and went to sleep like a beautiful silky kitten," Van Wyck Brooks had said of her after a dinner party ten years earlier, but now there was hardly a trace of beauty or silkiness. Her face was emaciated and twitched as she talked. Her mouth, with deep lines above it, fell into unhappy shapes. Her skin in the lamplight

looked brown and weatherbeaten, except that on the left cheek
there were four parallel red streaks where she had raked it with
her fingernails, so that she made me think of a starved Indian
in war paint.

After we said good night to her, Scott installed me in a
worn green armchair, the only one in the living room. On the
table beside me he put a pint of whisky from his bootlegger. It
was all mine, he said, since he wasn't drinking. He went out to
the kitchen for a glass of water. By that time the cook had gone
home with all her relatives and little Scottie had gone to bed. I
noticed suddenly how every sound was magnified by the absence
of carpets and furniture. The armchair creaked like a ship in the
night, the bottle thumped on the table, the kitchen faucet
squeaked, the door slammed like the iron door of a dungeon, and
Scott's footsteps when he returned had the hollow ring of
chains that a ghost was dragging over the bare floor.

He stood in front of me holding his glass. "That girl had
everything," he said. "She was the belle of Montgomery, the
daughter of the chief justice of the Alabama Supreme Court. We
met at the governor's ball. Everybody in Alabama and Georgia
knew about her, everybody that counted. She had beauty, talent,
family, she could do anything she wanted to, and she's thrown
it all away."

"That sounds like something from one of your own stories,"
I said.

"Sometimes I don't know whether Zelda isn't a character
that I created myself. And you know, she's cuckoo, she's crazy as
a loon. I'm madly in love with her. Excuse me for a moment, I'm
thirsty tonight."

Scott disappeared again; I heard the door slam and the faucet squeak. When he came back he started talking about himself
and his family background. "I have a streak of pure vulgarity
that I like to cultivate. One side of me is peasant and one aristo-
cratic. My mother was a rich peasant, Molly McQuillan. She kept
telling me, 'All this family is a lot of shit. You have to know

where the money is coming from.' She was as realistic as Karl Marx. I've been reading him; Bunny Wilson made me do it. My father belonged to the same Baltimore family as Francis Scott Key. What if they tore down the monument to the author of 'The Star Spangled Banner' and instead built one for me because I died for communism—a monument to the author of *The Great Gatsby*?" He looked down at me in the armchair and said almost shyly, "What did you think of *Gatsby*?"

I hadn't read *Gatsby* at the time, although I had admired Fitzgerald's stories in *The Saturday Evening Post*, which most of my literary friends regarded as beneath their notice. He didn't want to talk about the stories, except to boast of how much he was paid for them—$4000 each, at his best rate. "I'm a professional," he said. "I know when to write and when to stop writing. But wait till you read my new novel."

He took me to his study behind the dining room, first stopping in the kitchen for another glass of water, and showed me a pile of manuscript nearly a foot high. "I've written four hundred thousand words of that novel," he said—of course it was *Tender Is the Night*—"and thrown away three-quarters of them. Now I have a hundred thousand words in finished shape and only fifteen thousand more to write. It's good, good, good." There was a misty look in his eyes. "When it's published people will say that it's good, good, good."

We went back to the living room. Some time later his mood changed, I suspect because he had been brooding over my confession that I hadn't read *The Great Gatsby*. "I tell you Max Perkins of Scribner's is a real man," he said truculently. "You don't know he's a real man. If you don't know that, you don't know anything." Sitting on a stool he leaned forward, bringing his face close to mine, so that I felt like a criminal being examined by the district attorney. "What do you know anyway?" he asked as if for the benefit of a jury. "What do you know about people? What do you know about writing? Did you ever write a book half as good as *The Great Gatsby*? I tell you that's a book

you can't touch." He paused, and a moment later his face broke
into a bad-boyish smile. "You know this water I've been drinking?" he said, raising the glass. "It's only half water. The other
half is grain alcohol."

I wanted to say "Surprise!" but instead I managed something
between a grin and a yawn. It was nearly three o'clock. Scott
said, "You must be tired," recovering his natural courtesy, and
then escorted me to my room.

I don't know when he went to bed that night, if at all, but
by the time I came down for breakfast his secretary had arrived
and he was working in his study. Zelda, looking vastly younger
by daylight, took me for my first horseback ride in twenty years
and tried to teach me how to post; then we let the horses walk
side by side and chatted amiably. Scott's work was finished at
twelve and, leaving Zelda at home, the two of us drove into Baltimore to visit John Dos Passos, who was in the Johns Hopkins
Hospital recovering from a bout of rheumatic fever. During the
visit I noticed another side of Scott's character, his considerateness
of friends who suffered from any sort of misfortune. We must
have returned to La Paix, because I remember driving off in the
late afternoon when Scottie was home from school, with all
the Fitzgeralds standing on the porch to wave good-bye.

I drove fast to New Market, in the Valley of Virginia, where
I spent the night in a tourist home. Sitting there alone I forgot
the pleasant morning, but remembered the brown hunting lodge
at night, when everything rustled and squeaked and clanked in
the echoing rooms. It seemed to me the setting for a ghost story
of the Jazz Age, with Scott and Zelda as the ghosts: the golden
boy from Princeton and the belle of two states, both frozen in
the moment when they met at the governor's ball. I made a long
entry in my notebook, as I sometimes did in those days. Forty
years later I regretted all the entries that hadn't been made.

# 17.
# The Meriwether Connection

On my first morning at Cloverlands there was a tick-tick, tick-tick, as if a stranger were knocking timidly at the outside door of my bedroom. " Come in," I said almost in my sleep, but nobody came, and in a moment I was listening wide awake to what I suspected must be a bird. After putting on my clothes I found the stranger in a pecan tree outside my window. It was a red-headed woodpecker, the first I had seen, looking like a little man dressed for a masquerade: he had dipped his head in red ink and had slipped a swallowtail coat over a white cotton night-shirt. When I came nearer he flew away, not quickly, but as if he were strolling in air, till he lit on a gatepost. Beyond the post was a lane bordered by small telephone poles from which the wire had been removed. I followed him down the lane from one pole to another. At each of them he stopped to give two taps, then rose and coasted down to the next, always keeping ten paces in front of me. When we reached the big fishpond fringed with willows, he made a quick sideward flight and left me alone in the wide land.

It was a gentle and cultivated land, *un pays doux* that made me think of the Ile de France, except that instead of hills it had undulations like those of a coverlet spread over sleeping children.

Looking northward into Kentucky and southward into Tennessee, I could see sheep meadows like immense playgrounds worn bare in patches, then wheatfields already turned a paler green, with hints of gold, then cornfields pin-striped with the first bright-green shoots, and among them level tobacco fields now ready for planting, after being disk-harrowed and rolled and, it seemed to me, sandpapered as smooth as the floor of Madison Square Garden. The east and west horizons were broken lines of forest. Except for Cloverlands, there were no houses in sight, but only three or four unpainted tobacco barns standing like sentries in the fields. The only token of the twentieth century was the cloud of dust that followed a distant motorcar.

Cloverlands itself survived from another age, or rather from two different ages. The house, which was of brick painted dark red, had been built in 1830, I was told, but it looked much older. That was because the builder, dreaming back to his childhood east of the mountains, had followed the style of Virginia houses built around 1750, before the time of high white porticoes that proclaimed the owners' pride. The central portion had a steep-pitched roof with dormer windows, overhanging a broad porch, and there were one-story wings on either side. It was a large house, with more space inside than many Southern mansions, but with the exterior so unpretentious and well proportioned that it had the air of being a cottage. Off to the right was a row of four weatherboarded cabins that seemed old enough to have been built for slave quarters.

There was only one clock at Cloverlands. It had been wound in honor of my arrival, then after a week it ran down again, and we lived partly by our watches, but chiefly by the sun. We rose at dawn, or rather the Meriwethers did; as a guest I slept perhaps an hour later. I was wakened not by the woodpecker any longer, but by the firmer knock of a very black woman bearing a pot of black coffee on a tray. Breakfast was a family meal, with Cousin Henry—as I heard him called so often that I couldn't think of him by another name—back from feeding the stock, with his wife Cousin Clyde, who had been to Radcliffe, eager to talk about books, and with the two well-mannered boys getting ready for school (later they both became doctors). After breakfast Cousin Henry went to the fields in the already blinding light; he was setting out tobacco plants with his Negro helper. I retired to my two rooms in the east wing, where I worked all morning.

Dinner was served after the sun had reached the zenith, and supper was served at dusk. Mostly the table was set with what the farm yielded, that is, with too much of everything in season: first asparagus, then strawberries, then snap beans in an avalanche, always with pitchers of cream and platters of hot biscuits or cornbread. The meats were fresh-killed lamb, country hams that were the pride of the neighborhood, milk-fed chickens, and sometimes bass from the pond—if I caught them—or squirrels from the woodlot. The Meriwethers seldom went shopping that spring when money was scarce, and they never went to the movies. After supper we sat on the dark porch telling stories, if there were visitors, or simply enjoying the coolness from the fields till we yawned our good nights.

We were fourteen miles from the railroad station at Clarksville, three miles from a telephone, and a mile from the mailbox at the end of the lane, which last was our principal connection with modern America. There was no radio in the house, and the only newspaper, which arrived a day late, was the Clarksville *Leaf-Chronicle,* devoted chiefly to local doings and the price at auction of dark-fired leaf tobacco. It had little to report about measures debated in Washington, even when they were bold ones like the Agricultural Adjustment Act and the Emergency Farm Mortgage Act, both signed on May 12, or the Tennessee Valley Authority Act, signed on May 18. Those three laws would utterly change the countryside, but they were leaf-chronicled in less space than the hundred-pound buffalo fish that somebody caught at a lock in the Cumberland River.

Sometimes I made a trip to town, where there was other reading matter. One national story I enjoyed and managed to follow was that of the second bonus march. For Roosevelt it was a victory gained by excessive kindness. When two thousand unemployed veterans reached Washington on May 9, he had them convoyed across the Potomac to Fort Hunt, where they were issued army blankets, were fed by army cooks, and were housed in a tent city with showers and electric lights. The navy band gave them a concert. Mrs. Roosevelt came to see them and led them in singing "There's a long, long trail a-winding." Roosevelt himself issued an executive order permitting veterans to enroll in the Civilian Conservation Corps. The bonus marchers grumbled at being asked to do reclamation work with boys from the city streets, but most of them ended by accepting the offer. Soon they were dispersed to various camps, including those on the Florida Keys.

I didn't carry the story back to Cloverlands, where we seldom talked about national affairs. One reason for not discussing them may have been that the Meriwethers suspected me of holding strange opinions and were too polite to tempt me into making statements with which they might have to disagree. As a guest I tried to match their politeness, with the result that our conversations on the porch, though sometimes literary, were usually confined to sempiternal topics: tobacco growing, the shiftlessness of tenant farmers, and how soon it would rain. When visitors came they told stories. Most of these dealt either with the Negroes of the vicinity, who seemed to lead colorful lives, or else with the vast Meriwether connection. I listened absorbedly. Much later I decided that this habit of telling stories, as developed in a countryside where there were not many other forms of entertainment, helped to explain why the South was producing so many good novelists. Those I met all rehearsed their books by talking about curious episodes from the lives of their relatives and about the other race, familiar but mysterious, that lived on the same land. Each of them could draw on an immense store of characters and situations. Among the stories I heard on the porch at Cloverlands, many were told by Caroline Gordon, and most of these would be retold in one or another of her novels.

I saw Caroline or Allen Tate, her husband, almost every day, sometimes alone and sometimes with literary friends of theirs

from Nashville. They had a noble Southern way of inviting people to visit them, even when both of them were trying to finish
books and no money was coming in. That spring their porticoed
house on the Cumberland River had been rented to strangers,
and the Tates were staying with Caroline's grandmother at Merry
Mont, an old farmhouse badly in need of paint. It was north of
the Kentucky border, but was only two miles from Cloverlands
by a path that led through Cousin Henry's back fields. Often we
fished or swam together in the blazing afternoons. As we drove
home over roads that shimmered like desert sands, the Tates told
me most of what I learned about the economic and social geog-
raphy of the neighborhood.

Cloverlands and Merry Mont had both been parts of the
original Meriwether Grant, which had consisted of thirty
thousand acres north and south of the state line. Some of the
land had been sold to strangers, including foreign tobacco buyers
and one or two enterprising Negro farmers. Some of it had been
seized by the banks for unpaid mortgages, but much of it, in
1933, still belonged to the Meriwether connection. There were
very few small holdings in the neighborhood. Most of the land
was divided into big farms—Cloverlands, with 250 acres, was of
less than average size—each dominated by a big house, usually
built before the Civil War of home-fired brick, that stood on
high ground in a grove of very old trees.

All the houses had names, some of which were taken from
the Waverley novels; there was a Woodstock, for example, and
there may have been a Kenilworth. The owners were responsible
men, not a few of them Latin scholars, who worked beside and
dressed in the same fashion as their hired hands. From an earlier
visit to the neighborhood, in 1930, I remember one drive with
Allen and Caroline. We stopped outside a crossroads store covered with rusty tin signs that advertised Nehi and 666 and Clab-
ber Girl Baking Powder. Several men in blue overalls were talking
and spitting on the porch. The tallest of them rose and came
down the steps as if he were following a plow, but still with a

look of authority. When he stopped outside the car window, he was introduced to me as Cousin Gus. He started talking about his crops; then he recited several lines from Virgil's *Georgics*. I only knew they were Latin verse. It was Allen who recognized them as Virgil and said they were to the point. But even Allen, a Latin scholar himself, couldn't have capped the lines.

The cash crop of Cousin Gus and his neighbors and their tenants had always been dark-fired tobacco. Since this was too strong for American city dwellers, most of the crop had been sold abroad and especially to the Italian state monopoly. The result was that the neighborhood, for all its air of being self-contained, was colonial in its economy and peculiarly dependent on what happened in foreign capitals. Among these it regarded Washington as the most dangerously unpredictable. When Congress passed and Hoover signed a new tariff bill in 1930, the Italian monopoly had stopped buying dark-fired leaf, and prices at auction fell disastrously. That was the time when telephones disappeared from many of the big houses. It was as if Congress had sent an expeditionary force to strip the wires from the little poles that bordered the farm lanes—and to seize the farms as well, for most of them were mortgaged, and the owners could no longer pay interest on their debt to the banks. Once I went to the post office in Trenton, Kentucky, at the northern edge of the Meriwether Grant. I found on the bulletin board a typed list of every person in Todd County who had paid an income tax for 1932. There were only three names on the list, and I took them to be lawyers, not landlords. As for the tobacco sharecroppers, black and white without distinction, they had never had telephones to be taken out or land to lose, and they were now trying to survive on cash incomes of perhaps fifty dollars a year.

Some of the Meriwether connection had a fierce possessive feeling for the land; they fought the government, the banks, the weather, and the foreign tobacco buyers to hold and extend it. Caroline Gordon's first novel about the neighborhood, *Penhally* (1931), ends with a believable act of violence: the hero shoots his brother for selling the ancestral farm. I remember a gay swimming party toward the end of which I found myself alone on a rock in the middle of the creek with a very attractive young woman. Since her father's death she had been running a farm of fourteen hundred acres; of course there were several tenants and hired hands. She wanted to talk about herself. Once, she said, blinking her dark eyes, she had wanted to *create*—I winced at the word—but now all she wanted to do was get land, land, more hundreds and thousands of acres, all the farms in the neighborhood. She closed her fist as if she were squeezing the farms together. "I want all the land that my grandfather owned," she said. "That was more than five thousand acres, and it's all I want in the world."

"Who'll get it when you're dead?"

"I don't care. I'm all there is." Her eyes frightened me as they glowed in the dusk. "It all comes down to me. I don't care what happens to it after I'm gone."

Part of the Meriwether Grant was "crawfish land," a sort of hardpan, good for nothing but sheep pasture. Most of it, however, belonged to the Nashville Basin, an undulating limestone plain that has always produced rich crops, and therefore it was Confederate country. If one compares soil maps of Kentucky and Tennessee with historical maps showing which counties were Southern or Northern in their sympathies, one finds that the two sorts of maps coincide. The small farmers of the Cumberland Plateau and the Highland Rim were for the most part Unionists. Only the Bluegrass, the Nashville Basin, and the river bottoms had the broad fields that made slave labor profitable to their owners. In Meriwether country the heroes mentioned with a catch in the breath were still Robert E. Lee, Stonewall Jackson, and the brilliant cavalry leader Nathan Bedford Forrest, who said that the secret of victory was to "git thar fustest with the mostest." Some of his "critter company" had been enlisted in Meriwether country. But although the landowners still talked about the Civil War, they seldom mentioned slavery, for they had come to think of the war as having been fought between indus-

trialism and agrarianism. The latter had been defeated by numbers in the war, and then by Wall Street and the tariff, but the
Meriwethers and their friends continued to defend the agrarian
way of life. Any visitor from the North had the smell of
factory smoke about him, which to some was the smell of brim-
stone.

All this created difficulties for a young man whose family
came from Pittsburgh. The Tates and I both held to the notion
that literature was more important than region or politics, so that
as long as we agreed in our judgment of poems or of what constituted a good prose style, we could forget our different back-
grounds most of the time; but at moments they were brought
home to me. The Tates introduced me to their grocer. "We'd
like you to meet our Yankee friend," they said, as if prepared to
add in the same tone of voice, "Don't be afraid of him, we've
taken out the fangs." Another day I made an expedition with the
Tates and their cousin Marion Henry to Fort Donelson, on the
Cumberland, where a Confederate army of thirteen thousand men
had been captured after a brave defense. We stood in an embra-
sure of the old fort and took pictures of the bend of the river,
round which the Federal gunboats had appeared one by one and
had one by one been disabled or sunk; a relative of Marion
Henry's had commanded the Confederate battery. She refused to
enter the Union cemetery, saying, "I wouldn't be seen alive or
dead in a Yankee burying ground."—"But they're all *dead* Yan-
kees," Caroline said. Then we drove to the Confederate monument, where Allen and I were photographed solemnly shaking
hands: the Blue and the Gray. On the drive home in the dusk we
sang plantation melodies: "Old Black Joe," "Swanee River," "My
Old Kentucky Home." At last I said weakly, "You know those
songs we've been singing? They were all written by a Pittsburgh
boy."

Toward the end of May Allen took me to Nashville for a
reunion of the Fugitive group. *The Fugitive* was a little magazine,

founded in 1922, that had presented the work of several new and unusually gifted poets: four of them were John Crowe Ransom, the oldest of the group and a guide to the others, Donald Davidson, Allen Tate, and Robert Penn Warren, who was the youngest. At the time they were rebels in poetry, with little to say about politics, but after the magazine ceased publication, in December 1925, these four became increasingly concerned with the problem of recovering and maintaining a Southern tradition. They found a number of allies, academic and literary, and in 1930 they contributed to a symposium "by twelve Southerners," *I'll Take My Stand*. The stand they took was in the Southern countryside. All twelve contributors—it was announced in an introductory "Statement of Principles"—"tend to support a Southern way of life against what may be called the American or prevailing way; and all as much as agreed that the best terms in which to represent the distinction are contained in the phrase, Agrarian *versus* Industrial."

Besides those four poets of the early Fugitive group, other contributors to *I'll Take My Stand* were present at the meeting in Nashville. I remember Andrew Lytle, with his gift for telling backwoods stories and singing ballads, and Frank Owsley, then a professor of history at Vanderbilt, and John Gould Fletcher, who had started brilliantly with the Imagist poets in London, then many years later had gone back to Arkansas, his native state. We were all invited to dinner at John Crowe Ransom's house. One of his relatives, who owned a farm, had provided a country ham for the occasion, and I remember that Ransom carved it with the air of performing a sacrament. Afterward we went to another house and reconvened in the big room where the Fugitive group had held its first meetings. As in those earlier days, Dr. Sidney Mttron Hirsch served as an informal chairman. I had expected a discussion of verse from masters of the art, but Dr. Hirsch kept steering them toward metaphysics. He was a mystical philosopher of sorts, and he insisted on finding Rosicrucianism, Hermeticism, or Pythagoreanism in every great work of literature. Gradually his voice acquired a prophetic ring, as if it were sounding at midnight from Domdaniel's cave. Subdued by the voice and poached by the steaming heat of the Cumberland Valley, I fell asleep in my chair.

Next morning I talked with several of the Agrarians. Fletcher, gaunt and dejected, thought that the editors of *The New Republic* were plotting against him, but after a while he decided that I wasn't part of the conspiracy. Most of the others were jubilant about the defeats suffered by the industrial system during the last four years. The system had shown that it was unable to support its own workers, they said, and now the workers were leaving the industrial cities and streaming back to the farm at the rate of half a million each year. Perhaps these families rejected by industrialism would all discover that it was—I am quoting Andrew Lytle—"impossible for any culture to be sound and healthy without a proper respect and proper regard for the soil, no matter how many urban dwellers think that their victuals came from groceries and delicatessens and their milk from tin cans." Listening to the Agrarians, I felt they were trying to make a Northern convert, and for all my radical opinions I agreed with them on many points. I too had been raised in the country and was never happy for long where I couldn't feel the soil under my feet. Moreover, my weeks at Cloverlands had given me a more favorable notion of the order that the Agrarians were trying to preserve. Like them I sometimes pictured an ideal society, and it was never situated in a metropolis ruled by workers each of whom had an equal share in the products of aseptic factories; rather it was an open landscape where the houses were not too thickly scattered in groves of very old trees. I thought of Yeats's Ireland and of the prayer he offered for his daughter:

> *And may her bridegroom take her to a house*
> *Where all's accustomed, ceremonious.*

At the same time I could not forget that this pleasant society, with its traditional culture and good manners, was threatened not only by Northern industrialism but also—as the Anglo-Irish landlords had been—by the meager life it offered to the sharecroppers who produced most of its wealth. The question of social injustice was one that the Agrarians had avoided in their symposium, partly, I thought, because they could not agree on what to say about it. Robert Penn Warren came closest to discussing it in his chapter about the Negroes, which he called "The Briar Patch." In spite of that condescending title, Warren said clearly that Negroes must have wider opportunities and be paid more money, since their wages would determine what was earned by white labor. That seemed to me self-evident; but would the principle be accepted by the stiff-backed Confederates among his colleagues? I suspected that some of them clung silently to John C. Calhoun's dream of an Athenian democracy in the South, supported and given leisure by a subject race. Andrew Lytle, whose chapter "The Hind Tit" is the one that best stands rereading, evaded the question by celebrating only the "plain people," that is, the Southern yeomen who owned and cultivated their own farms. There were more of those yeomen than Northerners realized, but most of them were confined to middling-good land at the edge of the hills. The truly good land of the river bottoms and the limestone plains was owned by landlords and was cultivated mostly by tenants, white and black, who were as ragged and destitute as the Irish peasants had been.

In the year 1933, and in a border state, the injustice of the system appeared to be economic more than racial. White families "of the tenant class"—a phrase I heard often—had a few more opportunities than Negroes, or at least their children had; they could get more schooling and, if they showed ambition, could move into town and become small businessmen or politicians. If they stayed in the country, though, their pride of race was a disadvantage. Most of the landlords preferred Negroes as tenants, saying that they were less shiftless than the whites and more willing to take orders; also their women would work in the kitchens of the big houses. That was "nigger work," and white women refused to accept it even when they were hungry. Considering that both races suffered from the system, if in slightly different ways, the wonder was that they didn't unite against it, as some of the tenant class had already shown a disposition to do. Those were the days of the Sharecroppers' Union, which tried to enlist both races. If the depression continued, I thought that the union might spread, not without violence, from Arkansas to other parts of the South. If the depression ended, I guessed that all the younger and more vigorous tenants would stream toward the Northern cities as soon as they had money enough for their fares.

I did not foreguess how soon the big plantations would be mechanized or turned into cattle ranches (partly as a result of the New Deal), or how many of the tenants would be evicted long before they made up their minds to leave. I was merely a fascinated observer, not a prophet, but even then I could see no future for Southern Agrarianism. It seemed to me that the Agrarians themselves had been forced off the land by their talents and training, which they had no scope to exercise in rural life (as others like them had scope before the Civil War). They could not carry their theories into practice. Condemned by their superior abilities to live in cities, they might celebrate an earlier way of life, with its good customs, and might gather in sacramental feasts over a country ham, but meanwhile they belonged to the underpaid white-collar staffs of the new educational factories.

In June the summer heat set in at Cloverlands. I started work earlier each day, knowing that I should have to stop at eleven, when the sweat began to drip on my manuscript. In the lonely afternoons there was time to remember that I had been away from my wife for a long time. But work was going well in the morning hours, and I stayed at the farm till the middle of July; then I packed my books and papers into the rumble seat of the Ford roadster. The Meriwethers waved good-bye, and I felt that something good had ended. Although I might come back to Cloverlands, it would never again be the same as in that last spring of another age.

I drove east by secondary roads that ran straight through

the Bluegrass, with its miles of white-painted wooden fences, then zigzagged into the Kentucky Barrens. To the left of the road, halfway up a steep hillside, I saw a bright-yellow shack that stood alone in a gallows orchard of dead trees. I stopped the car for a moment. The shack was yellow because it was built of logs so freshly peeled that the sap had not yet dried. It had a square black hole for a window and an oblong hole for a door, as in a child's drawing. Above the shack, under the dead trees, there was a corn patch in straggling rows. Three children and a starved-looking dog, all playing in the dirt outside the door, rose to their feet and stared at me as I drove on. A mile up the road was a second yellow shack, just like the first. I passed dozens of others, some only half-built, as I climbed higher into the hills, then coasted into the valley of the Tug Fork and crossed a toll bridge into West Virginia. Not one of the shacks was bigger than a New England woodshed. Almost the only variation was in the roofs, some of which were covered with tarpaper, some with boards, some few with shingles riven out of oak blocks, and some with hammered-out tin cans.

I asked about the new log cabins at service stations and at a roadside eating place where I stopped to order a fried-chicken dinner for twenty-five cents. They were being built, I was told, by men who had given up hope of finding work in Detroit or Toledo or in the Harlan coalfields and who, if they had to go hungry, would rather do so among their own people. Some of them, the lucky ones, still owned a few hillside acres on which to build. The others made an arrangement with a coal company that had acres to spare, or with a lumber company that had no use for slopes from which the saw timber had been removed; or they dickered with a farmer to squat on his land while they "made a crop" on shares.

"But how do they eat?" I asked the restaurant keeper's wife.

"Well, I don't rightly know. They raise some garden stuff, and they shoot squirrels if they have money for shells, and maybe the Red Cross helps out a little with grocery orders." She looked up at the fly-specked ceiling. "Some of them are keeping a hog that they'll kill next fall, and they all have their little patches of corn. But I reckon they don't eat good," she said as she took away the plate of chicken bones.

These cabin builders, I reflected as I drove eastward, were among the beaten soldiers of industrialism that the agrarians had told me about exultantly. They were indeed streaming back to the land, but not to the good land of the limestone plains and the river bottoms that produced more food than Americans could eat; instead they were going back to the hill country that was unsuited for tillage. They were "deadening" the trees on three or four steep acres, burning the brush, and scratching the soil between fire-blackened trunks with a one-mule plow; or perhaps they hadn't a mule and simply grubbed in the ashes with their hoes, as the pioneers had done and the corn-planting Indians before them. Their first crop was likely to be a good one, but unlike the earlier pioneers they had no hope of finding an increasingly better life on the land. Next year their crop would be smaller, for half the fertility of the soil would have been exhausted. After three or four years the hillside would be so eroded by the rains that it would raise no crop at all—and there was no use trying to keep it fertile, since in most cases it belonged to others.

Everything that men had done in these hills was another step toward destroying their beauty and their wealth. First came the hunters to butcher the game, then the lumbermen to butcher the forests, then the coal companies to poison the bright streams and tempt the hillmen into filthy mining camps by the promise of high wages—which were paid for a time, but then the miners were left to starve or go back to the hills. This new migration was not an agrarian movement that would help to rebuild a stable society; instead it was completing the destructive work of two centuries. It was destroying the land itself by clearing trees from hillsides that were never meant to be cleared and by planting corn on slopes so steep that they would soon be washed away to bare shale.

Beside an abandoned coal tipple I stopped for two hitchhikers, natives of Harlan County. One of them said, "Pretty soon we'll have this country plumb worked out." He couldn't have guessed how soon that would be, since he was speaking before the days of strip mining. The other hitchhiker said, "If the Indians have any sense, they won't ever take this country back."

# 18.
## The Scream of the Blue Eagle

Home at last in the world of morning papers, I found that the excitement and yo-heave-ho of Roosevelt's first hundred days were persisting into the summer, though not for everyone: Wall Street was beginning to stand aloof, and my Communist acquaintances were shouting, "Fascism is here!" But there was a happier feeling in the streets and in the newspapers too, where one read more and more dispatches from Washington, signed by old and new correspondents and mostly concerned, in those days, with the programs and personnel of the new alphabetical agencies: AAA, CCC, FCA, FERA, HOLC, NRA, PWA, TVA, all dispensing hope to the formerly hopeless. NRA, the National Recovery Administration, was receiving vastly more attention than the others. Partly that was because of its director, General Hugh S. Johnson, a former cavalryman from Oklahoma, bull-necked and with satchels under his eyes, who could outcurse, outdrink, and, on occasion, outwork anyone else in the government. But the correspondents did not forget that NRA, with its aim of giving a degree of self-government to industry while putting "a floor under wages and a ceiling over hours," was the heart of the recovery program.

Johnson believed in NRA as if it were a new religion of which he was the divinely appointed prophet. Once he told an audience of businessmen, "Nothing like it has ever happened in the history of the world. It is as important as the Council of Nicaea or the Treaty of Verdun." At the same time he doubted whether this extra-historic treaty to be signed by industry, labor, and the government would be ratified by the Supreme Court. He wanted to keep it out of litigation and have it based on a series of agreements, one for each industry, to be reached by a process of free discussion and general consent. To obtain such consent and then to enforce the agreements, or codes, he needed what he called "a strong surge of public opinion." Therefore he planned a vast campaign for NRA, to be conducted in the same fashion as the wartime effort to sell Liberty Bonds.

The campaign was launched a few days after I returned from Tennessee, under the new emblem of the Blue Eagle. Permission to display the emblem would be granted to every employer who signed a blanket agreement not to use child labor and to pay not less than a specified minimum wage for not more than a maximum work week. The special codes for each industry could be signed at the same time or later. In the blue-collar trades the minimum under the blanket code was forty cents an hour, and the maximum week was thirty-six hours. White-collar workers would receive a minimum of $12 to $15, depending on the locality, for a maximum week of forty hours. The floor under wages was not a high one, even for 1933—though many employers had been paying less—but Johnson hoped that the ceiling over hours would lead to the rehiring of millions. Roosevelt devoted a fireside chat, his third, to praising the blanket code and the Blue Eagle. "In war," he said, "in the gloom of night attack, soldiers wear a bright badge on their shoulders to be sure that comrades do not fire on comrades. On that principle, those who cooperate in this program must know each other at a glance."

The Blue Eagle as an emblem was copied from the Indian thunderbird, but it bore a sheaf of punitive lightning bolts in the talons of its left foot and a cogwheel, to symbolize industry, in those of the right. Beneath it was lettered a slogan: "We Do Our Part." Soon it could be seen in shopwindows, on cartons of breakfast food or soap flakes, and high on factory chimneys. There were Blue Eagle lunch wagons, some of which would survive after forty years, Blue Eagle delicatessens, and Blue Eagle bar-and-grills (though as yet they served only beer). There were also, in that first summer, parades, brass bands, razzmatazz, and patriotic shorts in movie houses with sound tracks dubbed in by four-minute orators. The Blue Eagle screamed and soared. On Saturday, September 13, parades were held in Boston, New York, Schenectady, Tulsa, and dozens of smaller cities. Boston assembled its schoolchildren on the Common, where Mayor Curley administered a Blue Eagle oath: "I promise as a good American to do my best for NRA." In New York the parade started north from Washington Square at two in the afternoon and lasted for ten hours. There were a million and a half spectators, by police estimates, and a quarter of a million marchers, some of them royally sozzled. The contingents included 35,000 city employees, 20,000 dressmakers, 10,000 from banks and brokerage houses, and 6,000 motion-picture workers led by Al Jolson. Boys from the new CCC camps marched in olive-drab uniforms with sprigs of hemlock in their caps. Dozens of bands played "Happy Days Are Here Again." Two Howard Chandler Christie models, chosen as Miss Liberty and Miss Nira (for National Industrial Recovery Act), blew kisses to the crowd. After darkness fell, the brewery workers marched with red flares and unquenchable patriotism. The last two contingents, of Chinese waitresses and artificial-flower makers, passed the empty reviewing stand at midnight. They left Fifth Avenue to the street sweepers, who cleared it of waste paper and ticker tape at a cost to the city of $4,980.70.

That was the climax of the Blue Eagle's flight and the beginning of its descent. Having persuaded two million employers to sign the blanket code, Johnson went back to the task of drawing up separate codes for thousands of industries and the even more complicated task of enforcing them. The patriotic enthusiasm of the summer was dissipated among questions of administrative procedure and technical arguments that had to be conducted without the help of brass bands and Miss Liberty. Still, Johnson found scope for his own histrionic talent. He sat at ease in the midst of wild confusion, "coat off, blue shirt open at the neck, red-faced, and looking uncannily like Captain Stagg in Stallings' and Anderson's *What Price Glory*," so Jonathan Mitchell reported in *The New Republic*. "Like captured peasants, squads of sweating businessmen . . . were led in before him." Confused, exhorted, bullied, the businessmen signed their codes in the end—or all of them did but Henry Ford, who further complicated the situation by paying his workers more than the code minimum. By no means all of the others honored their pledges. Some of them quarreled with the code authorities about what the pledges meant. Some of them disregarded the codes, lowered the floor under wages, raised the ceiling over hours, and let it be understood that any worker who complained would be dismissed. Johnson threatened daily to "crack down on chiselers," but he still didn't know what the courts might say. Mostly the lightning bolts in the left talons of the Blue Eagle stayed where the artist had drawn them.

Many of the disputes centered on section 7a of the National Industrial Recovery Act, which started by saying, "Employees shall have the right to organize and bargain collectively through representatives of their own choosing." But how should the representatives be chosen? Would each employee have the right to select his own, or would the representatives speak for the whole working force of a factory after receiving a majority of votes in a general election? Would they be chosen from the workers in that one factory organized in a company union under the proud paternal eye of management, or would they be delegates from a craft union belonging to the American Federation of Labor?—or perhaps from a new industrial union that included all types of workers, skilled, unskilled, and white-collar? There was scope for protracted arguments, litigation, intimidation, and finally strikes, three times as many in 1933 as in the previous year. One thing certain was that almost all the workers wanted to join some sort of union. All they were waiting for was someone to organize them, give them union cards, and collect their dues.

But organizers were lacking in most industries. There was no machinery, there was no money in union treasuries, and most of all there was little wish to send them out. The AFL was appalled by the unruly millions who clamored to join its ranks. Most of its leaders belonged to craft unions whose members had served an apprenticeship and regarded themselves as aristocrats of labor. Now they were being asked to admit unskilled workers, a vast hoi polloi of Negroes and Polacks. They did their best to discourage the newcomers. When the rubber workers in Akron set up a union of all the workers in each factory, the AFL organizer promptly divided them into nineteen separate unions, from Blacksmiths to Teamsters. The rubber workers dropped out by thousands, as the automobile workers, also divided by crafts, were doing in Detroit and the steel workers in Youngstown and Pittsburgh.

It was a grand opportunity for the Communists to step in. Unlike the old-line unionists they had zeal, they had persistence, and even more to the point they had hundreds of devoted missionaries as willing to accept martyrdom as the Jesuits had been when they tried to convert the Iroquois. What chiefly hampered their efforts was a conviction that NRA was a full-scale model of American fascism: how could they conscientiously make it the basis of an organizing campaign? "The Blue Eagle is a blue buzzard for the workers," they kept repeating to every crowd they could gather; the crowd seldom agreed. But the Communists were also hampered at the time by their policy of trying to form separate unions like the one on whose behalf we had gone to Kentucky. All those little penniless unions were banded together into the Trade Union Unity League, or disunity league, which served as the labor department of the party. They had a record of always losing strikes, as in Kentucky, and the workers stayed away from them.

In the AFL, however, there were a few leaders who took full advantage of Section 7a. John L. Lewis of the United Mine Workers had always been known as one of the more conservative and dictatorial of the union presidents. He had watched his union dwindle away from a membership of more than four hundred thousand in 1920 to less than one hundred thousand in 1932. He had refused to help the Kentucky miners because they couldn't pay dues, and when the Illinois miners revolted against him, he had fought them with gunfire and dynamite. During the Blue Eagle days he was seized with an access of public feeling. Risking every penny that remained in the union treasury, he sent his organizers out to preach the gospel that "The law is on our side. . . . The United States government has said LABOR MUST ORGANIZE." The result was a religious revival that swept through the coal-mining country from Pittsburgh to Birmingham. By November the Mine Workers had four hundred thousand members again—even the Harlan County mines were organized—and they had forced the operators to observe the code for the coal industry by winning a number of hard-fought strikes.

Lewis found two allies in the garment industry: Sidney Hillman of the Amalgamated Clothing Workers and David Dubinsky of the International Ladies' Garment Workers, both of whom seized the chance to expand their unions. The Amalgamated, which had retained most of its members during the depression years, now managed to organize some of the biggest nonunion shops. The Ladies' Garment Workers, starting from a weaker position, tripled in membership within a few months. These two, with the United Mine Workers, were already industrial, not craft, unions, and together they would provide most of the money that was spent three years later by the Committee for Industrial Organization (CIO) in its successful campaigns to organize General Motors and Big Steel.

Several new unions were started in the autumn of 1933 without much help or sympathy from the AFL. Though most of them soon disbanded, a few were to have a long life. The most interesting to writers was the Newspaper Guild, founded by Heywood Broun, who had been known till that time as a crusader for lost causes. He had tried to save Sacco and Vanzetti (and had resigned from *The World* when the publisher refused to print one of his columns about them); he had cheered for Al Smith in 1928, for Norman Thomas in 1932, and had been the wittiest spokesman for the liberals who offered advice that was never taken by the public or by those in power. Now at last he had a cause that was not hopeless, since newspapermen had grievances and were, for the most part, eager to be organized. As a group they were overworked, underpaid by comparison with the unionized printers, and notoriously insecure in their jobs. Their craft or calling —it could hardly be called a profession at the time—was regarded as one for romantic youngsters willing to work for next to nothing while waiting to make their mark in some other field, often literature or Wall Street. Old newspapermen, unless they worked for *The Times*—or unless they were celebrities like Broun—were likely to be drunken "boomers" who wandered from paper to paper after each disastrous spree.

Broun, who loved the newspaper world and was loved by most of his colleagues, determined to change the situation. In August he began inviting groups of reporters to his penthouse apartment, where he argued with them, planned with them, and told them stories in his soft old-family New York voice (much like that of Mary Heaton Vorse, another tireless crusader). There seemed to be a tremendous lot of him in height, girth, features, appetite, rumpled clothes, untied shoelaces, and social conscience, all of which, except the shoelaces, were beyond the ordinary human scale. His newspaper friends, quoting Westbrook Pegler, called him "the one-man slum," but they listened to him and agreed with what he said. By the end of October the New York Newspaper Guild had enlisted five hundred members and adopted a constitution. Other guilds were being formed in what my wife, as a native New Yorker, used to call "out-of-town cities." Soon they were negotiating pacts with some big newspapers, while star reporters were being discharged by others for union activities. Each new case of the kind was referred to the Newspaper Industrial Board, set up under the code authority, which found itself deadlocked on every important issue.

While the Blue Eagle teetered on its perch, Roosevelt looked for other means of restoring prosperity. A new crisis was impending. After rising sharply in the spring of 1933, the index of business activity had been falling since midsummer. Agricultural prices fell in September, and once again the farmers were on the point of armed rebellion. In Iowa they barricaded roads and set bridges on fire; in Wisconsin they stormed butter and cheese factories. Something had to be done fast to raise the dollar value of commodities. Roosevelt, who seldom felt the need for intellectual consistency and was guided by aims rather than ideas, which last he borrowed from several conflicting schools, was willing to try anything so long as it promised to work toward the aims and so long as it could be persuasively explained to the public.

He had first turned to the national planners, including Rex Tugwell and Raymond Moley, for the ideas embodied in the National Industrial Recovery Act and the Agricultural Adjustment Act. It was still uncertain whether these would work in the end, though Triple-A, in spite of the farmers' new revolt, already promised to be more effective than NRA under Hugh Johnson. But Roosevelt couldn't afford to wait, and he next turned to the cheap-money men, a powerful faction whose ideas would be tested in practice. Starting late in October, Henry Morgenthau, Jr., the acting secretary of the treasury, and Jesse Jones of the Reconstruction Finance Corporation met at the president's bedside every morning to drink coffee and fix the daily price that the government would pay for gold. The price was raised in irregular steps—so as to fool the speculators—from

$20.67 to $35 per fine ounce, thus reducing the dollar to 59.06 percent of its former gold value. At that point the experiment was broken off. It had improved the position of American products in the export market, but domestic prices failed to rise.

Meanwhile Roosevelt had also been listening to the various advocates of government spending. Some of these were frightened by the rebellion in the farm belt; some—like Harry Hopkins of the Federal Emergency Relief Administration (FERA)—were moved by the sufferings of the unemployed; and some were disciples of John Maynard Keynes, the British economist who first contended that a nation could spend its way into prosperity. Roosevelt never fully accepted the Keynes theory or any other. There was always an economizer whispering into his right ear while the spenders were shouting into the left; that explains the intermittences in his spending program. He was convinced, however, that government money would have to be used, in his own phrase, to "prime the pump" before wealth again started to circulate. The farmers were his first concern. He directed Henry A. Wallace, the secretary of agriculture, to hasten the payment of government bonuses to those who agreed to reduce the acreage they would plant to wheat, corn, tobacco, and cotton. By December the farmers' revolt had died away.

Harry Hopkins was rushing ahead with his new program to help the unemployed. It was estimated at the time, rather than proved, that the National Industrial Recovery Act had led to the rehiring of two million workers. But there were still more than ten million unemployed, most of whom had exhausted their last resources, and the winter of 1933–34 promised to be the bleakest they had known. Hopkins undertook, if given the necessary funds, to put four million of them to work by December 15. He wanted to give them work, not simple cash payments, in order to maintain their self-respect, and the projects he had in mind were of the sort that required no mechanical equipment; they were pick-and-shovel jobs, for the most part, such as repairing roads and building small airports, though unemployed professional persons would be given a chance to exercise their own skills. The wage he considered offering was $50 a month for working thirty hours each week. Roosevelt promised him a billion dollars, partly taken from the appropriation that the secretary of the interior, Harold Ickes, had failed to spend for his Public Works Administration. Hopkins moved faster than Ickes, and though he missed his target date, he had more than four million at work by the middle of January—the coldest January, it happened to be, when the temperature fell to fifteen degrees below zero in New York City. Among the millions were three thousand writers and artists, who were paid for writing and painting: "Hell, they have to eat like other people," Hopkins said. It was a foreshadowing of the Federal Arts Projects, which were to be the largest subsidy to practicing artists as a group that had ever been offered by a government.

From the old house in Chelsea I watched these and other domestic developments with what seems to me now an amazing lack of interest. I wasn't even much excited by the Twenty-first Amendment to the Constitution, repealing Prohibition, when it was finally ratified at the beginning of December 1933. After the intense arguments of previous years, repeal was almost a non-event for New Yorkers I knew. Liquor was now a little easier for them to buy, but at first it wasn't much better, and—after paying federal and state taxes—it had become more expensive. We missed our favorite speakeasies, some of which closed, while others transformed themselves into respectable dull restaurants.

As for events in Washington, they had the defect for us of not fitting into an ideological pattern. We were all ideologists in those days, from Hoover on the right to the Trotskyites on the far left—all except Roosevelt, who was the only convinced and happy experimentalist. Because he lacked preconceptions; because he tried one policy and then another, or both at the same moment, his administration and the country at large had become a vast arena for struggling factions and conflicting theories. It was no longer a question of capital against labor, as in the plain reader's Marxism that was popular at the time: it was new Western capital, represented by Jesse Jones of Texas, against the Eastern bankers; it was craft unions against industrial unions; it was big farmers against small farmers; it was producers against processors (and often both against the consumer). In addition it was national planners, devoted to bigness and direction by government, against the apostles of smallness and competition; it was spenders against budget balancers; it was inflationists against sound-money men; and it was international free traders like Cordell Hull, the secretary of state, against believers in autarchy.

The legislation that Congress had passed during the Hundred Days provided a book of rules for these contests. But the outcome of each was decided not so much by law as by the actual strength and skill of the two sides. Thus, in the battles fought within Triple-A, the big farmers proved stronger than the small farmers, while the tenants not only lacked influence but could not even claim that their work was essential. Already they were being displaced by new agricultural machines—the mechanical cotton picker, for example—that only big farmers could use effectively. All the farmers together, as producers, were driven back by the financial power of the processors, that is, of the millers, packers, textile manufacturers, tobacco companies, and milk distributors. There were also the consumers, most numerous of all groups, but they could muster no organized force and had to suffer like Christians in the arena. Sometimes a national policy depended on the careers in government of its leading advocates and was defeated largely by their weaknesses. Among the national planners, for example, Moley was self-important, Johnson talked a good battle, but then went off on a spree, and Tugwell, a steadier man, let fall remarks that frightened conservatives, who regarded him as a threat to the Republic. Harry Hopkins, the spender, was a more effective administrator for all his raffish manner, and therefore his undertakings had a better chance of success. Meanwhile the great civilian departments—State, Treasury, Agriculture (then the largest), and Interior—were like vassal states ruled over by Lord Secretaries who had all sworn fealty to the sovereign, but each of whom intrigued against the others (and of course against the New Deal agencies) to extend his own domain.

I might have watched those gladiatorial combats as if from a privileged seat in the Colosseum. I might have found, moreover, that they were still more fascinating than the Russian experiment, which, for all its changes in direction, or party line, was based on a single theory of the human future. My own country was conducting scores of experiments, based on dozens of theories, and their outcome might determine the shape of Western culture for a hundred years. Like the Russians, however, and like many American intellectuals at the time, I insisted on thinking in terms of either-or: either peace in a world that was ruled by the workers or war between rival imperialisms. I differed from the Communists in being mildly attracted to Roosevelt, because he had planted trees and wanted to save the countryside, but still he was defending capitalism; therefore his social experiments were directed toward the wrong goal and they would fail. Assured of what the end must be, I turned to other spectacles as if selecting a more dramatic program. The political struggles in France and Spain, the foreign invasion and civil war in China, the second Russian Five-Year Plan, the cataclysm in Germany: all these seemed more crucial for the world revolution than the upward flight and broken-winged fall to earth of the Blue Eagle.

# 19.
## Privatation and
## Publication

Since my return from Cloverlands, I had been trying to finish the manuscript that I carried home. There was not much time for it in the midst of crises in the world and weekly press days, each a little crisis at *The New Republic*. February 1934 was an especially crisis-ridden month. On Tuesday the sixth, before the paper went to press, we read in dispatches from Paris that an immense rally of right-wing demonstrators had tried to storm the Chamber of Deputies. Fifteen of the rioters had been killed and fifteen hundred injured. Within three days, the parties of the left had rallied in their turn and France had returned to an uneasy truce under a Cabinet of National Union. Our attention shifted to Vienna, where Chancellor Dollfuss had been trying to impose a right-wing dictatorship by suppressing the Socialists. The Socialists waited till the last moment, then rose against him on the morning of February 12; for the next four days they defended themselves against the whole Austrian Army. Our hearts were with them, but there was nothing we could do except read the papers.

In New York the Socialists organized a mass meeting in Madison Square Garden to excoriate Dollfuss. They took special pride in their Austrian comrades because the Communists, who derided them, had failed to rise in Berlin. Their meeting, held February 16—a day after the last of the Vienna rebels had been killed or captured—was invaded by thousands of local Communists, who shouted down the speakers, threw folding chairs from the balcony, and started fights all over the floor. Hundreds of policemen stood by, happily watching the battle. It was a spectacle that revolted Dos Passos, and he joined with others in signing a letter of protest that was printed in *The New Masses*. When the editors chided him—but gently, because he had been an honored ally—he wrote an open letter of his own. "What happened in Madison Square Garden," he said, "was shocking to me because it indicated the growth of an unintelligent fanaticism that, in my opinion, can only end in the division of the conscious elements of the exploited classes into impotent brawling sects." He would never again be a friend of the Communist Party.

I sympathized with his feelings, but kept out of the dispute, not having attended the meeting. Also I was wrapped up in my own project, which seemed to be nearing its end. By the beginning of March, however, I still had most of a long chapter to write, and I carried my books and papers to the little town of Riverton, Connecticut, for sixteen days of lonely work.

Riverton, known to antiquarians as the birthplace of the Hitchcock chair, had been sleeping since the chair factory closed in the nineteenth century. During most of my visit I was the only guest at the inn, which faced the Farmington River. I rose early, wrote all morning, and had my lunch alone in the big dining room. In the afternoons I took long walks, sometimes nine or ten miles in the wet snow, while I dreamed about or mumbled the words I should write the following day. The weather had turned warm and sunny after that coldest of Januaries. In the evenings after dinner I stood for half an hour at the little bar and talked with two old men who were waiting for the ice to go out. One of them remembered the spring of 1875, when it had carried away the bridge. This time he was afraid it would go out in the night when he was asleep.

"I been here fifteen years," the other said, "and I ain't seen the ice go out but twice."

Except for a letter from Muriel, that was as much intercourse with the world as I needed for the day. I went upstairs, answered the letter, and was asleep by ten o'clock. Sometimes I woke in a cold bed to hear the ice groaning in the river, but it would still be there in the morning when I first looked out the window. I thought I was leading an ideal life for a man of letters. I was writing about the suicide of Harry Crosby, partly because it came at the end of an era which had also, in a way, committed suicide, and partly because I couldn't yet bear to write about the death of a closer friend, Hart Crane. I had Crosby's diary for guidance, and the typed pages piled up in a reassuring way.

On the second weekend Muriel paid me a visit. We went for a walk downstream on a lumberman's road that bordered the river as it flowed through a state forest; here it was swift and already free of ice. But snow was falling again, and we watched the flakes as they vanished into black water, then, after a time, began forming little gray rafts that merged into larger rafts as they sailed downstream. Talking excitedly, but not about the return of winter, we went back to the inn for dinner and bed. On Sunday I took Muriel to Winsted, where she caught a bus for New York, and I also managed to write two pages before falling asleep. On Monday I wrote four pages, then rambled in the ghostly woods where every twig was heavy with new snow. Once when I shouted out some words that came to mind, the branch above my head released its burden as if in applause.

I went back to *The New Republic* a week later, with the Crosby chapter finished and a comfortable feeling that my book would be ready for the publisher after a few more days or working nights. When I said good-bye to the two old men, they were unhappy about the ice in the river. "But maybe it's just as well that it didn't go out," one of them conceded. "It would have carried away the abutment at the chair factory. Now the ice'll just wear away."

The other nodded. "Yeah, and I'm sort of sorry. I been here fifteen years and I ain't seen the ice go out but twice."

Publication was rapid in those days when printers were eager for work. Before the last week in April I had corrected the galley proofs of *Exile's Return*. Then the publisher, Warder Norton, a conscientious man who bore himself like a retired British major, told me that he had doubts about the end of the book. To stop with a suicide was too abrupt. Couldn't I write an epilogue that explained my story and expressed some notions about the future of American writing? If I went to work on it immediately, I could send it back with the page proofs as late as May 1, but that was truly the last day.

I worked on the epilogue over the weekend. "So the story is ended," I began, "and I have written a longer book than I meant to write without saying half the things I wanted to say." I mentioned some of the events passed over in my narrative, and then, having dismissed the past, I started discussing problems that seemed to preoccupy the writers of a new age. I was trying to strike a reasonable and persuasive tone, but it was hard to maintain when the deadline was very near.

May 1 was Tuesday. That year the Communist parade, somewhat larger than it had been in 1933, started north from the Battery at 10:45 in the bright sunshine. The first marchers reached Union Square at 1:55, and the last not until 6:25. They carried banners denouncing Roosevelt, Hitler, Mussolini, and the Blue Buzzard of NRA. There was also a yellow Dragon of Capitalism, fifty feet long, which came apart at one point in the parade; but the bearers managed to reunite the fiery head of capitalism with its venomous tail. The line of march was guarded by 1171 uniformed policemen, and also by three hundred plainclothesmen, who later mingled with the immense crowd in Union Square. . . . That was the account I read on Wednesday morning in the capitalist press. I had missed the parade, as well as an editorial meeting at *The New Republic*, while writing my final pages. But I could not forget the meaning of the day, and I hoped that

I was doing my part in solitude to institute the new order of the ages.

Because of that hope, I wrote with more vehemence than I might have felt at another time. I pleaded with artists to take the workers' side in the class struggle. It can actually promise them, I said, much more than it seems to promise:

> First of all, it can offer an end to the desperate feeling of solitude and uniqueness that has been oppressing artists for the last two centuries, the feeling that has reduced some of the best of them to silence or futility and the weaker ones to insanity or suicide. It can offer instead a sense of comradeship and participation in a historical process vastly bigger than the individual. It can offer an audience, not trained to appreciate the finer points of style or execution—that will come later—but larger and immeasurably more eager than the capitalist audience and quicker to grasp essentials. It can offer the strength of a new class.
>
> And it can offer something else to the artist. Once he knows and feels the struggles of the oppressed classes all over the world, he has a way to get hold both of distant events and those near at hand, and a solid framework on which to arrange them. . . .

That "solid framework" was among the strongest appeals of Marxism in the 1930s, not to artists primarily, but more to those with an interest in world affairs. Vincent Sheean, as I have said, would discuss it persuasively in his *Personal History*, published the following year, and would call it "the long view." It explains why many foreign correspondents who adopted it, including Sheean himself, wrote with more breadth and clarity in the 1930s—and also with a capacity for making greater blunders —than they would display in their later work, after they had adopted shorter views.

But I had not yet finished my epilogue. I said:

> Values exist again, after an age in which they seemed to be lost; good and evil are embodied in men who struggle. It is no longer possible to write, as did Joseph Wood Krutch only a few years ago, that "we have come, willy-nilly, to see the soul of man as commonplace and its emotions as mean," or to say that the tragic sense of life has been lost forever. Tragedy lives in the stories of men now dying in Chinese streets or in German prisons for a cause by which their lives are given dignity and meaning. Artists used to think that the world outside had become colorless and dull in comparison with the bright inner world they so tenderly nourished; now it is the inner world that has become enfeebled as a result of its isolation; it is the outer world that is strong and colorful and demands to be imaginatively portrayed. The subjects are waiting everywhere. There are great days ahead for artists if they can survive in the struggle and keep their honesty of vision and learn to measure themselves by the stature of their times.

I remember that day as the high summit of my revolutionary enthusiasm. On the last page of the completed manuscript I wrote, "New York, May 1, 1934," as if to say, "I too have marched in the parade." Then I decided that the date was ostentatious and crossed out the "1." Late in the afternoon I carried the page proofs and the epilogue to Warder Norton. He showed less than a proper enthusiasm, it seemed to me, for what I had written that morning, but still he said that the book could go to press.

I find in my notebook a long entry which, though undated, may well have been written in May 1934, when I was waiting for the first bound copies of *Exile's Return*. Perhaps it will suggest the atmosphere of radical circles in what afterward seemed a transitional year. It reads:

"I walk in the drizzling rain to a dinner meeting that the National Committee for the Defense of Political Prisoners is holding in the grill room of a second-rate hotel. The dinner, which will be followed by too many speeches, is abundant, badly cooked, and costs eighty-five cents. I sit near the head of the table facing Orrick Johns, my relative by divorce. Between us are Alfred Hirsch, the secretary of the Committee (Harvard '26), Allan Taub, who was beaten by vigilantes during our mission to Kentucky, and Agnes Smedley, the guest of honor. Hirsch tells how he spent two or three days in jail for picketing. Taub presides at the dinner; he is learning to be a better chairman now and not to make such long speeches. I remember how astonished I was to hear a young woman, one of the comrades, say on another occasion, 'Aren't we lucky that we got Allan Taub to speak!' for Allan had bored and embarrassed me by not knowing when to stop; he'd ask for 'just one minute,' then talk for half an hour; but he can make good stories out of what he has seen, and he gets into the craziest scrapes of any living lawyer."

I was writing as a weary connoisseur of political dinners. "Agnes Smedley is fanatical," I continued. "She grew up in a Colorado coal-mining town, she came to New York and lived with a Hindu revolutionist, she was in Germany during Spartacist times, she somehow landed in China as correspondent for the *Frankfurter Zeitung*, she wrote militant speeches for Mme. Sun Yat-sen, and she stayed in Shanghai after the counterrevolution at a considerable risk to her life. The only thing that saved her from arrest, but narrowly, was her close association with the widow of the Chinese national hero. Now she is here for a visit, after crossing Siberia and recuperating at a sanitarium in the Caucasus. Her hair grows thinly above an immense forehead. When she talks about people who betrayed the Chinese rebels, her mouth becomes a thin scar and her eyes bulge and glint with hatred. If this coal miner's daughter ever had urbanity, she would have lost it forever in Shanghai when her comrades were dragged off one by one for execution.

"This is the first time I have seen Orrick Johns," who was my first wife's first husband, "though Peggy used to tell me stories about him. In the stories he was always a dandified little man with an artificial leg who wrote lyrical poems—

> *But a light tan cow in a pale green mead,*
> *That is very beautiful, beautiful indeed.*

—got drunk, and did crazy things. Once a friend of Orrick's had an argument with him about panhandling: Orrick said that the more prosperous you looked, the more money people would give you. They started around Washington Square in opposite directions, the friend dressed to look hungry and pathetic, Orrick in evening clothes with a cane and a topper; both men were to see how much they could beg. When they met on the other side of the Square, Orrick had two dollars and the friend had fifteen cents. They pooled their resources and went home with a bottle of scotch.—But that was a long time ago, and Orrick doesn't now look dandified or drunken. He gives a talk about the suppression of labor unions on the West Coast," which would soon lead to a general strike in the Bay Area, "and he speaks with conviction. He has a thin black mustache over what seems to me a cruel mouth.

"Sitting below us at the long table are the people who usually attend meetings of Communist sympathizers. I'm in the category too, and I can't help feeling that there is something false and ridiculous about the position of the whole bunch. We have proclaimed our loyalty to the working class while holding on to our comfortable places in the bourgeoisie. We give money, not too much of it, but we don't get slugged in the picket line, and if we go to jail for two hours or two days, it makes a funny story of the same type as Orrick's begging for money in a top hat. We send too many telegrams, sign too many protests. It's hard to stay in such a position forever—either one has to go on from it, plunge actively into the Communist movement, or else slowly and imperceptibly draw back. I know I'm going to do one or the other.

"This evening I'm drawing back, that much seems clear, into personal concerns and projects for writing another book. Will this one have even a moderate success? I don't enter much into the discussion of how to save Angelo Herndon from lynching when he is bailed out of Fulton Towers Prison in Atlanta. I don't write a postcard to Governor Talmadge of Georgia. I don't wait to hear Agnes Smedley give her speech, which will be more convincing than the others, as if each phrase of it were dyed in the blood of her Chinese friends. Instead, very tired from the work of the night before, I slip away and walk home through dark streets that are cool after the rain."

I think most authors feel an immense contrast between the writing of a book, which is a private undertaking, and its exposure to the judgment of whoever is willing to read. Publication: there should be another word to set against it, "privatation," as describing an earlier stage of authorship. Sometimes the passage from one stage to the other is so abrupt that it leads to private disasters.

For me the contrast was sharper, perhaps, than it has been for most others. *Exile's Return* was my first book in prose. Although it deals in large part with friendships and joint activities, and although it had been started at Yaddo, a writers' colony, in company with such good friends as Kenneth Burke, Matthew Josephson, and Jack Wheelwright, it had been continued in more than the usual seclusion, that is, on lonely weekends in New England, and in a Tennessee farmhouse, and later in the empty inn at Riverton. Most of it had been composed—tramped out, one might say—on walks in the woods or along farm lanes, as a sort of dialogue between the inner poet or maker and the inner critic or listener. Sometimes when the critic approved of a phrase, the maker had spoken it aloud to a respectful audience of trees. Now human beings were about to listen, or fail to listen, and I wondered and feared what they would say.

A circumstance that made me still more apprehensive was

that I had taken the risk of speaking candidly about my own life. I had my share of that almost universal but also specifically American weakness, the craving to be liked—not loved, not followed but simply accepted as one of the right guys. Any judgment of the book would be a judgment of my private self. When it went on trial I should look unconcerned, as every author tries to do, but I should feel like a timid nocturnal animal suddenly exposed to blinding sunlight, while shapes loomed over me and voices argued about whether to cage me and put me on display or let me scuttle back under the weeds.

*Exile's Return* appeared on the last Monday in May. Late Sunday night I read the bulldog edition of *The Times* and, having learned that John Chamberlain admired the book, if with reservations, I fell asleep reassured. On Monday I bought all the other New York papers—half a dozen in those days—that carried book reviews. It was a dead season in the publishing world when reviewers hadn't much to talk about, and either that day or the next they all devoted their columns to *Exile's Return*. Unlike Chamberlain, all the others had a grand time demolishing the book. Most of them said that it was a trivial story, intermittently amusing, that dealt with unimportant persons. They deplored and derided my political enthusiasms, as might have been anticipated, but they objected at greater length to my notion that the men of the 1920s had special characteristics and that their adventures in Paris were a story worth retelling. "Nobody wrote great books in the last decade," William Soskin said in *The American*. "Mr. Hemingway is growing dim. So are his colleagues." Lewis Gannett, writing in *The Herald Tribune*, described the exiles as my "little group of serious thinking drunkards. . . . They felt there was something superb in starving for three days while waiting for papa's next check." When Gannett read my statement that "they were a generation, and perhaps the first real one in the history of American literature," he found himself "snorting like a graybeard."

All the forty-year-old graybeards were snorting, and their indignation spilled over into F. P. A.'s column, "The Conning

Tower," also in *The Herald Tribune*. There he enlarged on his opinion that Gannett, his neighbor on what was then called the page-facing-editorial, had treated the book all too mercifully. Gannett's mistake was thereupon rectified by Burton Rascoe, who filled "The Conning Tower" of June 8 with a sterner excoriation. It proved to be somewhat too stern for his readers' taste, and also he made the tactical error of involving the ghost of Herbert Croly in my derelictions. Croly, so he claimed, completely lacked a sense of humor and had proved as much by failing to appreciate the ironical essays of his early colleague on *The New Republic*, Frank Moore Colby. Distinguished names and signatures were being tossed about like lethal bouquets, each hiding a hand grenade. Soon there were two more contributed columns in "The Conning Tower": Walter Lippmann in defense of Croly and Malcolm Cowley in defense of Cowley. A few days later Harry Hansen summed up the results in *The World-Telegram*, "from the standpoint of a highly diverted outsider":

> 1. Burton Rascoe restores "The Colby Essays" to circulation, unfortunately too late.
>
> 2. Malcolm Cowley proves conclusively that an editor of the *New Republic* can have a sense of humor.
>
> 3. Walter Lippmann comes down from Sinai and shows awareness of something besides the state of the country.
>
> 4. F. P. A.—the lucky dog—gets another vacation from work.

John Chamberlain in the *Times* offered another summary:

> The most-argued-about book of the Spring [he wrote] seems to be Malcolm Cowley's "Exile's Return." Everyone seems to be spilling critical blood over this story of "the lost generation" that dissipated itself for a while in the worship of art. A curious thing about the reviews of this book is that no one under 35 attacked it and that no one over 35 praised it. Is this an example of

the age war in criticism? Clifton Fadiman of The New Yorker, Bernard Smith of The New Masses and R. Blackmur of The Hound and Horn, all of them younger than Mr. Cowley took the book very seriously, whereas J. Donald Adams, Isabel Paterson, Lewis Gannett, Burton Rascoe, Harry Hansen and Hershel Brickell, all of them older, tore it to pieces. I don't know what this proves, but the sociologists may be glad to have the fact.

A sociologist would have noted, however, that older reviewers commanded more space, in magazines and newspapers of wider circulation, so that the weight of hostile opinion seemed overwhelming. A leading article that Bernard De Voto wrote for *The Saturday Review* did nothing to redress the balance. De Voto was then thirty-seven, just two years beyond Chamberlain's dividing age for critics, but he made up in vehemence what he lacked in gray whiskers. An amiable and entertaining man in company, he assumed a different character when alone at his typewriter; often he wrote as if he were the only solid citizen of the republic of letters, bombarded and besieged in his study by a cultured mob of lunatics. He was outraged by *Exile's Return* in all his prepossessions. Subjecting the book and its author to what he called an "easy exercise" in Freudian analysis, he found in them obvious symptoms of infantile dread, the castration complex, fugue, "vocational narcism," exhibitionism, and megalomania. He made me feel like a friendless man accused of being Jack the Ripper.

It all seems amusing in retrospect, but the impression it gave me of being exposed and helpless, a criminal chained and taunted in the marketplace, was a shattering experience while it lasted. Seventeen years later, when the book was reissued with a new last chapter to take the place of the May Day epilogue,[1] it was

1. For the curious, that epilogue is reprinted in *Think Back on Us* (Carbondale: Southern Illinois University Press, 1967), pp. 56–62.

received with as much enthusiasm as the first edition had been with abuse. From this one might infer that the reaction to the book in its earlier form had more to do with politics than with the relative gray-headedness of reviewers. Wide praise of the revised edition was a vindication of sorts, but it gave the author much less pleasure than the abuse had given him pain. Perhaps that is a general rule about reviews, explained by the vanity and insecurity of authors. When their work is reviewed favorably, they are merely confirmed in their good opinion of themselves: "That critic is a perceptive man," they think. A fusillade of hostile reviews has a deeper effect on them, since it calls into question their entire scale of values. I am not thinking here of those other unlucky authors whose first book has been too widely praised and who, still insecure, can't bear to finish a second for fear that the critics will find it disappointing. They feel safer resting on their withered laurels, as it seems to me now that I rested on my thorns. I reviewed for *The New Republic*—with rather more kindness to authors than I had shown in the beginning—I wrote essays and poems, but for years I couldn't bring myself to finish another book.

After being the most-argued-about book of the spring, *Exile's Return* had a total sale for the first year of 983 copies.

That disastrous record might cast some light indirectly on the old question whether the 1930s were a "red decade" in the publishing world. It has been the contention of some—and notably of Eugene Lyons in his book *The Red Decade* (1941)—that many publishers of the time, with most of their editorial assistants, were under Communist influence and therefore promoted radical authors, while suppressing the work of those who told the truth about Soviet Russia. If anti-Russian books managed to appear, Lyons tells us, they were attacked and massacred by a Red Indian band of reviewers (including the literary editor of *The New Republic*), who also came whooping to the defense of any book that exalted the Communists. Lyons' picture is not confirmed by my own experience or by anything I learned about the publishing record of others then writing from the left. With the exception of Clifford Odets and possibly Granville Hicks, nobody gained a paying audience or a more appreciative press by marching in the May Day parade.

# 20.
# Let Sleeping
# Dialectics Lie

Toward the end of July 1934 a voice on the telephone invited me to meet Willi Muenzenberg, the German Communist publisher, who was in New York for a short visit. "You know who he is," the voice said. "People call him the five most interesting men in Europe."

I found all five of him and another German exile established in two big rooms that smelled of dust, in an off-Broadway hotel. It was the day after a band of Nazis had tried to seize the Austrian government, had murdered Chancellor Dollfuss, and then had surrendered to the police. Muenzenberg was gloating in German over the failure of their putsch. He was a man of forty, short but not small, with a woodchopper's shoulders, a very large head, and a square chin that he carried in boxing style, half an inch from his chest. He said that the Nazis were "*dumm, dumm, dumm,*" as if each *dumm* were a bullet from an executioner's pistol.

When he excused himself for a moment, the other exile, who served as interpreter—and might have passed for his younger brother—told me about Muenzenberg's early life. He was born in Thuringia, the heart of the old German Empire, and was put to work young in a shoe factory. Even before the Great War, he was active in the International Socialist Youth Movement, which was agitating against conscription. In wartime he escaped into Switzerland, and while there he was one of the youngest men to attend the Zimmerwald Conference, at which left-wing Socialists of many countries drew up their program for a revolutionary peace. He met Lenin at the conference, and later, during the Spartacist revolt in Germany, he served directly under its soon-to-be-murdered leader, Karl Liebknecht.

All those details—the proletarian background, the apprenticeship as a left-wing Socialist, the laying-on of hands by Lenin himself—had become as it were compulsory in the youth of any European destined to become a Communist leader. But Muenzenberg had soon distinguished himself from others by a special talent for promotion and organization that would have earned him a quick fortune if deployed in Wall Street. During the postwar famine in Russia he had organized Workers International Relief, which at one time had millions of members over the world. Then he had launched into all sorts of publishing ventures and had become one of the German press lords, though he ranked well after Hugenberg and the Ullsteins. His principal competitor and, in a sense, his model was Alfred Hugenberg, a right-wing conservative, who had founded a magazine empire like that of Henry Luce. For every Hugenberg paper that appealed to the solid middle classes, Muenzenberg started another that appealed to the workers—an illustrated weekly, *A. I. Z.* (*Arbeiter Illustrierte Zeitung*), a sports magazine, a women's magazine, two Berlin newspapers, and thirteen other dailies, weeklies, or monthlies.

The most successful weekly in the Muenzenberg group, *A. I. Z.*, claimed a circulation of five hundred thousand, only a modest one by American mass standards. Magazine publishing had never been one of the big German industries. There was, however, a very wide audience for books, and some of the German publishing houses were giants by comparison with their

American counterparts. Neuer Deutsche Verlag, Muenzenberg's house, was among the larger ones, and he was especially proud of having published most of the naturalistic writers who had been trying to create a new German literature. There was a story spread by the Nazis that the publisher had lived in capitalistic luxury. The truth was—or so his friend assured me—that Muenzenberg had received only a small salary and that the profits from all his enterprises had gone to maintain the Communist Party.

He had also served as a Communist deputy in the Reichstag and had found time to address hundreds of public meetings. There was, however—though his friend did not mention it—a romantic or even impish quality in most of his exploits, and sometimes a stockjobber's disregard for the danger of being caught in a rearrangement of the truth. Many solemn Communists mistrusted him for his cynicism and also, I suspect, for his making too many jokes. The lines in his still youthful face were those of laughter rather than suffering or zeal; one thought of Till Eulenspiegel. Or should he be called a company promoter for the cause, as in an earlier age of faith he might have been a juggler for Our Lady?

While his friend was talking, Muenzenberg had come back from the other room. I asked him about his escape from Germany when the Nazis were making a countrywide search for him. Was it true, as I had heard more than once, that he had crossed the Danish border disguised as a capitalist, wearing a cutaway stuffed with little pillows and smoking a big cigar, while riding behind a chauffeur and a footman in a black Mercedes limousine? "*Nein, nein,*" he exploded. With the friend translating, he said that the story was another lie about him spread by the Nazis. There was not a Mercedes limousine in the German Communist Party or its connections. He had escaped in the biggest car he could find—"This big," he said, extending his arms to not quite their full reach. The passport he carried was that of a nineteen-year-old boy. When the border guard remarked that the photograph was not a good resemblance, Muenzenberg explained that he was feeling tired. He had been enjoying the carnival at Cologne, and a few white nights made him look older. The guard nodded, and Muenzenberg drove on into Denmark.

He paused to welcome three or four reporters who had straggled in with their notebooks. Now provided with a larger audience, he began talking about the German illegal press. He had managed to revive three of his papers: *A. I. Z.*, now appearing in Prague, *Gegenangriff*, a newspaper, in Strasbourg, and a political magazine, *Unsere Zeit*, printed in Paris. Besides their circulation among the exiles, *A. I. Z.* and the newspaper were photographed down to shirt-pocket size, printed on very thin paper, and smuggled across the German border. In Germany itself, scores of clandestine newspapers were being published. Many hundreds of people had been killed for distributing them, ten thousand aggregate years of prison sentences had been imposed, yet they continued to appear on schedule. Some of them were mimeographed in Storm Troop barracks. On one occasion the police confiscated the typewriters in a whole district of a German city, carried two thousand of them to headquarters, and tested them all to see which one had been used to cut the stencils of two illegal papers. They did not find the right machine, because it belonged to the son of a manufacturer prominently identified with Hitler's party.

As one of his own contributions to the struggle, Muenzenberg had edited and published *The Brown Book of the Hitler Terror*, an illustrated catalogue of crimes that had been translated into seventeen languages and also distributed throughout Germany in a shirt-pocket edition. He had organized the international commission that met in London to investigate the Reichstag fire. At present he was preparing another "Brown Book," this one dealing with the blood purge of the previous month, during which hundreds of Storm Troop leaders had been shot without a trial. He said that this massacre of June 30 was Hitler's St. Bartholomew's Eve.

The reporters were busy taking notes. Muenzenberg told

them that Hitler had been immeasurably weakened by the blood purge, that his government was coming to pieces, and that the putsch in Austria was proof of its disorganization. It was certain that the putsch had been organized in Germany, he said, but he doubted whether Hitler himself had any part in it. Rather, it bore the earmarks of Arthur Rosenberg's romantic foreign policy, and it showed that one faction in the government could take an important and perhaps fatal step without the approval of the so-called supreme leader. Those people were *dumm, dumm, dumm,* he repeated. "Why, Italy was the only friend they had, the only power that took their side against France and England, and now Italy is mobilizing against them."

Muenzenberg glowed with optimism that afternoon. A few years later he left the Communist Party when he was ordered to report in Moscow. He had reason to suspect that he would be executed there, like thousands of others. In the summer of 1940 his body was found hanging on a roadside tree in Unoccupied France, and it was generally assumed that he had been murdered by Stalin's secret agents. (The Nazis would have killed him too, but first they would have tortured him in an effort to learn the names of his German collaborators. Stalin merely wanted him out of the way.) In 1934, however, Muenzenberg was a faithful Communist expounding the party line, and he seemed utterly persuaded that a Communist government or—he made this concession—a coalition government of Communists and Socialists would seize power from Hitler in the not very distant future.

He invited the reporters to come and see him in Berlin *"in drei Jahren,"* and he held up three fingers. He begged them to impress upon American bankers and businessmen that a Communist government in Germany would be better to deal with than Hitler's government, because Communists had a record of keeping their word and paying their debts.

Though Muenzenberg's optimism was possibly sincere, the Communist movement had not been making the sort of progress it confidently expected in those years of worldwide crisis for its enemies. Instead it had been undergoing a series of defeats that were due in large part to its uncompromising militance and isolation.

The policies still followed, in 1934, as the "general line" of the party were those of the so-called Third Period of international Communism. The First Period, from 1917 to 1921, had been a time of civil war in Russia and of romantic dreams about carrying the revolution to the rest of the globe. Good Communists everywhere had preached and conspired and improvised as if the day of judgment were at hand. When it become manifest that the day would have to be postponed, communism entered its Second Period, which was that of the New Economic Policy. In effect it was a state of truce with the capitalistic world and even with the Socialists. But the truce ended in 1928, when the Communists abandoned their attempt to make temporary alliances and to "bore from within." During the Third Period they insisted that anyone, radical or conservative, who opposed the general line of the party was a class enemy fighting on the other side of the barricades. Meanwhile they were trying to build "socialism in one country" at a considerable cost in lives.

The usual explanation of those policies is that they were an adroit tactical move by Stalin. He had to confirm his position as dictator of Russia and pope of the Communist faith, which was threatened by enemies both on the right and on the left. First he formed an alliance with the right that enabled him to defeat the leftists and send their leader, Trotsky, into exile. Then he consolidated the defeat by adopting most of the extreme policies that Trotsky had been advocating. It was a maneuver that not only outflanked the remaining leftists but also allowed him to turn against his former allies on the right—Tomsky, Rykov, Bukharin—and destroy their influence.

But that explanation in terms of Russian politics, though partially correct, leaves an important question unanswered. Why was Stalin's move followed with a degree of enthusiasm by Communists in other countries? Of course the older ones had learned that they had to obey Stalin in order to rise in the party or merely keep from being expelled as deviationists. But what about the new men attracted to the movement, those still rosy with enthusiasm and innocent of personal designs? Why did they too support the extreme policies of the Third Period and treat the Socialists as pariahs, as "social fascists," to use a slogan of those years?

One answer seems to be that the new men were eager to be good Marxists, and that the Third Period expressed something fundamental in the Marxist habit of thought. Its extreme policies were accepted not only because Stalin enforced them but also because they were in keeping with what might be called the theological side of the Marxian dialectic. Of course the dialectic had its practical side as well: it served as a taxonomy of revolution, a descriptive method based on Marx's study of social changes. His close friend Engels once defined it as "The great basic thought that the world is not to be comprehended as a complex of readymade *things*, but as a complex of *processes*, in which thoughts apparently stable, no less than their mind-images in our heads, the concepts, go through an uninterrupted change of coming into being and passing away." So far the definition expresses a scientific attitude toward the world, but Engels departed from science when he added that "in spite of all seeming accidents and of all temporary retrogressions, a progressive development asserts itself in the end." How can that be proved? The progress of history toward a classless society is a theological notion, an article of faith that all good Marxists accepted. They believed in accelerating the historical process, since it was leading to a desirable consummation, and they believed that the Nazis were only a seeming accident, a temporary retrogression, perhaps even a step in advance. As late as April 1934 the Presidium of the Communist International declared that Hitler's dictatorship, "by destroying all the democratic illusions of the masses and liberating them from the influence of Social Democracy, accelerates the rate of Germany's development towards proletarian revolution."

"After Hitler, our turn!" the Communists said. On the other hand, they regarded the Social Democrats (and the British Labor Party and the New Deal) as obstacles to progress, since these were trying to soften the conflict between capitalism and the masses, between thesis and antithesis, that would lead to a happy new synthesis. The Socialists, not the Nazis, were the real enemies of the future. That was the chain of reasoning, or of blind feeling, that had led to such incidents as the Communist invasion of Madison Square Garden when the Socialists were trying to hold a dignified protest meeting. On a world scale it had led to a series of disasters for the Communist movement— in Germany, in Austria, almost everywhere. The parties of the left were everywhere disunited and were being crushed one by one. Since the leaders of international communism had a practical side, as well as being theologians of a sort, it was not hard to foresee that the Third Period would come to an end. Willi Muenzenberg had learned to keep his ear to the ground. When he prophesied that the Nazi dictatorship might be replaced by something hitherto unthinkable, a coalition of Communists and Socialists, he revealed that a change in tactics, or at least in language, was already under way. But the message was slow to reach his American comrades, including those engaged in conflict on the literary front.

# 21.
# Waiting for Lefty

Two literary arguments of the years 1933–35, both conducted with zealous acrimony, were about proletarian literature and Marxian criticism. On the first question I had a divided mind. The so-called proletarian writers, inspired by what they thought was happening in Russia, were dealing with aspects of American life that had never been fully explored. I hoped they might end by vastly extending the subject matter of American literature, but their performance had so far been disappointing. I didn't want to discourage them and preferred to have their books reviewed in *The New Republic* by others. About Marxian criticism I felt more enthusiasm. It seemed to enforce the great principle that art is not separate from life but grows out of it, reveals its conflicts, and returns to it as well, in the sense that honest books give us a different picture of what it means to be "I" or "we"; hence, indirectly, they change our patterns of conduct. As long as Marxian criticism studied the "we" of writers—that is, their class loyalties—and what such attitudes implied in action, I was on their side and even in their ranks. But I could not join them in abusing middle-class writers for telling the truth about themselves, and I sometimes scolded the critics for being intolerant.

Granville Hicks, whose honest and orderly mind I respected, was one of my victims. He had written a history of American literature since the Civil War, *The Great Tradition*, which appeared in October 1933; that was three months before he became literary editor of *The New Masses*, which was being transformed from a monthly into a weekly. My *New Republic* review of his book took the form of a letter to the author. "Dear Granville," I said. ". . . Both of us believe that the central feature of modern life is a struggle between classes which is also a struggle of the working class against all forms of exploitation. . . . Both of us are convinced that literature and politics, art, science and education, all are departments of life, and that no artist or writer can divest himself of his role in life. He takes, or eventually will be forced to take, one side or the other, and both of us have made the same choice.

"This doesn't mean at all that we agree on every subject. . . ." Ah, no, we had our comradely differences, and I find in rereading the review that I devoted only one paragraph to the considerable virtues of the book, as against seven paragraphs that enlarged on what I held to be its harshness, narrowness, and dogmatism. Faults like these, I said in my peroration,

> are not at all inherent in our position. It is our business, I think, to leave them to our opponents. Let them, lacking in sounder arguments, heap abuse on people with whom they disagree. Let *them* be stingy of praise [I adjured, forgetting that the reviewer had not been generous]. . . . Let *them* be harsh, arid, one-sided and dogmatic. Let them, in a word, write propaganda; they need it in order to justify things as they are and make people accept the bleak world toward which they are leading. Generosity and human warmth are fighting on our side. We need simply discharge our responsibility as critics, we need simply find and set down the truth in its human complexity, being confident that the truth is all the propaganda we need.

That is what I believed in those innocent days, but still there were limits to my credulity. I would not grant that Marx had answers to everything. A year after reviewing *The Great Tradition* I wrote a little essay on the limits of Marxian criticism. I said that literary subject matter included the emotions aroused by various biological events including sexual desire, walking in the country, growing old, and dying. I said that poems and stories dealing with such events might still embody social judgments, but that some of them, at least, belonged to a vast neutral area of literature that was neither revolutionary nor counter-revolutionary. "About the only thing that Marxian critics are justified in saying about that area—within the limits of the Marxian method—" I concluded, "is that if a writer confines himself permanently to neutral subjects he will narrow his scope, impoverish his sympathies and, in the end, diminish his literary stature."

This mild statement called forth a number of furious answers. One of them was from a young man, let us call him Wiggins, whom I remembered for his hungry-looking face, and his very big, almost colorless eyes. He had grown up in the coal country among Welsh miners, he had earned his way through the state university, he had been graduated with honors, but without money, and he was trying to survive as a revolutionary journalist. On various occasions he had elected to serve as my political conscience. The letter he wrote me reflected the spirit of the times, as Wiggins' remarks always did, and it glowed with Marxian fervor as an altar with candles.

"The history of our literature," he said, "is marked with the bones of those searchers after neutrality. Why are they bound to perish? 'Socialism looks at us from a thousand windows'; we see it foreshadowed in a thousand institutions; the need for it broods over us in the very material characteristics of the societies in which we spend our lives. We can only deny it by closing our eyes to the clamorous realities. Your artist who hopes to find a neutral area won't merely suffer because he has impoverished his sympathies or narrowed his scope. He will suffer psychologically what he would suffer if he deliberately put out his eyes, amputated his arms and legs, destroyed his means of perception. He would *decay*, and decay, no matter what sort of front it puts to the world, is a terrible and painful process of rotting away."

Two years later, when Wiggins was offered a well-paid magazine job, he changed his opinions unterribly, without losing arms, legs, or eyesight. Ten years later he was a Republican, and twenty years later he was a vestryman of St. Somebody's Episcopal Church. In those early days, however, he was following the party line in literature, before it suddenly veered off. He was trying, like many others, to write a great proletarian novel.

In theory proletarian literature was based on the principle that each work of art enforces the values of a social group and ultimately serves as a class weapon. This has been true—so the left-wing critics said—of the art produced under every social system. For example, the art of feudal times exalted the sort of ideals—courage, loyalty to one's overlord, and rewards or punishments beyond the grave—that would strengthen the nobility in its unremitting warfare against the peasants. The artists, in other words, were serving as men-at-arms of the barons and the bishops. But then a new class came forward, the bourgeoisie, and it called for another sort of literature to express its own ideals of thrift, enterprise, calculation, sobriety, and domestic rather than courtly love. That led to the development of new literary forms—the novel, the sentimental tragicomedy—in which the hero was rewarded on earth for his middle-class virtues by making or marrying a fortune.

The left-wing critics all said that bourgeois literature, after two centuries in which it refined its methods and vastly flourished, had entered a period of violent decay. Even the strictly bourgeois writers were turning against it, although their revolt had assumed the corrupt forms of bohemianism, aestheticism, or withdrawal into ivory towers. The result in any case was an art that fed the pride of the leisure class. But once again a new class was rising, the soon-to-be-victorious army of workers, and these in turn were demanding a new art to express their revolutionary ideals. Proletarian literature was taking shape among the earthquake-shattered ruins of bourgeois literature and the relics of feudalism.

But exactly what shape would it assume? The left-wing critics found it easy to agree among themselves when they were explaining the past or attacking their present enemies, but they each had a different notion about the writing of the future. It raised questions to which they found conflicting answers. Should the term "proletarian literature" be confined to works by certified proletarians? Or might college graduates, even those from the Ivy League, be proletarians too, if they wrote about the workers or specifically *for* the workers? Or again, might their books deal with and be intended for their own class, the petty bourgeoisie, yet still have a special attitude that earned them the right to be called proletarian novels?

This last was what Edwin Seaver, a Harvard man, strongly asserted at the first American Writers' Congress, in 1935. "It is not style," he said, "not form, not plot, not even the class portrayed that are fundamental in differentiating the proletarian from the bourgeois novel. . . . It is the present class loyalty of the author that is the determining factor." But Martin Russak, a labor organizer who had gone to work in a textile mill when he was only thirteen, and who in 1935 was writing a never-to-be-published novel about the silk weavers, rejected Seaver's inclusiveness. He said, "The proletarian novel has got to be, and is already becoming, a novel that deals with the working class. . . . If we completely understood the nature of class division, we would not say that all people are the same. In the working class we have a distinct kind of human being, a new type of human being, with an emotional life and psychology that is different, and distinct." Seaver and his ilk would never get past the membership committee of Russak's working-class club.

Another question was whether proletarian writers could

profit from the technical experiments of bourgeois writers such as Joyce and Eliot, for instance, and even Henry James, or whether they should confine themselves to straightforward narrative, clear political messages, folksong, mass chants, and other forms of writing that would stir the workers to action. There was a continued bitter argument between *Partisan Review*, founded in 1934 as an organ of the John Reed Club, and *The New Masses*, which was more directly controlled by the Communist Party. *Partisan Review* advised its readers to study the new bourgeois writers as examples of technique. *The New Masses* spoke in several voices, but usually it said, in effect, "Down with technique and hurrah for writing that follows the party line." One of its editors, Mike Gold, was applauded when he said in a public debate, "There is no 'style'—there is only clarity, force, truth in writing. If a man has something new to say, as all proletarian writers have, he will learn to say it clearly in time: if he writes long enough."

Most of the left-wing writers must have agreed with *Partisan Review*, at least in their hearts. In public meetings, however, they often became so dizzy with religious enthusiasm, so eager to lead the other neophytes, that they offered to renounce their patiently acquired skill, together with everything they had learned about middle-class life, if only the sacrifice would bring them into communion with the workers. They made me think of the Florentine burghers in 1497, when hundreds of them cast their wicked books and paintings into Savonarola's bonfire. A few of the new enthusiasts had followed the example of young Leftwich, the poet with whom I drove back from the national hunger march, and had abandoned any thought of a literary career in order to become party organizers. Whittaker Chambers, after writing four widely translated stories, had given up his identity as well as his reputation when he joined the Soviet secret service, but Chambers' case appears to have been unique.

The usual sacrifice was to walk in a local picket line, to be carried off in a paddy wagon, to sing "The International" with the other jailed pickets—Mike Gold would carry the bass—to be tried before a judge who obviously wanted to dismiss the prisoners, while the Communist attorney for the defense was doing his best to get them convicted, and then, after the judge had overruled the attorney, to rush home and write a turgid account of the strike as the first red glow of a revolutionary dawn. There were other writers, however, who played a part in serious strikes like those in Minneapolis and San Francisco, where pickets were likely to be slugged and given stiff sentences. At the first American Writers' Congress, Robert Gessner, usually a sensible man, advised his fellow poets to go farther; he wanted them to submerge themselves in the mass of workers, lead the lives of workers, and learn about the workers' problems at first hand. "Leave your technique on the fence," he said. "It will come trotting after you with its tail between its legs."

This eagerness on the part of some to renounce the art of making patterns out of words for the easier task of writing cautionary tales and artless sermons might possibly be explained by a parallel that was seldom mentioned, although it must have been present in many minds. Communism was antireligious, true, but even party members often pictured it as the new scientific faith that would take the place of Christianity. Hence, the two might bear the same resemblance as the opposite poles of a magnet. The millions who had already died for communism would be like the early Christian martyrs, while the works of the first proletarian writers would be like the Christian art of the catacombs. Still more they would resemble the writings of the first church fathers, which were stiff, graceless, even barbarous by the standards of a classical style, but which were redeemed by their power and fanaticism. "Like all new art," Joseph Freeman said in his introduction to a big anthology, *Proletarian Literature in the United States*, "revolutionary art is bound to start crudely, as did the art of other classes"—and of other faiths, he might have added. Let it be crude then; crudeness was a virtue to be cultivated, so long as it was combined with the savage vigor that had enabled church fathers to overwhelm the pagan rhetoricians. There would come a day when communism was like the church triumphant. Then proletarian art would give way—as it already promised to do in Russia—to a universally human art endowed with the harmony and complexity of later Christian works like *The Divine Comedy* and the Cathedral of Chartres. Such was the dream that sustained not a few of the embattled theorists.

Others were seized upon by a different dream, that of finding personal salvation—and perhaps literary salvation also—as a reward for undergoing the perilous experience of joining the Communist Party. A few of these described the experience in language that suggested St. John of the Cross and his dark night of the soul. "With your own powers," St. John writes, "no matter how well you might have used them, you would never have been able to work so efficiently, perfectly, and securely as now, when God takes your hand and guides you in darkness to a goal and by a way which you would never have found with the aid of your own eyes and feet." In the same spirit, but invoking the proletariat instead of God, Meridel LeSueur, a young Minnesota writer of good family, wrote in *The New Masses* of her conversion:

> It is difficult because you are stepping into a dark chaotic passional world of another class, the proletariat, which is still perhaps unconscious of itself, like a great body sleeping, stirring, strange and outside the calculated, expedient world of the bourgeoisie. It is a hard road to leave your own class and you cannot leave it by pieces or parts; it is a birth and you have to be born whole out of it. In a complete new body. None of the old ideology is any good in it. The creative artist will create no new forms of art or literature for the new hour out of that darkness unless he is willing to go all the way, with full belief, into that darkness.

A few quite promising writers followed LeSueur with full belief, but they did not emerge from that darkness with new forms of art or literature for the new hour. I cannot think of one truly distinguished work that any of them produced while still regarding himself as an all-the-way party member. A very few produced such works years after they had lapsed from the faith. Perhaps the works were enriched by the quasi-mystical experience that their authors had undergone years before. In its general effect, however—on literary careers and often on personal lives as well—that venture all the way into the darkness proved to be an unmitigated disaster.

In practice the proletarian or revolutionary literature of the early 1930s was broad in its geographical range, which was roughly from Penobscot Bay to Puget Sound and from New Orleans to Minneapolis, with forays into Germany and China. It was excessively narrow, though, in its range of emotions.

The principal emotion would seem to be anger, whether it was felt by workers in a story or was meant to be evoked in the reader by the misdeeds of the exploiting classes. Often it took the form of revulsion and was expressed by the incantatory use of such terms as "bloated," "cancerous," "chancres," "diseased," "distended belly," "fistula," "gorged with," "maggots," "naked" (almost always used in a bad sense by proletarian writers, as in the phrase "naked greed"), "nauseating," "pus," "putrefying," "retching," "rotted flesh," "spew forth," "syphilis," and "vomit." One message which all the terms conveyed or chanted was that a young writer, or anyone else who turned against the bourgeoisie, was fighting his way out of a charnel house.

The other emotions that recur in proletarian writing could be expressed in more appealing images. Second to anger (or standing before it, in many cases) was the yearning for comradeship, for a sense of communion to be obtained by merging the lonely and helpless "I" in a great fellowship of the dispossessed. Third was the burning faith that this "we" must rise by hundreds and thousands, then by millions against the exploiters; "Strike!" was always the message here. Fourth and last was the hope that "we" could march arm in arm across the battlefield and into the golden future. Meanwhile there was not much place for such gentler feelings as sorrow and romantic love. These could either be mentioned in passing as additional reasons why the workers must UNITE and FIGHT for every RIGHT, including that of loving and grieving at leisure, as rich people did, or else they could be deferred from consideration till the last battle was won.

The result of ruling out so many emotions was a monotony of tone that becomes even more evident in proletarian fiction than in poems and plays of the same school. Most of the proletarian novels were cast in one mold, and the fact is that many of them deal with the same events, usually a Communist-led strike like the one in the cotton mills of Gastonia, North Carolina. Within three years after the strike was fought and lost in the summer of 1929, it had become the subject of four published novels—*Strike!*, by Mary Heaton Vorse; *To Make My Bread*, by Grace Lumpkin; *Gathering Storm*, by Myra Page; and *Call Home the Heart*, by Fielding Burke—besides contributing to the background of Sherwood Anderson's *Beyond Desire*. Strikes in the lumber mills of Aberdeen, Washington, would be the subject of three novels: *Lumber*, by Louis Colman (1931); *The Land of Plenty*, by Robert Cantwell (1934), which can still be admired; and *Marching! Marching!*, by Clara Weatherwax (1935), which reads like a parody; nevertheless it won a prize offered by *The New Masses* and a publishing house, the John Day Company, for the best proletarian novel submitted in manuscript. There were ninety other novels in the contest, all of which, to the best of my knowledge, remained unpublished and unregretted except by their authors.

As for the published novels, most of them have essentially the same plot. A young man comes down from the hills to work in a cotton mill (or a veneer factory or a Harlan County mine). Like all his fellow workers except one, he is innocent of ideas about labor unionism or the class struggle. The exception is always an older man, tough but humorous, who keeps quoting passages from *The Communist Manifesto*. Always the workers are heartlessly oppressed, always they go out on strike, always they form a union with the older man as leader, and always the strike is broken by force of arms. The older man dies for the cause, like John the Baptist, but the young hero takes over his faith and mission. Escaping from Herod's soldiery—usually with a sturdy young woman who has also been converted—the hero swears that his life will be devoted to organizing the workers for greater battles to come.

Proletarian poetry was more diversified in manners and messages than proletarian fiction, but most of it has become almost as hard to read. I do not think that its failure in this country was due to lack of talent among the poets. Some of them had, or seemed to have, more than enough to carry them through. Besides Alfred Hayes, already mentioned, there was Sol Funaroff, an editor of *Dynamo*, who often signed himself Charles Henry Newman, He was a sallow, gangling, shy, but fervent young man with a gift for bold musical constructions and another gift for interrupting them with terse imperatives or angry questions. Thus, he addressed the landlords of the world as a single watchdog with a hundred heads:

> *Howl, Cerberus,*
> *hell-hound of war*
> *defend your hell,*
> *howl and hiss your hate.*
>
> *Of those who have power*
> *I have hatred.*
>
> *You, thieves of today,*
> *what can you steal*
> *from those whose possessions*
> *are in the future?*

There was Edwin Rolfe, who preferred the older iambic measures. Often he celebrated the daily lives and festivals of Communist Party members in blank verse that read smoothly and effectively, until the reader stumbled over a party slogan left standing like a baby carriage in his path. ("But why not put the slogans into your own words?" I asked when he submitted a poem to *The New Republic*. "You don't understand," he said. 'Slogans are the poetry of the new age.") There was Kenneth Fearing, who invented a style of his own that was halfway between Whitman and Damon Runyon. Often he wrote with a sardonic chuckle, as when he recounted the death of a white-collar man in "Dirge":

*Denouement to denouement, he took a personal pride in the certain,*
*    certain way he lived his own, private life,*
*        but nevertheless, they shut off his gas; nevertheless, the bank*
*        foreclosed; nevertheless, the landlord called; nevertheless,*
*        the radio broke;*
*And twelve o'clock arrived just once too often,*
*        just the same he wore one grey tweed suit, bought one straw hat,*
*        drank one straight scotch, walked one short step, took one*
*        long look, drew one deep breath,*
*    just one too many,*
*And wow he died as wow he lived,*
*        going whop to the office, and blooie home to sleep, and biff got*
*        married, and bam had children, and oof got fired,*
*    zowie did he live and zowie did he die. . . .*

Fearing was less successful when he wrote in a lyrical mood and in a style that was closer to Whitman's. Still, I am tempted to quote his "Lullaby," because it might be taken as another answer to my warning about the limits of Marxian criticism. In suggesting that there was a neutral area of literature, neither revolutionary nor counterrevolutionary, I had mentioned poems and stories that dealt with such biological events as "birth, puberty, sexual desire, eating, walking in the country." "Lullaby" is a poem about walking by moonlight on a country road.

*Wide as this night, old as this night is old and young as it is young,*
*    still as this, strange as this,*

*filled as this night is filled with the light of a moon as grey,*
*dark as these trees, heavy as this scented air from the fields,*
    *warm as this hand,*
*as warm, as strong,*

*Is the night that wraps all the huts of the south and folds the empty*
        *barns of the west;*
*is the wind that fans the roadside fire;*
*are the trees that line the country estates, tall as the lynch*
        *trees, as straight, as black;*
*is the moon that lights the mining towns, dim as the light upon*
        *tenement roofs, grey upon the hands as the bars of the Moabit,*
        *cold as the bars of the Tombs.*

For readers of another generation, the poem has to be translated into prose. Holding his girl's hand, Fearing thinks first about the beauty of the summer night, but then he is seized again with his passion for social justice. He remembers that the same gray moon shines down on Negro cabins in the South, on starving farmers in the Dust Bowl, on vagrants camped beside the road, on rich men whose estates are bordered with trees that make him think of lynched Negroes, on mining camps in the Kentucky hills, on tenements, and finally on the bars of the Tombs prison in New York, and of the Moabit prison in Berlin, where Communists were held before execution. There is no neutral area. The struggle for justice goes on everywhere in the world, and Fearing implies that it should be echoed in every line of verse. Echoed it was, in so many poems by others and often in such a dull fashion that it ceased to be heard.

Fearing's later poems lacked the force of conviction he had shown in the early 1930s. He died in middle age, as did Edwin Rolfe, and Funaroff died young, all three without giving more than a foretaste of what one had hoped they would do. Among the poets who once belonged to the proletarian school, Muriel Rukeyser—more of a student than the others and with more music in her language—was the only one whose work developed over the years, though not in its early direction. Revolutionary verse belonged to a revolutionary period and would have declined in any case as the period drew closer to its end, but we are left to wonder why it wasn't better while it flourished—in this country, I mean; some of it was very good in England and France.

One reason may have been that although there were several talented poets in the proletarian school, there was no outstanding talent like that of Aragon and Eluard in France or Auden in England. The presence there of such leaders, too self-assured to be jealous of rivals, helped to form something more than a group of poets; one might call it a poets' community. Auden in particular—"Uncle Wiz," as he was called by younger men— attracted others into the revolutionary school by his faults as well as his virtues, but chiefly by his power of invention, which inspired others to make inventions of their own: to emulate rather than imitate. We had no poet in the United States like the Auden of the early 1930s—not even Auden himself, when he finally came to New York.

But we did have a playwright who was admired and emulated, for a time, in almost the same fashion. I am thinking of Clifford Odets in 1935, the year of *Waiting for Lefty*.

He was then a young man of twenty-eight, the son of a Jewish immigrant, a Litvak, who had gone into the printing business and had mildly prospered over the years. Odets himself was born in Philadelphia and was raised mostly in the Bronx. After leaving high school at the age of fifteen, he had quarreled with his parents, who wanted him to be a businessman, and had lived on the edge of hunger while trying to become an actor. Twice he had speaking parts in Theatre Guild shows; then he became a member of the Group Theatre, a talented company that had been assembled by Harold Clurman and others without much thought of how it could survive. Somehow it struggled on from season to season, paying its actors when a show was running and at other times providing them with food and a place to sleep. The Group was devoted solely to art, but many of its younger members had begun to dream of being political revolutionists; Odets was one of these. In Boston during the lean theatrical season of 1934, he confided his dreams to Clurman, who had become his closest friend in the company. "He wanted comradeship," Clurman says; "he wanted to belong to the largest possible group of humble, struggling men prepared to make a great common effort to build a better world. . . . None of my homilies could have the slightest effect on him. He was driven by a powerful emotional impetus, like a lover on the threshold of an elopement."

The New Theatre League (formerly the League of Workers Theatres) had announced a prize to be given for a one-act play without scenery, designed for workers to produce at their ordinary meeting places. Odets, as he explained to Clurman, had a plan for meeting those conditions. A few days later he locked himself in a hotel room and set to work on his play, which he finished in three nights. *Waiting for Lefty* could be performed in less than an hour, and was afterward printed in less than thirty pages, but it gives the effect of having more than its actual length—and this for a simple reason, because it presents not only the emotions but the typical characters and most of the messages that were scattered through fifty longer works.

> *As the curtain goes up we see a bare stage. On it are sitting six or seven men in a semi-circle. Lolling against the proscenium arch down left is a young man chewing a toothpick: a gunman. A fat man is talking directly to the audience. In other words he is the head of a union and the men ranged behind him are a committee of workers. . . .*

The first stage direction shows how Odets has solved the problem of writing a play that requires no scenery and almost no stage properties except six or seven folding chairs. He has simply borrowed the technique of the blackface minstrel show.

His interlocutor is the union president, Harry Fatt, who also doubles as a villain, and the gunman is Mr. Bones. The committeemen, described as being "seated in interesting different attitudes," are the company of minstrels, each of whom will rise to do his turn. But Odets has introduced a brilliant variation into his minstrel show by preparing to draw the spectators into the action and by giving them parts to play. They must imagine themselves to be taxi drivers assembled in their union hall to hear arguments from both sides and finally vote on the question "Shall we strike?"

Fatt has been speaking against a strike. He tells the hackmen that they should trust their friend in the White House, who has been working day and night. "For who?" says a voice from the audience. Other voices cry, "We want Lefty! Where's Lefty?" Fatt pounds with his gavel and says, "That's what I wanna know. . . . You elected him chairman—where the hell did he disappear?" One of the committeemen, Joe Mitchell, rises and steps forward to defend the absent leader, who "didn't take no run-out powder," he says. "That Wop's got more guts than a slaughter house." Then the lights go out, except for a white spotlight that plays on Mitchell and his wife, Edna, as they act out their story.

Mitchell has been unable to support his family on what he earns by driving a cab. He comes home to find that most of his furniture, bought on the installment plan, has been taken away and that his two children have gone to bed hungry. Edna tells him that she will sleep with another man, for money, unless the union goes on strike. "We gotta go out," Mitchell calls to the audience as lights come on again. Next a very young committeeman, Sid Stein, tells his story in the same fashion. He and Florrie are desperately in love, but they can't get married on the money a hackman takes home. He talks about his brother, a college graduate who has enlisted in the navy. "They'll teach him to point the guns the wrong way," he shouts—that is, point them at other workers instead of shooting the bosses at home. A moment later Sid kneels in despair and sobs with his head in Florrie's lap. Blackout.

A third episode is played with the house fully lighted. Tom Clayton, an older man from Philadelphia, tells how a taxicab strike was broken there and the strikers put on a blacklist. "The time ain't ripe," he says. A voice from the audience—that of his own brother—exposes Clayton as a labor spy, and he escapes down the center aisle. Two more episodes follow, both preaching the message of anger and revolt. Then, as the lights come on after a last blackout, we hear the end of a speech by another committeeman, Agate Keller, who is proud of being a Red. Fatt and the gunman try to throw him out of the hall, but he breaks away, and his fellow workers protect him. With his shirt torn to rags, Agate faces the audience again and cries, giving the clenched-fist salute, "Don't wait for Lefty! He might never come. Every minute—"

A man runs down the center aisle and jumps on the stage. "Boys," he says, "they just found Lefty."

From the audience rises a confusion of voices: "What? What? Shhh. . . ."

MAN. They found Lefty. . . .

AGATE. Where?

MAN. Behind the car barns with a bullet in his head!

AGATE (*crying*). Hear it, boys, hear it? Hell, listen to me! Coast to coast! HELLO AMERICA! HELLO. WE'RE STORM-BIRDS OF THE WORKING-CLASS. WORKERS OF THE WORLD. . . . OUR BONES AND BLOOD! And when we die they'll know what we did to make a new world! Christ, cut us up to little pieces. We'll die for what is right, put fruit trees where our ashes are! (*To the audience.*) Well, what's the answer?

ALL. STRIKE!

AGATE. LOUDER!

ALL. STRIKE!

AGATE and OTHERS on Stage. AGAIN!

ALL. STRIKE, STRIKE, STRIKE!!!

*Waiting for Lefty* won the prize for which it competed, and it was produced on January 5, 1935, at a Sunday benefit performance for *The New Theatre Magazine*. Harold Clurman, who was there, reports in his memoirs, *The Fervent Years* (1945), that "a kind of joyous fervor seemed to sweep the audience toward the stage. The actors no longer performed; they were being carried along as if by an exultancy of communication such as I had never witnessed in the theatre before. . . . When the audience at the end of the play responded to the militant question from the stage: 'Well, what's the answer?' with a spontaneous roar of 'Strike! Strike!' it was something more than a tribute to the play's effectiveness, more even than a testimony of the audience's hunger for constructive social action. It was the birth cry of the thirties."

The cry, whatever its nature, resounded in all parts of the country. Very soon *Lefty* was being produced on other stages, and in union halls, and even on Broadway, where it ran for months. To make a full evening it had to be combined with another play by Odets, *Till the Day I Die*, which he wrote in one night after reading a news report from Germany in *The New Masses*, and which he should have had the good sense not to print in his collected works. But it was fairly effective on the stage, and at one time the combined bill was being played simultaneously in thirty-two American cities. Then *Lefty* went to England, where it roused the same joyous fervor. At one performance even H. G. Wells raised a plump fist and was heard to cry "Strike, strike!" in a militant squeak.

But I cannot agree with Clurman that *Lefty* was the birth cry of a new era. In spite of its immense popularity, it was not followed by many other effective plays for the workers' theater, and there would be none that unified actors and audience in the same exultancy of communication. Proletarian literature as a whole was to be pushed aside after a change in the party line; the new model was "socialist realism." Nobody any longer repeated the slogans that had been reworded by many earnest young writers: "Roosevelt is working day and night for capitalism"; "The New Deal means fascism in America"; "Soldiers, turn your guns against the bosses!" By June 1936, even Joseph Freeman would forget what he had said in his introduction to *Proletarian Literature in the United States*, published in October of the previous year. Writing in *The New Masses*, he would now speak in a casual way of "those radical writers," not admitting that he was among them, "who in the 'sectarian' days were engaged in advancing what used to be known as 'proletarian literature.'"

Later the ideals of the sectarian days would have an indirect and delayed effect on the work of several writers, including Steinbeck and Hemingway. Looking back on the earlier time, however, I suspect that *Lefty*, for all its faults, comes as close to being a classic as anything that directly emerged from the proletarian school. It is still easy to read and even to admire in a dispassionate way, though not with enthusiasm. To recapture the effect of its first performance, either one would have to rewrite *Lefty* in terms of a later era, or else one would have to reconstitute an audience that remembered five years of depression, the banks closing, the landlord at the door, and that shouted "Strike!" with a sense of release, a dream of brotherhood—then again, louder, "Strike! Strike!"—as it raised a thousand clenched fists.

# 22.
# The New Republic
## Moves Uptown

In January 1935, shortly after the first performance of *Waiting for Lefty*, *The New Republic* moved away from its old brownstone house in Chelsea. Etienne and Lucie, the butler and the cook, retired to northern Italy with their modest savings. Although there wasn't much new construction in the 1930s, the house was torn down soon afterward, with its neighbors on either side, and was replaced by a drab apartment building.

I had spent five happy years in the house, always stimulated, in the midst of the depression, by new crises in the world and the need for making new decisions. When new talents appeared in literature, they liked to be printed in *The New Republic*. John Cheever sent us his first narrative, written when he was seventeen; "Expelled from Prep School" was its original title. I found it in a pile of unsolicited manuscripts, was charmed by its candor, and persuaded my senior colleagues to accept it—"But first cut it down by half," Bruce Bliven said. A year later John appeared at the office, a fresh-faced boy with an engaging smile and a stubborn jaw. He was determined to become a professional writer while living on an allowance of $10 a week from his older brother. Soon he was publishing stories in magazines that didn't pay for contributions. "Your stories are too long for other magazines to accept from new writers," I told him one Friday evening after dinner. "Tomorrow, try writing a story of not more than a thousand words, say three and a half of your pages. Write another of the same length on Sunday, another on Monday, and still another on Tuesday. Bring them all to the office on Wednesday afternoon"—that was my time for receiving callers—"and I'll see if I can't get you some money for them."

John wrote the four stories on schedule, a feat that not many young writers could have performed. *The New Republic* seldom printed fiction, but one of the four could be regarded as a "color piece" about a burlesque theater, and I passed it along to my colleagues. "Yes. Lively and short," Bruce said. The other three stories, plainly fictions, I sent to Katharine White of *The New Yorker*. She accepted two of them, and that was the beginning of John's professional career.

I must have offered good advice to many of those who came to see me on Wednesday afternoons, but I was ashamed of giving only that to callers some of whom plainly needed a meal. By selling books that we hadn't space enough to notice, I established a reviewers' loan fund and was able to dole out a few dollars in emergencies. Young writers had a hard time of it in those early depression years before the Federal Writers' Project. Whenever possible I gave them books to review, and I was often pleasantly surprised by their work. At other times I had to recast and retype a grubby manuscript before the reviewer could be sent a check for it; that was the cost of being softhearted.

Joe Gould wasn't young or really a writer, but he got a dollar every Wednesday. Joe, whom I had known for years, was a little man with a goatee whose clothes were spotted with ketchup; he sat apart from the others (or perhaps it was the others who sniffed and moved away from Joe). He sometimes uncapped a fountain pen and scribbled an entry in one of the half-dozen greasy notebooks piled beside him on the floor. He claimed to be compiling a history of the world from oral sources. He also said that he lived mostly on ketchup, which was free at the Automat, and that his address was the Hotel Entrance. Once or twice I tried giving him a book for review, but that was a failed experiment; I suspected that he had sold the books before reading them.

There was always a book for Robert Cantwell, who, in his writing, showed a gift for broad perspectives. His reviews were full of anger or admiration based on his feeling that everything in literature was connected with some great historical movement, usually the struggle for socialism. Soon we found him a place on the *New Republic* staff. While there he finished a second book, *The Land of Plenty*, which still seems the best of the proletarian novels, and he laid ambitious plans for a third book. Then Lincoln Steffens, white-haired and soft-spoken, came to the office bent on hiring him away from us. He wanted Cantwell to become the well-salaried biographer of his friend the Boston philanthropist E. A. Filene.

I was against the project on the ground that Cantwell was a born novelist who shouldn't waste his time writing biographies. With Bruce assenting, I suggested an arrangement by which he would stay on *The New Republic* at a higher salary, but only for six months each year, while devoting the other six months to his novel. Cantwell refused; he said that writing the life of Filene would give him a chance to demonstrate the utter failure of philanthropy, even when it was guided by the best intentions. He went off to Boston to start his researches. The biography was written, so I heard, but it was never published and Cantwell wouldn't talk about it. Later he went to work for *Time* at a still higher salary. The ambitious third novel died in embryo.

Cantwell's place on *The New Republic* had been taken by Otis Ferguson, whom I first met in the autumn of 1933. He was a black-haired, sharp-featured, rather saturnine young man with decided opinions, often spoken from the corner of his mouth. He didn't talk much about himself, but he told me that he had served four years in the navy after enlisting at seventeen.

He then worked his way through Clark University, in Worcester, Massachusetts, where he was editor of the senior yearbook, besides winning one of the first prizes in a *New Republic* college-writing contest. Now that he was trying his luck as a freelance, he wondered whether we wouldn't give him a book to review. . . . I gave him a book, one that other reviewers were praising extravagantly. Otis reported the following Wednesday that its author had, in his words, laid a precious egg.

When an untried reviewer disagrees violently with the whole critical press, an editor has to decide whether he knows what he is talking about. I discussed the book with Otis for nearly an hour, not without heat; people rarely succeeded in being calm with him. He would rise from his chair, shouting and waving his arms, and often his victim shouted back, but there were no hard feelings afterward. This time Otis won his point. I didn't agree with his opinions, but felt that he had good reasons for holding them and that it was our job to print what he wrote.

In December, when books for review were scarce, Bruce Bliven suggested that he try his hand as a critic of movies and radio. He wrote lively reports about both of them. The following summer, if I remember the time correctly, he became a salaried member of the staff. He later broadened his audience by writing a series of articles on swing music and musicians. The boys in the big name-bands, who were reading *The New Republic* for the first time in their lives, and the last, told him he was the only writer who came anywhere near expressing what they were trying to do. He was in fact creating a new literary genre, but he never bothered to collect the articles into a book.

Otis was one of the people who could write for deadlines, and only for deadlines. At *The New Republic* in those days, the final moment when copy could reach the printers' in Brooklyn was ten o'clock on Monday morning. Otis would sometimes arrive there in a taxi at 10:05, unshaven and smelling of whisky, after sitting up all night over his article. He would make final corrections standing over the linotype. If he had more time, he would simply make more corrections, in hope of attaining an ideal that pre-existed in his mind. The ideal was to be, not a man of general ideas—he distrusted them—but, in his own words, "a writer, a clean writer with discipline, with the true flash which can make a thing suddenly tender or explosive."

He was a good editor, as might have been expected; he could take a vastly overwritten manuscript and trim it down into something terse and effective. He was also a continual problem to his colleagues, who sometimes felt that he had been possessed since childhood by the imp of the perverse. If you said "white" to him, Otis said "black." If you made the mistake of saying "genius," quick as a flash he answered "phony." He was a genius himself at letting the sawdust out of stuffed shirts, but there were times he missed his target and drew blood instead.

He resented the older editors, especially Bruce, whom he suspected of being pompous. "Did you hear what Buster said to me?" he would almost snarl. Bruce had hired him and was always tempted to fire him, but that didn't matter to Otis. Many times I had to defend him at editorial meetings to which he wasn't invited. Outside of the office, if he met someone with influence, someone who could give him a bigger job or make his reputation, he was likely to become profane, gob fashion, perhaps spilling drinks on the oriental rug. By contrast he was never anything but kind to the timid or suffering or penniless, including many of the young writers who appeared on Wednesday afternoons. I know there were several of these for whom he revised manuscripts, bought meals, or found jobs.

That summer and fall of 1934, when Otis went to work for us, were a busy time for me. They were the time when Jim Thurber, separated from his first wife, was living alone at the Hotel Algonquin and wandering about the city in taxis. When he visited friends, he usually stayed until three or four in the morning, as if putting off the moment when he would have to open the door of an empty room. Once inside the room, he might spend the rest of the night typing a letter. One of those he sent me, on the subject of literary communism, which he detested, was fifteen pages long. I don't know how I found leisure to answer him or what I said beyond asking him to review books. He wrote only two or three reviews, but they were full of strong opinions buttressed with examples.

That was also the time when writers appeared from Vassar, Mary McCarthy first, then Muriel Rukeyser with her revolutionary poems, then Eleanor Clark and her tall sister Eunice, both strikingly handsome. They made me feel that the Vassar classes of 1933 and 1934 had been exceptionally brilliant and opinionated, an army or a daisy chain with banners. It was the time when Hamilton Basso came up from the mountains of North Carolina, where he had been writing novels that didn't sell and a biography of Beauregard that was published on the day when every bank in the country was closed. Ham worked on the staff that year, and we were sorry when he went back to the mountains to write another novel. He had skill with words, and more than that a personal warmth that radiated through our shabby offices.

Alfred Kazin appeared that summer at the age of nineteen. In the front parlor—it was really that and not a reception room— Otis Ferguson examined him, read a scrawled introduction from John Chamberlain of *The Times*, and sent him upstairs with a favorable verdict; later they became friends. Kazin had finished his third year at City College, had written essays on the English metaphysical poets, and had formed a diversity of literary judgments, which he delivered in a heavy Brownsville voice with an engaging note of eagerness. Even his first reviews didn't have to be edited. Sometimes he joined in the hot games of deck tennis, usually mixed doubles, that we played in the backyard on summer afternoons, or watched from under a striped umbrella while drinking Tom Collinses or emptying a pitcher of Lucie's special iced tea with oranges and mint. Betty Huling played the hostess and referee; we called her Mrs. New Republic.

Of course there was no deck tennis in the late autumn, but

there was Ping-Pong or sometimes an evening party in the Cowleys' two big rooms on the top floor of another old house, just
across Ninth Avenue. Always there was hard work performed
with a sense of responsibility to the new world that was painfully in birth. Now all this pleasant but challenging family life
of ours was to be left behind: not only the games and laughter;
not only the streets of Chelsea, through which I used to wander
south past the Old Homestead, still a saloon, where Edwin Arling-
ton Robinson in his early drunken period used to live on nickel
beers and the free lunch, till I reached the Hooverville on Abingdon Square; not only Chaffard's French restaurant with its ancient
waiters and its big room upstairs for meetings, and the Italian
former speakeasy on Twenty-sixth Street where table wine was
a dollar a bottle, but *The New Republic* house itself with its
scratched heirlooms, its worn carpets, its editors' offices like mas-
ter bedrooms, and its dining room with the round enormous
table. There we used to sit in Windsor chairs discussing the crisis
of capitalism with our luncheon guests from abroad, while sometimes feeling that we were being watched and judged from the
parlor wall by the stern faces of Lincoln and his cabinet.

Our new offices were shared by three other magazines also
supported by the Elmhirsts: *Asia, Antiques*, and *Theatre Arts*;
together we occupied two floors of an office building just east
of Madison Avenue. The two floors had been remodeled by a
modernist architect, William Lescaze, who, by using a great deal
of blue enamel, caramel-colored mahogany, and butterscotch
leather, had made them look like the tourist-class lounge of an
ocean liner. We still had a dining room, but without the round
table or Lucie or Etienne; a merely passable cook now appeared
once or twice a week. My great scarred desk, which had once
been Francis Hackett's and Robert Morss Lovett's and Edmund
Wilson's, had followed me uptown, but only after being sandpapered and painted horizon blue. It occupied so much of my
smaller office that callers liked to sit on it and talk down to me.

They were now a different type of callers, somewhat more

carefully dressed. Only a few of the out-at-elbows reviewers and proletarian poets appeared on Forty-ninth Street. Joe Gould came regularly, but others may have been intimidated by all the leather and mahogany. I was a little uncomfortable myself, not only in the office but downstairs in the streets where rows of little shops glittered with treasures I had no wish to buy. And those shoppers crowding the sidewalks, those carefully tanned businessmen, those admen flagging down taxis with their Mark Cross briefcases: they were not my people. After spending so many years downtown among rebels, I felt like a spy in enemy country, unsafe in my disguise as a junior executive. I had to admit, though, that the enemy's women were beautiful. That year most of them seemed to be tall hatless girls appearing fresh from the hairdresser's with shoulder-length bobs like golden helmets. Two or three of them came to the office to ask for books, among a little stream of polylingual German refugees. One beautiful girl sat on my desk and let her legs dangle. "Cheese-cake," Otis Ferguson grumbled as he passed the open door.

*The New Republic* gave its first cocktail party to celebrate the move uptown. It invited all the regular contributors, ranging in age from the patriarch John Dewey through an assortment of scholars, liberal lawyers, and labor economists, to John Cheever, then twenty-one. Muriel, leaving the new baby with a practical nurse, had come to the office the day before and had joined with Isobel Soule and Ebie Blume to make jugs of martinis, which they left in the refrigerator. That is a dangerous way to prepare for a big party, since the very cold martinis are slow to melt the ice over which they are poured; the liquor is undiluted. Almost everyone drank the martinis fast, then shouted to be heard by his neighbor. John Dewey got into an argument, made a sweeping gesture with his arm too low, and swept the cloth off the new square table, sending fifty glasses crashing to the floor. More glasses appeared and the din rose higher. A young matron was sitting happily on Stark Young's well-tailored lap, where few women had sat before her. George Soule was beaming through rimless spectacles. Bruce Bliven, a temperate man, looked more and more unhappy. "Why don't you go home?" Otis said to him, and almost added, "Buster." We missed an artist friend and found him vomiting in the women's toilet with his wife holding his shoulders. A little crowd was waiting for the only elevator that ran after six o'clock. This wasn't Herbert Croly's *New Republic;* it was a midtown office party.

# 23.
## Assembly on the Left

The Communist movement was also, in a sense, preparing to move uptown. Already the Communist International showed signs of changing its policy, or "general line," and of modulating from the Third Period of sectarianism, exclusion, expulsion, and attack into a new period of inclusiveness and even tolerance of heretics if they proved willing to defend the Soviet Union; "defense" was to become a key word. After recklessly finding enemies, the movement would soon be looking everywhere for friends. All this had been decided in Moscow, but the extent of the change hadn't yet been grasped in New York. Inside the American movement there was soon to be a struggle, mostly in words, between zealots of the Third Period and open-armed adherents of what would soon be known as the People's (or the Popular) Front.[1]

That struggle seems to me, in retrospect, the most interesting feature of an American Writers' Congress that was held in New

1. I have always preferred "People's Front" as being a more accurate translation of *Front Populaire*. In this case *Populaire* has little to do with popularity in its English sense of "the state of being widely liked or admired."

York in the spring of 1935. A call for the congress had been printed in *The New Masses* of January 22. It began:

> The capitalist system crumbles so rapidly before our eyes that, whereas ten years ago scarcely more than a handful of writers were sufficiently far-sighted and courageous to take a stand for proletarian revolution, today hundreds of poets, novelists, dramatists, critics, short story writers and journalists recognize the necessity of personally helping to accelerate the destruction of capitalism and the establishment of a workers' government.

Here one notes such phrases as "proletarian revolution," "accelerate"—that word abused by Marxists—"the destruction of capitalism," and "a workers' government," all suggesting the zealotry of the Third Period. But a moment later one reads, "The dangers of war and Fascism are everywhere apparent; we all can see the steady march of the nations toward war and the transformation of sporadic violence into organized fascist terror." Here the emphasis is no longer on revolution, but rather on a defense of culture that would have to be undertaken by many writers, presumably of many different opinions. The very notion of holding a writers' congress, with a fairly broad composition, shows that the sectarianism of the Third Period was going out of fashion.

I might quote a few passages from the remainder of the call:

> A new renaissance is upon the world; for each writer there is the opportunity to proclaim both the new way of life and the revolutionary way to attain it. . . . The revolutionary spirit is penetrating the ranks of the creative writers. . . .
>
> Never have the writers of the nation come together for fundamental discussion.
>
> We propose, therefore, that a Congress of American revolutionary writers be held in New York City on May 1, 1935; that to this Congress shall be invited all writers who

have achieved some standing in their respective fields, who have clearly indicated their sympathy to the revolutionary cause, who do not need to be convinced of the decay of capitalism, of the inevitability of revolution. Subsequently, we will seek to influence and win to our side those writers not yet so convinced. . . .

We believe such a Congress should create the League of American Writers, affiliated with the International Union of Revolutionary Writers. . . .

By its very nature our organization would not occupy the time and energy of its members in administrative tasks; instead it will reveal, through collective discussion, the most effective ways in which writers, *as writers*, can function in the rapidly developing crisis.

Some further remarks on the text of the call:

A draft of it had been offered by Granville Hicks, then literary editor of *The New Masses;* he wrote in English, unlike many of his colleagues. The draft was discussed at a number of informal meetings held in Greenwich Village apartments. At one meeting I was depressed by the way some writers forgot their professional standards and tried to rewrite the call in Marxist jargon. One paragraph of the final text must have been supplied by a party official "from the ninth floor"; it was an agglomeration of party slogans: "Fight against imperialist war and fascism; defend the Soviet Union against capitalist aggression; for the development and strengthening of the revolutionary labor movement; against white chauvinism (against all forms of Negro discrimination or persecution). . . ." That seemed to me a syntactical jumble, but still I signed the document, as did sixty-two writers in all. Dreiser, Dos Passos, Caldwell, Farrell, Steffens, and Waldo Frank were then the glittering names, but most of the others had at least written books or plays. The call was also signed by two nonwriters: Earl Browder, secretary of the Communist Party, and Alexander Trachtenberg, head of its American publishing house.

Trachty, as everyone called him, was a short, round man

with a bald head, a fierce dragoon mustache, and a disarming manner. He was thought to have close connections with Moscow and served as a sort of cultural commissar. At later meetings of the informal committee, people asked him questions involving policy. His instructions from Moscow must have been vague, for he liked to temporize. "On the one hand," Trachty would say, ". . . but on the other hand—" Joshua Kunitz, who had written two books about Russia, called out at one point, "Trachty, we know on the one hand, on the other hand; what we want to know is which hand."

One question that continued to be argued was about the writers who should attend the congress. Should invitations be confined to those "who have clearly indicated their sympathy to the revolutionary cause," or should they also be extended to doubters and waverers? "On the other hand," Trachty said, "the time has come to count noses." What he meant, I suppose, is that the congress should apply political standards, as during the Third Period. Waverers might be invited—that was something new—but not declared enemies of the party leadership such as Max Eastman, Sidney Hook, or V. F. Calverton.

About another important provision in the call, I heard no discussion. It was that members of the congress should be "writers who have achieved some standing in their respective fields." This meant, in substance, that there were to be no invitations for the eager beginners, the kids, those in various cities who had flocked by hundreds into John Reed Clubs or Pen and Hammer Groups. Though nobody spoke of the matter, it had already been decided that such groups were to be dissolved, their meeting places deserted, their dozens of little magazines allowed to die. That whole field of activity was to be taken over by a new organization, the League of American Writers, composed of somewhat older men and women. Already one might have foreseen a new conflict of generations. Neglected by Communist leaders, many young writers would soon drop out of the movement or go over to the Trotskyites.

There were, however, few signs of dissension at the congress when it convened—not on May 1, that symbolic date, but on Friday evening, April 26. The first meeting, open to the public, was held uptown, in Mecca Temple, where the auditorium could seat four thousand people. Every seat was filled. On the stage were the writer-congressmen, 216 of them, assembled in rows of folding chairs. Granville Hicks, the chairman, looked out over the audience with an exultant feeling. "I assumed at the time," he reported thirty years later,[2] "that these four thousand people were passionately devoted to literature. Since then I've become convinced that the party simply loaded the meeting. It told various units that they had to turn out for this particular meeting, that they had to sell tickets for it, and they did." The party, small as it was, had a capability for putting things together, and selling tickets to finance them; that was one of its attractions for intellectuals used to protesting in lonely ineffectiveness.

Most of the speeches that evening were short and were intended to be stirring. The exiled playwright Friedrich Wolf delivered a brave message from the writers tortured in Hitler's concentration camps. Waldo Frank had prepared a longer and thoughtful address on "The Values of the Revolutionary Writer"; he had good things to say in his high voice, but I could hear chairs squeaking on the stage behind him. Earl Browder's speech received closer attention, since he was laying down the party line. Browder was a gray-faced man in a rumpled gray suit; he had the honest face of a clerk in a Kansas feed-and-grain store. His message was factual and conciliatory. He had noted that most of the writers present were not affiliated with the Communists and might have misgivings about the possibility of fruitful collaboration. Some of them feared that the Communists might tell them what to write and treat them as artists in uniform. Those fears were ungrounded, as they could learn from other writers who

2. In the symposium "Thirty Years Later: Memories of the First American Writers' Congress" (*The American Scholar*, Summer 1966).

were members of the party. "The first demand of the party," he said, "upon its writer-members is that they shall be good writers, constantly better writers, for only so can they really serve the party. We do not want to take good writers and make bad strike leaders of them." Browder was rebuking the zealots of the Third Period and he received something close to an ovation. Later, however, the zealots were to have their say.

The closed sessions of the congress were held on Saturday and Sunday at the New School for Social Research, in the Village. Here the speeches were longer and, in many cases, euphoric about the advance of revolutionary writing. "I don't think the fact is open to question," Edwin Seaver said, "that the most valuable contributions to the American novel during the last several years are to be found in the work of our writers in the left sector. . . . John Dos Passos, Robert Cantwell, Erskine Caldwell, William Rollins, Waldo Frank, Josephine Herbst, Jack Conroy, Edward Dahlberg, Grace Lumpkin, James Farrell—these and a score of others—we have only to consider subtracting these names to see that there is very little remaining worth mentioning, and that the sum total of this remainder is constantly diminishing." The playwrights' commission of the congress found that there were in the United States three hundred functioning workers' theaters and that they were springing up everywhere with tremendous vitality. "This new theater in America," the playwrights said, "is booming as is no other revolutionary art today. Write for it and help it grow."

There were also disputes, as always among writers, with more recriminations and bruised feelings than one would infer from reading the official report of the congress.[3] James T. Farrell, always a maverick, was hurt because his paper on the short story was to be read at the Sunday-morning session, when most of the

3. *American Writers' Congress*, edited by Henry Hart (New York, 1935). Farrell's embittered memory of the congress is recorded in his novel *Yet Other Waters* (1952).

delegates would be in bed. Several other speakers belabored the men of the 1920s "in their velvet jackets" (did anybody wear them?) who, as Jack Conroy said, "have been able to spend a year or two in the Paris Latin Quarter, where it is possible to learn the writing of proletarian literature in the technical manner of Marcel Proust and James Joyce." Conroy must have been reading *Exile's Return*. He was a hard-drinking novelist from Moberly, Missouri, strong in the workers' cause. "To me," he said, "a strike bulletin or an impassioned leaflet are of more moment than three hundred prettily and faultlessly written pages about the private woes of a gigolo or the biological ferment of a society dame as useful to society as the buck brush that infests Missouri cow pastures." *Exeunt* the works of Henry James and Edith Wharton. But other voices at the congress defended Jamesian techniques and the effort to reach a more sophisticated audience. The central dispute, for me, was the one aroused by Kenneth Burke's paper on "Revolutionary Symbolism in America."

Kenneth was and is my oldest friend, with memories of high-school days in Pittsburgh and of walking home together night after night from the Carnegie Library. For a long time we had lived near each other in Greenwich Village. Later I was to write of him as he was during those Village years:

> *This man strains forward in his chair*
> *to argue for his principles,*
> *then stops to wipe his spectacles,*
> *blink like a daylight owl, and shake*
> *his janitor's mop of blue-black hair.*
> *He can outquibble and outcavil,*
> *laugh at himself, then speak once more*
> *with wild illogic for the sake*
> *of logic pure and medieval;*
> *but all that night he will lie awake*
> *to argue with his personal devil.*

We had seen rather less of each other since 1932. I was busy with the book department of *The New Republic*. Kenneth, having left his job with The Rockefeller Foundation, had retired to a farmhouse in New Jersey three miles from a railroad station (no electricity, no running water). He chopped wood and wrote. When he sent me reviews, they were sometimes excessively long and too abstruse "for our readers," in the bureaucratic phrase I had learned to use. The reviews went back for revision and our friendship became a little strained. Though we had both "gone left," in the phrase of the day, we had progressed at different speeds along slightly different paths, and we argued by letter. I was more interested in day-to-day tactics and in problems of political behavior, whereas Kenneth kept his eyes on distant objectives.

Lately his literary interest had turned from construction to persuasion, from pure form to rhetoric. He had also emerged from the personal crisis of divorce from his first wife and marriage to her younger sister. He now worried about the effect of divorce on his three daughters. He worried about the state of the country. He worried about the risk of his family's sinking into destitution. He had written a novel, *Towards a Better Life* (1932), in which the hero declines into catatonic dementia, and that was another worry: mightn't he end as his hero did? Could he avoid that fate by joining with others to build a better world?

I am trying to set forth by one example the tangle of motives that sometimes lay behind the "going left" of American writers during the 1930s. The nationwide spectacle of breadlines, violence, injustice, and illogic was part of it, but there was also, in many cases, the personal specter of isolation and nervous breakdown. Those papers at the writers' congress often had a substratum of unexpressed emotions, and Kenneth's paper was no exception.

The paper dealt with myths or symbols as weapons in revolutionary propaganda. It made a simple point, but one with broad implications. "The Communists," Kenneth said, "generally focus

their scheme of allegiance about the symbol of the worker. . . .
The symbol I should plead for, as more basic, more of an ideal
incentive, than that of the worker, is that of 'the people.' . . . I
am suggesting fundamentally that one cannot extend the doctrine
of revolutionary thought among the lower middle class without
using middle-class values. . . . I recognize that my suggestion
bears the telltale stamp of my class, the petty bourgeoisie, and I
should not dare to make it, except for a belief that it is vitally
important to enlist the allegiance of this class." Kenneth was more
daring than he recognized; he was affronting all the habits of
thinking that had been formed during the period of revolutionary
dogmatism. He was exposing himself as a premature adherent of
the People's Front.

He was an innocent at the time, unused to speaking before
an audience, especially one with strong political convictions. "I
had a friend," he says,[4] "whom I took to be a member of the
party. I showed him the article before I read it at the congress. I
asked him to tell me what he thought of it, for I didn't want to
do anything that in any way would be considered wrong. I had a
terrific desire to belong; as they put it later in the mass media,
you know, 'togetherness.' My friend looked at it and told me
he didn't see anything wrong with it, so I felt reassured. But
after I had been reading for a while and was nearly finished, the
chairman, John Howard Lawson, announced that my time was up.
Holding up the two unread pages, I asked for a bit more time . . .
and was allowed to read the two pages. The audience gave me a
nice hand. Since I was greatly afraid of audiences, I sat down
feeling wonderful."

Another paper followed, to which he gave little attention, and
then came a discussion of all the papers. It was centered on Kenneth's suggestion. He says, "The boys got going. Oof! Joe Free-

4. In the symposium already mentioned, "Thirty Years Later: Memories of the First American Writers' Congress." As for the friend, Kenneth
never told me his name.

man gets up, throbbing like a locomotive, and shouts, 'We have a snob among us!' " Kenneth had become a snob by conceding that he would have to speak like a petty bourgeois. "Then," he continues, "Mike Gold followed and put the steamroller on me. A German exile, Friedrich Wolf, attacked my proposal to address 'the people' rather than 'the workers.' He pointed to the similarity between this usage and Hitler's harangues on *das Volk*. And so on, and so on, until I was slain, slaughtered."

I listened to the diatribes that morning and was disturbed by them, for Kenneth's sake, but was also amused. I had been attacked in much the same fashion, if with less violence, and hadn't been hurt by the abuse because I thought it was uttered chiefly to affirm the speaker's position as a loyal Communist. Kenneth felt wretched, though; his dream of fellowship was shattered. "I remember that when leaving the hall," he tells us, "I was walking behind two girls. One of them said to the other, as though discussing a criminal, 'Yet he *seemed* so honest!'

"I was tired out and went home," he continues. "There had been a late party the night before, after the meeting in the big hall uptown. I lay down and began to doze off. But of a sudden, just as I was about to fall asleep, I'd hear 'Burke!'—and I'd wake with a start. Then I'd doze off, and suddenly again, 'Burke!' My name had become a charge against me, a dirty word. After this jolt had happened several times, another symptom took over. Of a sudden I experienced a fantasy, a feeling that excrement was dripping from my tongue. . . . I felt absolutely lost."

But Kenneth went back to the congress for the sessions that evening and the following day. "On Sunday as I walked down the hall," he remembers, "I saw Joe Freeman coming and started to cringe away. I felt embarrassed at such a meeting. But Joe came up and smiled and shook hands with me and said, 'Well, I'm sorry, old man.' It was all over. The politicians had forgiven me.

"Some friends of mine had an aquarium with a big frog in it. There was a cover so he couldn't get out. Then somebody gave them a little frog, which they put in the same aquarium. The two frogs would sit there side by side. Maybe Joe Freeman was the big frog. One day my friends looked in—and by God they couldn't see the little frog. All of a sudden they spotted his feet sticking out of the big frog's mouth. So they pulled him out, and since he hadn't started to get digested yet, he was all right. All they could do was put him in the aquarium again. The next time they looked in, those two frogs were sitting side by side; all was forgiven. I often think about that story when I think about politicians."

At the last session of the congress, held on Sunday afternoon, the principal business was to organize the new League of American Writers. Jack Conroy announced the name of the man nominated for head of the league: Waldo Frank. The nomination was unanimously approved. Conroy then read, in alphabetical order, the names of those nominated for the executive committee: the first was Kenneth Burke, the third Malcolm Cowley, and the fifth Joseph Freeman. Those names, too, were unanimously approved. Waldo delivered his inaugural address. "With these words," he said, "I should like not to end this congress but to begin the League of American Writers. . . . Everything remains to be said. Everything remains to be done. Let us get to work."

After the applause died down, Jim Farrell offered a motion that the congress close its final session by singing "The International." Trachtenberg's face turned red. By then he must have received instructions to keep revolutionary communism in the background. Everyone rose to his feet, though. In a confusion of voices we sang "The International":

> *Arise, ye prisoners of starvation,*
> *Arise, ye wretched of the earth!*

# 24.
## The Summer of Congresses

"Let us get to work!" Waldo Frank had told the writers' congress at its last session. He was roundly applauded, but, for a time, hardly anyone followed his adjuration. The newborn League of American Writers was at first a body without the breath of life. It had a president, a national council, and an executive committee, and these would at least provide names for a letterhead, but nobody had gotten around to having one printed. So far the League had no office, no working secretary, and no need for a treasurer, since it had no money. There was little chance of convening the national council, whose members had scattered to various parts of the country. The executive committee was largely composed of New Yorkers, but even these proved hard to assemble in the bright spring weather. Waldo, the president, was sailing for Paris to address another congress, this one including famous writers from many countries.

It was Trachtenberg, representing the party, who managed to bring together the executive committeemen—not all of them, but enough to hold two or three meetings. I remember that much of the discussion centered on the new magazine that the League was to issue. It was to take the place of all the little proletarian magazines that had been published by John Reed Clubs in a dozen cities. It was to be an imposing quarterly. It was not to be concerned with left-wing politics, but rather with wider topics of interest to writers. It was to have distinguished contributors, some of whose names were suggested, but nobody offered to serve as its unpaid editor. Nobody volunteered to raise money for the printer's bill.

I listened to the discussion without enthusiasm, since I had work enough to do for *The New Republic*. Then I heard a low-voiced remark of Trachtenberg's: "We'll tell them to stop publishing the *Partisan Review*." I was indignant. "Listen, Trachty," I said, "the kids have done a good job. They've gotten out a lively magazine and they've done it all themselves. Let them go ahead with it." Others agreed with me, and Trachty changed the subject.

At the last of those summer committee meetings, there was talk of a larger meeting to be held after Labor Day, when more writers would be back in New-York. We could then plan activities that would give life to the League. Meanwhile we had before us the example of the Paris congress that Waldo Frank had attended as our chief delegate. It had been a Writers' International Congress for the Defense of Culture, and we all noted the absence of the word "Revolutionary." Apparently those zealous voices of the Third Period had not been raised in Paris, and early reports seemed to show that the congress had been a huge success.

Later I read many of the reports as printed in the French and English press. The congress had been organized by a left-wing group composed of Communist sympathizers, but this time all sorts of prominent writers had been invited, provided only that they were hostile to fascism. Not everybody accepted the invitation. Still, when the guests or delegates assembled at the Palais de la Mutualité on June 21, there were about two hundred of them, from thirty-eight countries, and they included many leading citizens of the world republic of letters. Especially brilliant were the French delegation (Gide, Barbusse, Malraux, Aragon,

Vildrac, and others), the Soviet delegation (with Pasternak, Babel, Ehrenburg, and Alexis Tolstoy), and the German delegation composed of famous exiles (among whom the novelist Anna Seghers was one of the few women on the stage). The English were represented by E. M. Forster, Aldous Huxley, and John Strachey.

The congress continued for five days, with public sessions every afternoon and evening. In spite of the interminable sticky heat, there was an audience of several thousand at all the meetings, a young audience partly composed of students and tourists, but chiefly drawn from the Paris working class. Communist Party units, once again, must have done their share in selling tickets. The delegates sat on a high platform barricaded with microphones. Flashlight bulbs exploded among them, caricaturists made sketches, reporters took notes at long, unpainted tables, and the speeches continued hour after hour, those in German, Russian, or English being followed by competent French translations.

Nobody spoke in favor of abandoning "bourgeois culture" for the sake of a proletarian culture still to be created. All writers of whatever political complexion agreed that the old masterpieces should be not only preserved but rendered available to a much wider audience. The old culture, however—this was a point made by many speakers—is not a fixed and definite object to be kept like a family heirloom. It is, said the novelist Jean Cassou, an *act* that must be continually renewed. In the closing speech André Malraux went further along the same path. "Art, ideas, poems, all the old dreams of man: if we have need of them to live, they have need of us to live again. . . . Whether or not we wish to do so, we create them at the same time that we create ourselves. . . . The cultural heritage does not transmit itself, but must be conquered."

In other speeches the term most often repeated was not "revolution" or "the toiling masses," but "humanism," which was redefined as a preoccupation with living and suffering persons and a hostility toward the abstractions and institutions that weigh them down. If there was one emotion underlying almost all the speeches and binding them togther more closely than any idea or slogan, it was a sense of *urgency*. No matter how high the speakers might soar into realms of disembodied thought or pure nonsense, they were brought down to earth by the feeling of what might happen tomorrow, in this city, in this street. Yesterday the fascists had triumphed in Germany. There were dozens of exiles on the platform; there were writers scarred with floggings received in concentration camps. Today France was threatened with the same disaster; and if France fell, nobody doubted that the rest of Europe would come tumbling after.

The Paris congress was the first public display of a policy that the Communist movement was getting ready to follow. Now the party was reaching beyond "the workers," though it still regarded them as its priesthood. It was trying to affect a larger group, "the people"—and perhaps the governing classes as well—by forming an alliance with respected men of letters. The alliance had to be loose, it had to be defensive, but within those limits it was being widely accepted.

In New York we were eager to join the grand alliance. We were, at the time, so dismayed by the jackbooted march of the fascists in Europe that, once more, we paid less than the proper attention to events in Washington. Much was happening there in the spring and summer of 1935. On May 27, in the case of A. L. A. Schechter Poultry Corporation *v* United States—by then known as the Sick Chicken Case—the Supreme Court ruled that the National Industrial Recovery Act was unconstitutional; the decision was unanimous. All the Blue Eagle parades of 1933, with their outpouring of confidence, were so to speak annulled. All the five hundred industrial codes that General Hugh Johnson had imposed on captive businessmen while he thundered against chiselers, all those rules about minimum wages, maximum hours, and uniform prices, all the rights conferred on labor unions by Section 7a of the act, were so much paper to be shredded. In some areas there would be new laws of more limited scope and more careful draftsmanship; in others there was hardly any salvage. Johnson said of various attempts to revive NRA, "Those poor, pale ghosts that spook around their ancient place have not even the dignity of the honored dead. They are just funny phantoms." The book he wrote after leaving government service was called *The Blue Eagle from Egg to Earth*.

Raymond Moley and Adolf Berle had retired to New York; Donald Richberg was about to establish a private law practice in Washington; and Rex Tugwell, shunted aside, would resign from the Department of Agriculture in 1937. Those four had been the principal architects of the first New Deal, that effort to plan the future of the country by forming a grand alliance of business, labor, and agriculture. The alliance had faltered well before the Sick Chicken Case. The Agricultural Adjustment Administration, Triple-A, had been vastly more effective than Johnson's circus and was thought to have a better chance with the Supreme Court, but Roosevelt himself wasn't certain. (Of course Triple-A would be stricken down in its turn, on the first Monday of January 1936.)

As for the Blue Eagle, Roosevelt believed that it had done its part and could be interred. He held to the same goal of vastly advancing the general welfare, but was now eager to pursue it by other means and with a less venturesome group of collaborators. Felix Frankfurter, Harry Hopkins, Tom Corcoran, Ben Cohen, and Marriner Eccles were among the spenders and regulators who fashioned the second New Deal. In general they would depend on the marketplace to adjust prices and would maintain purchasing power with infusions of government money. They would draft new laws to regulate business and restore competition.

Once again, as during the First Hundred Days, Congress was kept busy with legislation. The Emergency Relief Appropriations Act, providing $4.8 billion for the unemployed, had already been signed into law early in April. There was a battle over who would spend the money, but Roosevelt decided that most of it would go to Harry Hopkins' new Works Progress Administration (WPA), which could spend it faster. It was Hopkins who, in July, would initiate the Federal Arts Projects and thus largely transform the literary scene. The Wagner Labor Relations Bill had been debated for months, but the Sick Chicken Case gave it a new urgency; something was needed to continue the protection of labor unions that had been provided, after a fashion, by Section 7a of the Recovery Act. The Wagner Bill was signed into law early in July. The Social Security Bill, which had been the subject of still longer discussions, was passed in the middle of August.

Although Social Security was the most important, and revolutionary, of all the new measures, it was not the one that aroused the fiercest disputes. There was more of a battle over the Banking Act of 1935, which gave the Federal Reserve Board power to control the money market; this had become the favorite project of Marriner Eccles. Weakened in some respects, but not emasculated, the bill was signed into law on August 24. A bill to regulate public utilities and abolish holding companies, drafted by Tom Corcoran and Ben Cohen, was fought by a utilities lobby that spent millions in bombarding Congress with telegrams, many of them signed with fictitious names. The lobbyists succeeded only in softening the "death sentence" for holding companies before this bill, too, was signed on August 26. Softened in more respects was a bill designed to lay heavier taxes on wealthy individuals and corporations. Still, when Congress adjourned before the end of the month, it had laid the foundations of what we have come to call the Welfare State.

Another congress that summer was destined to have a perceptible influence on American political life, not to mention its effects and countereffects in the intellectual world. It was the Seventh Congress of the Communist International (Comintern), which convened in Moscow July 25. The Sixth Congress, in 1928, had adopted the uncompromising policies of the Third Period. These, it was now clear, had contributed to the disaster in Germany, as well as to defeats for the Comintern in other countries. Almost everyone in the movement was expecting a change. Almost everyone was waiting to hear what the new policies would be.

The important declaration at the congress would be made by Georgi Dimitrov, who, falsely accused of having plotted to burn down the Reichstag, had become the hero of the trial that followed. Now he was general secretary of the Comintern and was scheduled to speak on August 2. That morning delegates from all nations crowded into the Hall of Columns and gave Dimitrov a mass ovation before he launched into his prepared speech. It would last for several hours. Of course he started with the obligatory denunciation of fascism, which he defined in a familiar way as "the power of finance capital itself." Of course he blamed the Social Democrats once again for letting Hitler come to power, but also—this was something new—he admitted that the German Communists had made their own blunders. Then, after more than an hour at the microphone, he put forward the new proposal, which was "joint action with the Social Democratic parties, reformist trade unions, and other organizations of the toilers against the class enemies of the proletariat." Willi Muenzenberg had indirectly spoken of some such move. But this was the first time that the Communists, speaking as a world party organized in national sections, had offered to form an alliance with national sections of the Social Democrats.

Dimitrov foresaw a still broader alliance, a "people's anti-fascist front" that would include not only the organized workers but the peasantry and the lower middle classes. "Those masses must be taken as they are," he said, "and not as we should like to have them." He spoke of France as the country in which the Communists had set a bold example by cooperating with other parties. "If in France," he said, "the antifascist movement leads to the formation of a government which will carry on a real struggle," then the Communists, "while remaining the irreconcilable foes of every bourgeois government . . . will nevertheless, in the face of the growing fascist danger, be prepared to support such a government."

That in itself was a sensational statement for those days, but Dimitrov, speaking for the Comintern, had further suggestions to offer. Thus, he advocated the heresy lately condemned as "exceptionalism" by saying that a different policy should be followed in each country; during the new period it would be permissible to argue that each presented a different problem. The history of each country should be respected and, more than that, it should be carefully studied for the revolutionary lessons it embodied. He laid a good deal of stress on the question of words, saying that "we want to find a common language with the broad masses" (at this point Kenneth Burke would have applauded him). It was time, he implied, to dissolve the Communist labor unions that had been losing one strike after another: "We want one union in each industry." In the United States efforts should be made to found a powerful Farmer-Labor party that would represent the real interests of the workers. But Dimitrov mildly castigated his American comrades for their vituperations against the New Deal, reminding them that Roosevelt was also being abused by "the most reactionary circles of American finance capital," those which "represent first and foremost the very force which is stimulating and organizing the fascist movement in the United States." He had other chidings and urgings, but always he returned to his central proposal: that the Communists, in alliance with their old enemies the Socialists (no longer to be called "Social Fascists"), should reach out for other allies and create a broad antifascist front, a People's Front.

Dimitrov was telling his audience what it wanted to hear, and his speech was received with describable enthusiasm. For the most literal description, I quote from a stenographic transcript that was closely studied when it appeared, after some delay, in several American editions:

> The entire hall rises and gives Comrade Dimitrov a rousing ovation. Cheers coming from the delegates are heard on all sides and in various languages: "Hurrah! Long live Comrade Dimitrov!"

> The strains of "The International" sung in every language fill the air. A new storm of applause sweeps the hall.
>
> Voices: "Long live Comrade Stalin, long live Comrade Dimitrov!" "A Bolshevik cheer for Comrade Dimitrov, the standard bearer of the Comintern!"

Without receiving any such ovations here, the new program outlined by Dimitrov promised to have broad repercussions in the United States. It would, for one thing, put a stop to that silly abuse of the New Deal and thus permit Communists to take advantage of the social legislation passed by Congress; some of them—though not nearly so many as was later alleged—might help to administer the legislation, on government salaries. The dissolution of the ineffective Communist-led unions would release hundreds of tough, devoted organizers to join the new industrial unions, in which many of them would play important roles. (But say this for the Communist unions: they had fostered cultural activities, including those three hundred workers' theaters. With the unions dissolved there would be very few plays on the model of *Waiting for Lefty* performed in union halls.)

The party would soon find wider support for its international aims. By supporting democracy—by talking less about armed rebellion—it could stand on common ground with millions of Americans who would have been appalled by a Communist revolution, but who regarded fascism as a more pressing danger. These might be induced to join one of the mass organizations sponsored by the party, some cover-all such as—to mention only the largest—the League for Peace and Democracy, which sought affiliation with all sorts of church groups, peace societies, and even bowling clubs; at one time it would claim that those affiliated bodies had 7.5 million members. The party itself could flourish by "talking American," by celebrating Lincoln instead of Lenin, and by wrapping itself in the flag. It was attracting a new type of recruits, less radical than idealistic; they were likely to be young, native-born, and well-educated. Many of them were instructors in college English departments who did not pretend to be proletarians; no leather jackets. The party was destined to grow rapidly until 1939, but the new men and women would be less steadfast in times of doubt than many of the older missionaries.

It remains true that the 1930s were not a Red Decade in terms of numbers; the party would never lay claim to having more than a hundred thousand members. Still, the four years beginning with 1936 would be tinged with pink. Having adapted itself to international circumstances, communism was becoming almost respectable. In 1936 I said to Edmund Wilson, "It seems to me that the comrades are acting more sensibly these days." Wilson said, "I liked them better when they were crazy."

For the Cowleys that summer of 1935 was the second and last to be spent at Millstone Point, on the Connecticut shore between Niantic and New London. Millstone Point is now the site of two huge nuclear power plants. In those days it was six hundred acres of woods, rolling hayfields, and empty shorefront, besides an abandoned granite quarry, all belonging to a somewhat less affluent branch of the Long Island Gardiners. A big farmhouse on the property had been rented by George Soule and a group of his friends, four families in all. Two of the families spent weekends at Fish Widows, as the farmhouse was called. The other two, including the Soules, had houses in the back country near a trout stream and used Fish Widows for changing clothes when they went to what was, in effect, their private beach —and ours, for those two summers. Isobel Soule, that immensely fat, kindhearted woman, had persuaded the Gardiners' caretaker to rent us a quarryman's cottage, empty for years, at the now unbelievable price of $150 for the season. There Muriel kept house, and there I spent four magical days each week, fishing, diving from the rocks, brooding over things to be written, and feasting on lobsters.

Even the train ride to Niantic was magical, at dusk on a Thursday evening. I found a seat by the window, where I could look out at the shore. Between the ugly towns were flat salt marshes, pale green even in midsummer when most of the countryside was turning brown. Little islands of darker green rose out of the marshes; they were round compact clumps of oak trees growing on rocky soil, each island floating on its marsh against a background of gray-green twilight. Here and there were market gardens, straight rows of cabbages and onions in coal-black earth. Beyond New Haven two or three surviving farms descended almost to the water's edge; then we passed inlets crowded with sloops and speedboats, and again the salt marshes, the islands of trees, and far beyond them a row of cottages along the beach, where it loomed faintly in the twilight like an enchanted city. Muriel would be waiting at the Niantic station. "We have lobsters for dinner," she would say.

The world of congresses and conflicts was far away. One rainy July afternoon I started a letter to our son Rob, then seven months old. "You were lucky in your parents," I said after writing three pages, "and for this reason, that both of them love life and laughter and people, animals, children, landscapes, swimming, eating, working, making love. They have a good time, hold a high opinion of themselves, and are easy to get along with (your mother especially—your father, being a writer, has a writer's worries that make him inhuman part of the time). But there's a more important reason why you're lucky: your father and your mother love each other. All children whose parents aren't divorced are supposed to believe that Papa loves Mamma; it's one of those fictions that hold society together; but in your case it is simply and literally true. Your parents love each other and begot you so that their love would have an enduring sign. Your father is writing this upstairs at the pine table where he works; your mother is downstairs bathing herself at the pump in the kitchen—and your father thinks of her and loves everything from her curly blue-black hair and moist long laughing eyes and freckled eaglebeak nose down to the belly where you slept for nine months. You're lucky that way, to say nothing of your parents' being lucky."

The rain had stopped and I wanted to carry my elation outdoors. "I'm going fishing," I said to Muriel, who by then was getting dressed in the kitchen. "I'd like to try casting from the rocks."

"Don't be late for supper," she said.

That was a disastrous expedition. The pink granite elephant-backed rocks by the shore were drenched with spray and treacherous underfoot. When I tried jumping from one rock to another, I slipped and broke my left arm above the elbow. I couldn't rise to my feet. Another fisherman found me and got me back to the cottage, I don't remember how; then Muriel drove me supperless to the hospital in New London. There a doctor fitted me out with the most elaborate splint I had ever seen; my cantilever bridge, I called it. Steel rods formed a double arch above my shoulder and descended to the elbow, where they were held in place by heavy rubber bands that also exerted tension on the broken bone. I couldn't lie down with the cantilever bridge and for two months I slept as best I could, often sitting up in an armless chair. Still I continued my weekly pieces for *The New Republic;* there were ten of these, in all, that I typed with one hand.

During the week after Labor Day, I read about the hurricane that had swept the Florida Keys. Nearly a thousand homeless veterans of the Great War and the Bonus Army had been housed there in camps of the Civilian Conservation Corps, and nearly all of the thousand were drowned. There had been two days' warning of the storm, but officials in Miami had fumbled with red tape until it was too late to save them. A train finally sent to evacuate the veterans had been blown off the track before it reached the camps on Upper and Lower Matecumbe Keys. The track itself had been washed away, together with hundreds of men who tried to save themselves by clinging to the rails. It was a strange epilogue to the otherwise peaceful story of the second bonus march. The veterans who had returned to Washington in the springtime of the New Deal; who had been led by Mrs. Roosevelt in singing "There's a long, long trail a-winding"; who had been authorized by presidential order to enroll in the CCC, were now wiped from the books. "You could find them face down and face up in the mangroves," Hemingway wrote after visiting Lower Matecumbe. "In the sun all of them were beginning to be too big for their blue jeans and jackets that they could never fill when they were on the bum and hungry."

Hemingway was then living in Key West, which had escaped the worst of the storm. "Who Murdered the Vets?" was the title of the furious article that he wired to *The New Masses* because nobody else had asked him for it. "I would like to make whoever sent them there," he said, "carry just one out through the mangroves, or turn one over that lay in the sun along the fill, or tie five together so they wouldn't float out, or smell that smell you thought you'd never smell again, with luck. But now you know there isn't any luck when rich bastards make a war. The lack of luck goes on until all who take part in it are gone." It was the first time that Hemingway had published anything in a Communist magazine, and I guessed that the left-wing intellectuals would be jubilant. Had they found a still more prominent comrade to take the place of Dos Passos, who was slipping away as at a Village party, after leaving his hat near the door?

The League of American Writers was to hold its meeting on Tuesday evening, September 10, if I remember the date correctly. I chose that day for my first visit to *The New Republic* after six weeks' absence. On the crowded morning train from Niantic, I happened to sit next to one of the characters we had been taught to identify as labor skates. He was an official of a railwaymen's union and was active in local politics, of course on the Republican side—in other words, he was a traitor to labor's true interests, a henchman of the bosses, and I forget the other phrases applied to men of his stamp. He was kind to the stranger with a broken arm. He had me sit next to the aisle, to make room for my cantilever bridge; he talked to me about his union; when we reached Grand Central he carried my suitcase to the concourse and tried to get a cab for me, till I thanked him and explained that I was checking my suitcase and walking to the office, only five blocks away. Then he offered to meet me at the information booth and go back to Niantic on the same train with me, so he could carry my bag. I was staying in the city overnight, but his offer made me feel good on that hot September day.

I still felt good at the office, sitting once again at my big desk. Otis Ferguson had been running the book department during my absence and had run it well, besides carrying on his regular assignment of editing the correspondence page. He liked short, breezy letters from new correspondents, including even Joe Gould, the little man with the goatee. Joe still came to the office each Wednesday afternoon for the dollar I had always given him. Finally Otis laid down an edict: no weekly dollar except when Joe submitted something short for the correspondence page. The following Wednesday Joe appeared with a sheet torn from one of his notebooks. "Now you can give me my dollar," he said as he passed it over. The sheet contained a couplet which Otis recited from memory:

> *Dear God, save Malcolm Cowley from harm,*
> *Or at least break his neck instead of his arm.*

That evening the League of American Writers held its meeting in a little building on West Twenty-third Street. There may have been fifty or sixty members seated on those familiar rows of folding chairs. It was an argumentative meeting because the League was trying to revive itself and adopt a program for the coming year. How could it find money enough to rent an office and hire a secretary? I suggested a lecture series that might attract a sizable audience. Some members were opposed to the plan, and the discussion became embittered with jealousies. Finally the plan was adopted by a not very decisive vote. The meeting broke up into arguing groups.

I had my big suitcase again and carried it downstairs, with nobody offering to help. At the foot of the stairs were two doors to open successively before I reached the street. A little group of writers was in front of me arguing about the inevitable stages that would lead to a new society. They went through the first door and let it close in my face. I put down the suitcase, opened the door with my good arm, held it open with my foot, picked up the suitcase, backed through the door, and put the suitcase down again. Sweat was dripping into my spectacles. Another group of writers brushed past me and closed the second door in my face. I opened it with my good arm, held it open with my foot, picked up the suitcase, and backed into the street. I still had the dream of comrades marching shoulder to shoulder, but it was retreating into the deeps of my mind. There on the sidewalk, waving with my good arm for a taxi that didn't stop, I wondered whether the new society that my fellow writers were hoping to inaugurate would include in its manners any consideration for persons with broken arms. If it didn't include such minor courtesies, would it neglect greater ones as well? Would it be any more humanistic than the old society of robber barons and labor skates?

# 25.

# The High 1930s

That broken arm of mine had other sequels. On the day in mid-September when the cantilever bridge was finally dismantled, I ran to the beach for my first swim since July. There was a bare root across the path. I tripped over it, fell headlong, and broke the arm again in the same place. That second break was less disabling. Holding the arm I went on to the beach, past a little group of wives, and though I couldn't have the swim, at least I waded into the Sound; then Muriel took me back to the doctor's office. "Hello," he said, "I didn't expect to see you again today."

This time he fitted me out with a simpler, less uncomfortable contraption, a triangular wood frame that fitted under the elbow; I called it my balalaika splint. That too was removed after six or seven weeks, while we were still at Millstone Point, but then I came down with appendicitis and spent two weeks more in the New London hospital. My left ear kept ringing. "Tinnitus," the doctor called it, explaining that it was often a first symptom of deafness. I decided that Millstone Point, with its enchanted shoreline, had a curse for me like that of a fairybook castle. Henceforth we should spend our summers inland, and perhaps our winters too.

By the time I got back to New York, early in November, Muriel had found us a larger apartment where our son, now learning to walk, could have a room of his own. She had supervised the moving from Chelsea to the Village, besides hiring a carpenter to build bookshelves. That night we had a homecoming feast. Next morning I plunged happily into the work that had accumulated at *The New Republic*.

I learned that the most argued-about of the fall books was Sinclair Lewis's *It Can't Happen Here*—not much of a novel, I thought on reading it, but a vigorous antifascist tract. Many of the left-wing writers were delighted with its success and hoped that its author, the Nobel prizeman, would become their champion. Somebody in the League of American Writers conceived the notion of holding a semiprivate dinner with Red Lewis and his wife, Dorothy Thompson, as guests of honor. I wasn't enthusiastic about the proposal, knowing Red as I did, but still (with Henry Hart, who was in publishing, and the poet Genevieve Taggard) I signed the letter of invitation:

> You are invited to attend a small dinner in honor of Mr. and Mrs. Sinclair Lewis on Wednesday, November 13th, at seven o'clock. The dinner, arranged by a few members of the League of American Writers, will be held at John's Restaurant, 302 East 12th Street. We will discuss the subject of Lewis's novel, *It Can't Happen Here*. We hope that you will wish to take part in the discussion.
>
> We are limiting the group to twenty-five invited guests. Your dinner will cost you $1.00, wine extra. For the sake of informality, we wish to guarantee our guests no publicity, no uninvited persons, real talk for mutual benefit.

The dinner in the big room above John's Restaurant was a disaster, even though half a dozen speakers abounded in praise for Lewis and his novel. Lewis kept glancing round suspiciously; his face was like a rubber mask drawn tight over a skull. Had he been drinking again? Clearly he did not propose to be inveigled into joining the League. Dorothy Thompson, seldom a quiet woman, this time had few opinions to express. Finally Lewis burst out with a speech. I forget his words, but I was sitting near the poet Horace Gregory, who quotes him as saying: "Boys, I love you all, and a writer loves to have his latest book praised. But let me tell you, it isn't a very good book—I've done better books—and furthermore I don't believe any of you have *read* the book; if you had, you would have seen I was telling you all to go to hell. Now, boys, join arms; let all of us stand up and sing, 'Stand Up, Stand Up, for Jesus.' " The boys and girls stood up embarrassedly. Horace and I made our way to the door without saying good night to the guests of honor.

That was to be the only dinner given by the League or part of its membership. Otherwise it had been surviving in a state of suspended animation, like a bear in midwinter; but the bear lives on its fat, and the League had none. It did have a hundred members, but most of them hadn't paid their dues. Almost its only source of funds was the lecture series, at first meagerly attended, that had been argued against and barely approved in September. The one group that held regular meetings was the subcommittee on publicity of the lecture committee.

There were four of us in the group; the others were Harold Rosenberg, who later became a distinguished art critic, Marjorie Fischer, who wrote mystery novels, and my old friend Isidor Schneider. Each Saturday afternoon we crowded into my very small study to plan and publicize, if we could, the lecture to be given a week from the following Monday. We also looked for speakers, and that winter we hadn't much trouble findng persons who would work for the good cause without demanding a fee. "Let's try to get Max Lerner," I remember saying. "He might draw a paying audience." All four of us glanced at the green tin box on my desk. It contained our total wealth, which was a thin sheaf of greenbacks and a fistful of silver, net proceeds of the first two lectures.

"Max looks something like Mike Gold, doesn't he?" Hal Rosenberg said. "The girls will like him." Hal was tall, with heavy black quizzical eyebrows. He was a skeptic about the League and would resign from it the following year, but meanwhile he gave us hardheaded advice.

Marjorie Fischer was an unassertive madonna-tempered woman who did her work for us without complaining. I liked her and always intended to read one of her novels. Now she volunteered, "I'll speak to Max."

Isidor Schneider, with his mop of black-brown hair, seemed to be an amiable furry creature, easily wounded. He took out his pipe from under an untrimmed mustache and said, "I suppose it's my job to do the release." Isidor had usually earned his living as a publicity director, though he was better known as a poet, one of strong convictions and some imaginative power. Lately he had edited the poetry section of that big anthology, *Proletarian Literature in the United States*. He had also published a novel based on his boyhood in the slums, one that might have had a longer life if he hadn't permitted his convictions to intrude so often into his vivid storytelling; everything had to have a socialist moral. Isidor was an idealist and a believer. I had always felt protective toward him, surmising as I did that his transparent goodness would get him into trouble.

Hal Rosenberg gave me an inquiring look and said, "We'll put you down for a lecture too." I nodded.

The lectures were given in what had been the grand ballroom of a decayed hotel in the West Forties. Marjorie sat beside the door, selling tickets and making change from the green tin box. The audience, mostly young, was scattered through the inevitable rows of folding chairs. I remember feeling pleased that more of the rows were filled for my lecture. Some of the faces I recognized from those *New Republic* Wednesday afternoons. My subject was "The American Intelligentsia," which I defined, after consulting *The Oxford Concise Dictionary*, as "the part of a nation that aspires to independent thinking." "The audience here tonight," I said, "the chairman and the speaker, all belong to the intelligentsia, whether we like the word or not." I thought our class was growing in the United States; during that winter of 1935–36 it might amount to as many as three hundred thousand persons. Only a few of them had upper-middle-class incomes, for the time, of $10,000 a year. Professors earned $5000 a year if they taught at good universities, but most of the intellectuals struggled along on smaller salaries, or none whatever. As for the poets among us—I paused—it was a mystery how they lived at all.

There was a commotion, followed by laughter, in one of the middle rows. A poet brushed off his wife's arm and rose to his feet; it was Alfred Hayes. "We marry schoolteachers," he said. There was applause.

People seemed to enjoy the lectures. After each of them I went home by subway with the green tin box; subways were safe in those days. The box, with its sheaf of greenbacks that grew stouter week by week, became a symbol to me of an era of good feeling that seemed to prevail in the intellectual world (but how long would it last?). For a moment the intellectuals were drawing closer together, partly because of apprehensions roused by such events as Mussolini's invasion of Abyssinia, in October 1935, and Hitler's military seizure of the Rhineland in March 1936. France and Britain were like old men in wheelchairs, unable to rise. At the same time we noted the first signs of what might become a concerted resistance to fascism, something in which Spain was leading the way. After the February elections, Spain had installed a People's Front government supported by all the working-class parties, even the Anarchists. The new policy adopted by the Comintern was bearing fruit.

Perhaps the new mood in New York was a reflection in miniature, and with comic features, of those distant events. There was more tolerance among left-wing intellectuals, with less bickering than at the Writers' Congress of the preceding year. Even Granville Hicks, often abused for his critical articles in *The New Masses*—"I wish people would stop kicking me in the pants," he used to say—published a biography of John Reed and found himself very widely praised.

A new spirit, though of a different type, could also be sensed in the country at large. We had entered a brief period that I think of as the High 1930s, a time neglected by most historians, who tend to picture the decade as a time of uninterrupted misery. There was an interlude extending, say, from the summer of 1935 to the end of 1936. After the anger and confusion of 1932, the worst year; after the parades and euphoria of the first New Deal, with the disappointment that followed, most Americans had adjusted themselves to living on smaller incomes with a limited degree of security. They no longer had nightmares of falling into utter destitution. Many had found new jobs—there were six million more Americans employed than at the bottom of the slump —and they were somewhat less afraid of what would happen if they lost them. At worst they could go on relief, like many of their neighbors, or they could rake leaves for the Federal Emergency Relief Administration (or later for the WPA). Hoovervilles had disappeared from vacant lots, and nobody wondered what had become of them. Freight trains were no longer festooned with boys going nowhere; the boys stayed home and went to high schools, which now had more students than ever before. If the boys went on to college, they might be helped by part-time jobs provided by the National Youth Administration. If they came from families on relief, they could enlist in the Civilian Conservation Corps.

Marriages were still being deferred for want of income and the birth rate had steeply fallen. Young wives, for the most part, regarded pregnancy as a disaster. Older wives with children took pride in serving "better meals for less money," a slogan in popular cookbooks of the era; "new dishes from leftovers" was another. A big white refrigerator, often a new one when everything else was old, had become the center of the kitchen. Families had drawn closer together. With the five-day week, a legacy from darker days, they had leisure now for simple family diversions: picnics, dancing (for the kids), croquet, deck tennis, Ping-Pong, quoits, badminton, bridge (for older people), and the still-new game of Monopoly. Merchants carried new stocks of equipment for low-cost games. Bicycling had come back into favor. In the smaller cities, speakeasies, mostly for men, had been replaced with roadhouses for all the family.

There was always someone who kept snapping pictures; the production of American cameras grew by 157 percent between 1935 and 1937. Also there was a revival of interest in flower gardening. In 1938 a vice president of W. Atlee Burpee, the seedsmen, reported to me in a letter:

> It is true that there are more and better gardens now, especially flower gardens, than there were ten years ago. The general trend with the backyard gardener is for an increase in flower production; backyard vegetable gardens have suffered as a consequence. . . . Taking 100.0 as our business level for 1928, the level for 1938 would be 102.5. In 1932, at the bottom of the slump, the level was slightly lower, but the seed business was not as much affected by the depression as other businesses were.

In 1932 people had been growing and canning vegetables so they could be sure of something to eat. Three years later, with a little cash in their pockets to pay the grocer or the roadside stand, they were, as was widely observed, growing more flowers. Robert S. Lynd went back to Muncie, Indiana, in June 1935 with a staff of five assistants. It was ten years after his first "venture in contemporary anthropology," the one later described in *Middletown* (1929). He had chosen Muncie as the typical American city. In what ways had it been changed by the boom and the depression?

This time Lynd reported (in *Middletown in Transition*, 1937, written with his wife Helen Merrell Lynd) that Muncie had fallen more under the benevolent despotism of a single family. The family had prospered even in the worst years by making glass fruitjars, then a necessity for thrifty housewives, especially those with home gardens. Meanwhile the working class had suffered from the lack of other employment than making glass jars. People hadn't adjusted their habits of thought to the new situation, and Lynd felt that the city had remained stoutly Republican. At the same time he found that Muncie had become more attractive. There were those flower gardens in what had been bare yards, and larger improvements were visible.

Most of these had been made with the help of federal (that is, Democratic) money. One improvement was a new riverside boulevard across the city. The polluted river had been cleaned and dredged. Streets had been widened and repaved, the airport graded and drained. Public buildings had been enlarged (and in some cases decorated with murals by artists working at a federal subsistence wage). A park with a big municipal swimming pool had replaced a city dump near the center of town. Other parks were cleaner as a result of that ridiculed leaf-ranking, and they were often the scene of public dances (music by courtesy of the Federal Emergency Relief Administration). Good times were coming back, and Lynd reported that the streets were crowded with smiling people.

Those were indeed the high 1930s in small-to-medium cities like Muncie. In larger cities too, including New York, that period of eighteen months was a relatively happy time, at least for the middle classes. There was an easier feeling almost everywhere. The national income had risen from its low point by more than 60 percent and corporations were prospering once again. If all American corporations, to the number of roughly five hundred thousand, had issued a single balance sheet for 1932, it would have shown an aggregate loss of $5.6 billion. By 1936 their joint profit for the year was more than $5 billion. The Dow-Jones average price of industrial stocks had risen by 200 percent—from 59.93 at the end of 1932 to 179.90 at the end of 1936—and stockbrokers should have been exultant. Instead they were complaining about government interference and were inventing stories about the antics of that crazy man in the White House.

Even in New York, not much of the money trickled down to middle-class intellectuals. Our incomes were almost the same as before, but the little we earned went a long way in what was still a buyers' market. Food was cheap by later standards and rents were cheaper, with apartments easy to find (the Cowleys were then paying $85 a month for seven rooms in the Village). Restaurants always had tables, and waiters said "Thank you" for a 10-percent tip. Doctors made house visits. The streets weren't crowded and were reasonably clean, not to speak of being safe at night. There was no racket of riveting hammers. Parking places were easy to find and so were taxis (unless one had a broken arm). The subway was only a nickel.

And entertainment— That interlude in the depression years was the great age of swing bands. With Otis Ferguson as guide, we listened to Benny Goodman at the Café Rouge of the old Pennsylvania Hotel, or to Count Basie at the Famous Door on Fifty-second Street; or we could taxi to the Savoy Ballroom in Harlem on the chance of hearing Duke Ellington or Louis Armstrong. Racial animosities were muted in those years, and like many downtown people we had friends in Harlem who sometimes gave bottle parties. We didn't do much dancing any longer, since our tastes went back to the sweet-and-slow foxtrot era; it seemed to us that the new dances—the Lindy Hop, the Shag, and later the Big Apple—were designed for the limber knees of bobbysoxers. Neither did we attend such public spectacles as the 1935 championship fight between Joe Louis and Maxie Baer, when ninety-five thousand people with money to spend crowded into the Yankee Stadium (twenty-three thousand had so-called "ringside seats"). But we did go to the movies in those high old days of the Marx Brothers and W. C. Fields. If we preferred Broadway shows, tickets for most of them could be bought half-price in Gray's Drugstore at the corner of Forty-third Street. The Federal Theater Project was even cheaper, and furthermore it engaged our sympathies. By May 1936 it had five hits in New York (they weren't hits with Congress, which always mistrusted the project). The best of them were *Murder in the Cathedral*, *Macbeth* played for the first time with an all-Negro cast, and the Living Newspaper production of *Triple-A Plowed Under*.

Or were we planning a trip across the country? No reservations had to be made in advance, since there was always a room to be found. Domestic travel was easier in those days when trains went everywhere and traffic was light on most of the highways. There were pleasanter sights, too, with less suburban sprawl and no unbroken ranks of gas stations, motels, and fast-food outlets to hide the landscape. The real country began some thirty miles from New York (or Boston or Chicago), with cows grazing, untouched woodlots, and cornfields in tassel. Might it be that those high 1930s were the last American idyll? Not if one bears in mind the suffering that also continued through those years, though with less despair; there were still eight million persons out of work, and more than twenty million, counting dependents, were on relief. In retrospect, however, this country seems most attractive in times of relative danger or hardship, when it is less pushing, less crowded, more given to acts of kindness—"We're all in this together"—and less intent on grab-and-get-ahead.

My praise of the countryside as it then appeared is based on the Northeast and the Middle West, two regions I knew better than others. Here and there in my travels I saw brushpiles set afire as a sign that old fields were being cleared again. People were still moving back to the Northeastern land and they clung to it for security. West and south of the Missouri River the countryside had a different look. Especially on the High Plains the land itself was blowing away; no one could cling to it. The years from 1933 to 1936 were those of the great dust storms that turned the sky black at noon. The air was solid with dust; it filled the eyes and the nose. Dust went drifting through the fields like snow and rose in pyramids over farm machinery. It seeped under doors, even when the cracks were lined with rags soaked in kerosene; it lay in windrows on the kitchen linoleum. Crops failed year after year. Mortgages went unpaid and the denuded farmland was seized by the banks. Hundreds of thousands of farm families were "dusted out"; the tenants were the first to go, when they couldn't pay rent, and then the former landowners followed them. Still other tenants, in regions unaffected by dusters—notably the Deep South—were "tractored out" by new machines that made their labor superfluous; it was the end of an American peasantry. As *Fortune* magazine reported in 1939:

> It is an ironical sidelight that the government's crop-control program has abetted the dispossession. Crop restriction in itself reduces the labor need, and therefore causes some eviction. But more important, the benefit payments have furnished landowners with the capital to buy tractors. In addition, though the law requires that benefit checks be divided between owner and tenant, owners in many cases have secured the whole amount for themselves by dismissing the tenants and rehiring them as wage-workers. The disturbance in southeastern Missouri last January, when some 300 tenant-cropper families camped on the highways in public protest, were partly directed against this practice. But such isolated acts of treachery, however cruel, are merely incidental to the forces that are crowding the southern farm workers by the thousands off the land and into the army of migrants.

Part of the army would soon move northward, from Mississippi to Chicago, from the Carolinas to Washington and New York. Another part—consisting of 285,000 persons by official count, though there may well have been more—was already moving westward by highway into California; those were the ragged pioneers, the Okies and Arkies and Texicanos. At first we in the

Northeast didn't hear much about them. There had been no drought or dusters in New England and the Middle Atlantic states; country people there were living a little better than before because the Western drought had raised the price of what they produced. Farmland was still cheap, though, and its availability had revived in us an old dream of owning a house within reach of New York, but among fields and with its own garden. I didn't reflect at the time that this was a dream of self-subsistence, quite different from the dream of linked arms and raised fists that had possessed our minds in the early years of the decade.

During the spring of 1936 I was negotiating to buy an empty barn and seven acres of land in the little town of Sherman, seventy miles north of Grand Central Station. The price was $1300, if I could scrape that much together (starting with a bank balance of $300). If I could also negotiate a mortgage, the barn might be remodeled into a house. It was across the road from a cottage rented for $10 a month by Peter Blume, a gifted artist and a close friend. Ebie Blume and Muriel were also close friends and we were fond of other people in the neighborhood, including the biographer Matthew Josephson and the novelist Robert M. Coates; we shouldn't be lonely living in Sherman. There I could fish and hunt in season, grow a big garden, and still spend three days a week at the *New Republic* office.

By June, after a complicated series of transactions, our house was under way. I had borrowed $1000 from my secretary, who insisted on lending me the money, and thus had been able to pay for the barn in full. Using it as security, I had obtained a federally guaranteed mortgage of $6500 from the local bank. I had found a local architect, unemployed and not too bright, but willing to accept our ideas. I had found a contractor too, one who owned a lumberyard and was eager to dispose of his oak flooring and cedar shingles. Everything marched forward, though soon there would be further complications involving a second mortgage, a bank loan to pay for the oil furnace, and a bitter quarrel with the contractor. A new house always costs more than expected and there are always quarrels. In the end, after starting with goodwill and $300, I was to find myself possessed of, or by, a seven-room house, a cornfield, a brier patch, a trout brook, and a crazy edifice of debts to be razed stone by stone.

There would be time enough to worry about the debts. Meanwhile, the lecture series having ended, I turned over the green tin box with its fat, by now, sheaf of banknotes to Liston Oak, a gaunt Communist, who looked like one of El Greco's martyrs. He had agreed to serve as executive secretary of the League and I wished him luck. To celebrate the era of good feeling, and also our planned departure from New York, we decided to throw a big party and invite "everybody." That meant our literary friends of whatever political complexion: Communists, anti-Communists, New Dealers fresh from Washington, diehard liberals, all-for-artists, and dissenters of various types, including a brace of Technocrats and a said-to-be fascist. It would be a Writers' Front, even broader in composition than the People's Front government that had taken office in Paris at the beginning of June. Authors would mingle with critics who had slaughtered their books. There would be a truce to quarreling.

There wasn't exactly a truce, but neither were there many wounds. I had been a little worried about the said-to-be fascist. He was Seward Collins, a wealthy and once popular young man who had worked with Edmund Wilson on the staff of *Vanity Fair* magazine and had later become publisher of a literary monthly, *The Bookman*. When he used the magazine to express ideas that seemed close to those of Mussolini, his literary friends dropped away. He was delighted to attend a party at which some of them would be present. That evening he wandered from room to room, glass in hand, defending his ideas so mildly that nobody could abuse him. Jim Farrell, who had bludgeoned or shillelaghed me that spring in his *Note on Literary Criticism*, was now finding points of agreement. Everybody agreed with the New Dealers on this occasion; they were fulminating against the

Supreme Court. Its last ruling before the summer recess had been that the states had no constitutional right to fix minimum wages for women and children. Earlier it had ruled that the federal government had no such power. "Those venerable justices," a young woman said, "have taken the bit in their dentures." A novelist wondered loudly what would happen next in Spain. His audience scattered to reassemble at a table near the big bow window where bottles stood in disarray. John Chamberlain had lately joined the staff of *Fortune* against my urging. I said that the salary was too high and would tempt him to spend more and more, so that he might end as a slave to his standard of living. John blinked and said he would live simply while maintaining his right to hold his own opinions, no matter how radical. We drank to that. Jim Thurber, the foe of proletarian literature, was fraternizing with Joe Freeman, but he had to shout in order to be heard across the barricades. Our son slept soundly in his crib through the hubbub.

That was Thursday evening June 18. On Friday Muriel and I drove to Sherman and found that the well driller's rig was pounding away, though it hadn't yet found water. Progress on the house was exasperatingly slow. I remember that we had our first quarrel after four harmonious years of married life; it was about the location of the fireplace. The quarrel was pushed aside, though, as others would be for the rest of our days. Both of us had the feeling that, with the move to the country, we were about to enter a new era.

# 26.
## The Fading of
## a Dream

The 1930s would reach their highest point on election day, November 3, 1936. In the preceding weeks there had been enormous campaign rallies at which the president kept reminding voters that happy days were truly here again, and his words had been accepted with enthusiasm. Now it became apparent that the businessmen who feared and abused him had been talking mostly to one another. Nobody could forget that day when Roosevelt carried every state but Maine and Vermont. He even carried Muncie, Indiana, among other cities that had never before gone Democratic; it was a little revolution that amazed and puzzled the authors of *Middletown in Transition*. Stocks on Wall Street shot upward in spite of the brokers' long faces. Seventeen big corporations announced that wages were being raised.

But retail prices went up as well, a first sign that the high 1930s were ending. Labor had become confident and was growing restive. There was an epidemic of clearly illegal sitdown strikes, during which factories were occupied and held like captured fortresses. By May 1937 the epidemic had directly affected nearly half a million workers. Its climax was on February 3, at Fisher Body Plant No. 1 in Flint, Michigan, when a pitched battle between strikers and National Guardsmen was averted by the last-minute surrender of General Motors. The public was relieved by the outcome, but remained divided or hostile in its attitude toward sitdown strikes.

It was more bitterly divided by Roosevelt's effort to change the complexion of the Supreme Court, which had been over-turning almost every liberal law passed by Congress. Among the nine justices were four very old men of hidebound opinions who voted as a bloc and were likely to be joined by one or two others, thus creating a safely conservative majority. Roosevelt proposed to neutralize the conservatives by a bill providing that for each federal judge who reached the age of seventy and failed to re-tire, a new judge should be appointed as his colleague. The Su-preme Court might be enlarged in this fashion to a maximum of fifteen members. The bill, introduced in February, was hotly de-bated all spring while feeling rose against it; the newspapers called it a scheme for packing the Court. In July the Senate killed the bill by sending it back to committee. Before that blow to Roosevelt, the next-to-oldest justice, Willis Van Devanter, had retired at seventy-eight; after he was replaced by a younger man, a majority of the justices would be liberal. The president could thus claim a success in his real purpose, but his prestige had suffered.

It suffered still more from a decline in commerce and in-dustry. People hadn't money to buy the goods that were being offered them at higher prices. A further blow to their purchasing power was the president's new effort to balance the budget by holding down appropriations. Once again profits were falling and factories were closing. October 19, 1937, was Black Tuesday on the stock market, almost exactly eight years after the Black Thursday of 1929. Roosevelt had been trying to "restore con-fidence" among financiers, as his predecessor had tried; but what the money lords couldn't do for their friend Hoover, they wouldn't attempt to do for a man they regarded as their enemy. The army of unemployed grew by more than two million. Finally the president threw up his hands, forgot the balanced budget, and asked Congress for authority to spend $3 billion more for relief and public works. Federal money in circulation was showing its effect by June 1938. I am getting ahead of my story; the point is that recovery would be slower this time, with rumblings of doubt and dissension. The easier mood of 1935 and 1936 wouldn't return for a long time, if ever.

Nor would that brief era of good feeling in the intellectual world. Writers had drawn together, as I said, in response to the broad advance of fascism. The mood had been confirmed when the Communist International adopted a new and more realistic policy. "It was what we wanted," said Granville Hicks, speaking for many others, "and it seemed to us a great step ahead for the revolutionary movement." Now all the men of goodwill could work together against their common enemy. An opportunity for joint action was offered, furthermore, when the Spanish generals revolted against their government late in July 1936. Spain would become the test for us of moral attitudes, and anyone who supported the Loyalists was our comrade.

In those early days of the People's Front, it seemed to offer vast possibilities. It might bring together all factions on the left and then win over the wavering middle class. It might gain control of governments, as it had done in Spain and France. It might stop Hitler at the Rhine as well as undermining his power in Germany. It might introduce broad social reforms (and note the emphasis on reforms; the word "revolution" was losing its glamour). Then slowly the weaknesses of such a coalition began to appear. A People's Front could move only as fast or far as its more cautious elements were willing to move. It would have to surrender one bold policy after another (as in France Léon Blum had yielded in the crucial matter of sending arms to the Spanish republicans). Soon it might hesitate even to propose bold policies, fearing as it did that they might alienate too many voters.

In their effort to gain adherents, the members of a People's Front would often be tempted to sacrifice principles to propaganda. A homely example of that sacrifice had been the attempt to win over Sinclair Lewis. Nobody who helped to plan that "little dinner" in his honor had much private regard for Lewis as a writer; what everybody regarded highly was his standing with the public. Lewis showed that he had sounder instincts than the planners, who were being less than candid with him or themselves. Critical standards were likely to be relaxed in the People's Front days. There was not much original thinking about literature or politics; the emphasis was on public relations. Two years before that dinner I had written in my innocence, "The truth is all the propaganda we need." At the Writers' Congress I had given a speech, "What the Revolutionary Movement Can Do for a Writer"; I claimed that it could vastly strengthen his work. Gradually we should find that the movement might diminish a writer by giving him what seemed to be noble motives for concealing part of the truth.

In the course of time we should learn about another all-too-human result of the effort to establish a grand coalition at any price. The effort in itself was making the revolutionary movement too uptown and respectable. Many of its younger members were joining the establishment by finding responsible work in New York or Washington or Hollywood. Their motive was largely idealistic; that is, they wanted to change the establishment, humanize it, end by directing it toward the struggle against fascism; but they also enjoyed the higher standard of living and the modest exercise of power. When a crisis forced them to choose between the establishment and their ideals, most of them would surrender the ideals (though often that would prove to be a useless sacrifice). Sometimes they surrendered old friendships as well.

The People's Front, although proposed as a means of uniting the public in defense of peace and democracy (and the Soviet Union), was to end as the ground of new dissensions. These were inevitable, given the course of events in Europe.

Two dominant issues, both European, would create the mood

prevailing among generous-minded Americans during the later 1930s; one was the civil war in Spain and the other was the Russian purges. The first of these had a unifying effect in the beginning. Almost all writers, and a majority of their readers, supported the Spanish Republic. In 1938 the League of American Writers would send a letter to hundreds of literary figures asking two questions: "Are you for, or are you against Franco and fascism? Are you for, or are you against the legal government and the people of Republican Spain?" The questions were answered by 414 writers, of whom seven were neutral and one was for Franco, but with reservations; 406 were for the republic. That was something close to unanimity.

As for the Russian purges, their dreadful magnitude was still a secret even from Russians; here we had only printed reports and blurred newsreels of the various trials. There would never be unanimity about them, except in respect to the general uneasiness they created among left-wing intellectuals. Even those who believed that the defendants were guilty of the crimes to which they confessed couldn't help feeling that the evidence revealed a disheartening state of affairs in Russia. As one trial followed another, more and more persons rejected the confessions, and soon they would also reject the Communist Party. But there was no unanimity even among the rejecters. Those whose doubts about the party went back to the early days of Trotsky's exile distrusted those whose doubts were revealed after the first big Moscow trial, in 1936, while these in turn distrusted the apostates of 1937 and 1938 as unstable allies who had clung to their illusions. Each new trial sowed dragon's teeth for a new harvest.

The era of good feeling had been forgotten. Even the Spanish Republic, though it continued to engage the warm sympathy of American intellectuals, was soon to be the cause of new dissensions. The idealists who fought for the republic in the Abraham Lincoln Brigade had suffered more than their share of losses, and some of the survivors—by no means all of them—came home disenchanted. So did a few American visitors to

Spain, who complained of the part that Communists were playing in the government. (Liston Oak was one of them, and the League of American Writers lost an executive secretary.) Others reported that innocent persons had been secretly executed, including a Spanish friend of Dos Passos. The Gaypayoo, as everyone called the Russian secret service, was active in Madrid and more active in Barcelona. Then Barcelona fell, late in January 1939, and Madrid late in March; the war was over. But some of the quarrels continued among supporters of the republic, as they do after any great defeat; one faction always blames another.

American adherents of the People's Front also had a feeling of defeat in their political efforts at home, for all their success in winning over part of the public. Was that part truly won over, or did it merely accept a few of their aims, as notably the hope of preventing another world war? "Against war and fascism" had been their slogan, but this suggested two aims that couldn't always be harmonized: resistance to fascism might in itself bring the nation dangerously close to war, and at this point the pacifist sector of the public might stand in bitter opposition to the resisters. Meanwhile the New Deal had nothing new to offer, apparently, and was attracting less attention except from its enemies. There was dissension in Washington even more than "in the field," as officials called the rest of the country, and there was confusion in liberal circles. A widely prevailing mood would be one of suspicion, acrimony, and accusation, a foreshadowing of the McCarthy era.

As the bickering continued, what would happen to the dream of revolutionary brotherhood that has been mentioned often in this narrative? It faded imperceptibly for some dreamers, perhaps for most of them; the golden mountains receded into the mist. For others, who had been more ardent, the dream was shattered in a moment of deconversion. It had exerted such power, though; it had risen from such a depth of national and personal confusion; it had answered such a need for faith that even those others clung to fragments of the dream—sometimes only to the single word "revolution"; they wanted to think of themselves as revolutionists long after their essential feelings had become conservative. Those for whom the dream merely faded were likely to persist for some time in patterns of behavior that their faith had imposed on them. They still went to meetings, they served on committees, and they signed open letters in spite of being dubious about what the letters said. Some of them must have felt that there was an emptiness at the center of their lives; once I described it as "The white egg-shaped motionless, speechless No."

In the beginning the dream had been composed of several elements, all fitting together. There was the notion that capitalism and its culture were in violent decay and on the point of being self-destroyed. There was the idealization of "the workers" as the vital class, the only one fated to survive. There was the moral imperative: surrender your middle-class identity, merge yourself with the workers, suffer their common hardships, and be born again! That was the religious feeling exalted by Waldo Frank in his novel *The Death and Birth of David Markand*, and there it was combined, as in books by others, with a yearning for martyrdom. Untold numbers of people will be sacrificed in the struggle, but let us be among those victims if the need arises, since history is on our side. All of us joined in brotherhood, our right fists raised in the Red Front salute, let us march forward into the classless society. The Soviet Union has shown us the way.

Those elements of the dream in its early form were subjected one by one to the test of day-by-day living. One by one they were dimmed, eroded, put into question. Was bourgeois culture truly at the point of death, considering that in America it had shown unexpected powers of recuperation? Were the Russian workers creating an order that should serve as model to the rest of us? That second question exposed what seemed to be the weakest element of the dream. Even the Communists were apologizing for Russia in a quiet fashion, while continuing to thunder against its detractors. As for the American workers, did they share our hope of building a new society? They were encouragingly militant, as they had proved in the sitdown strikes, but was their militance aroused by anything nobler than the hope of driving a new Buick? And to merge our lives with those of the workers: would that mean we might truly be born again?

There must have been many who asked those questions, if not always consciously, but I suspect that most of us also asked another. One element that underlay the rest of the dream and would weaken the whole by its disappearance was an absolute faith that our side would triumph in the end. It was the faith that had given millions the courage to die for the revolution, not only in Russia but in China, Germany, Spain, many other parts of the world. Would history confirm that faith? The question began to afflict me in the later 1930s, when the Spanish Republic was falling. By then it was almost certain that there would be another world war, but its outcome was unpredictable. If America entered the war, as I came to feel it must do, we might win at the cost of submitting to a more or less autocratic government in our own country. If we failed to enter it . . . then Hitler's armies might triumph everywhere and his realm might endure, as he had promised, "for a thousand years." I thought again of those nameless martyrs—

> *for comrades dead, for having loved tomorrow,*
> *betrayed and bastinadoed, burned at the stake,*
> *slow-starved in prison or exile, buried alive,*
> *beaten insensible, roused at the day's break,*
>
> *then hurried through the snow to execution,*
> *shot down in Florisdorf or Chapei Road,*
> *and now reprieved from prison graveyards piled*
> *so high with victims that they overflowed.*

In the days of faith I had pictured the martyrs as a phantom army that would sweep the tyrants aside. I now began to wonder at moments, perhaps with many others, whether those millions had died in vain and whether the future might belong to their executioners.

That mood wouldn't come over me until the days when New York was full of German and Spanish and Austrian refugees. They were most of them clever and talkative persons, but sometimes they had the look of being reprieved from the grave. Some of them came to *The New Republic* with projects for articles. I kept meeting others at parties or at cafeterias on the Upper West Side where groups of them sat long over cups of coffee, as in Vienna. Each of them had a tale about his narrow escape, a theory to explain the collapse of Europe, and for me they gave a special atmosphere to the period; it was the dusk of a late-autumnal day, after the leaves had fallen. In some respects those final years of the 1930s were indeed a disheartening time, but they also had a different aspect, being full of drama, rumor, intrigue, and a feeling that the world hung in the balance. We had our grand adventures and misadventures, but they were no longer episodes in a confident dream.

# Index